MacGyver

FUGITIVE GAUNTLET

MacGyver

FUGITIVE GAUNTLET

'MacGyver' Created By Lee David Zlotoff

Written By Lee David Zlotoff & Tony Lee

Pencils / Inks - Will Sliney

Colors - Ciaran Lucas & Owen Jollands

Letters - Aditya Bidikar

Cover - Andie Tong & Ciaran Lucas

Consulting Editor - John Potter

IMAGE COMICS, INC.

Robert Kirkman - chief operating officer
Erik Larsen - chief financial officer
Todd McFarlane - president
Marc Silvestri - chief executive officer
Jim Valentino - vice-president

Eric Stephenson - publisher
Ron Richards - director of business development
Jennifer de Guzman - pr & marketing director
Branwyn Bigglestone - accounts manager
Emily Miller - accounting assistant
Jamie Parreno - marketing assistant
Emilio Bautista - sales assistant
Susie Giroux - administrative assistant
Kevin Yuen - digital rights coordinator
Tyler Shainline - events coordinator
David Brothers - content manager
Jonathan Chan - production manager
Drew Gill - art director
Jana Cook - print manager
Monica Garcia - senior production artist
Vincent Kukua - production artist
Jenna Savage - production artist

image

www.imagecomics.com

From: "B. Cornwell" <cornwell@cornwellinstitute.org>
Date: 18 July 2012 17:04:35 GMT+01:00
To: "MacGyver" <a.macgyver@phoenixfoundation.org>
Subject: Come and visit.

Dear Mac,

I realize it's been ages since we last spoke—for which, if I had any interest in social skills, I should apologize. But since, as you well know, my research has always come first, I will dispense with all that nonsense and say only that I wouldn't be contacting you at all if it weren't a matter of some urgency.

I am currently near completion of my most recent project—in Kenya of all places—and, though I've no right to ask, I'm hoping I can persuade you to come visit me here as soon as you possibly can.

I realize that I was by no means your favorite professor at Caltech, any more than you were one of my favorite students: frankly, your relentless questioning left me thinking you were generally a pain in the ass. But that's not to suggest I didn't respect your abilities, or what you've managed to do with them in these intervening years.

And it's those abilities I may be in need of now. My current project is nothing less than a game changer on a global scale. And, as is often the case with such paradigm shifts, it has aroused the interest and attention of some powerful stakeholders, not all of who have the most benevolent intentions.

I will apologize for being so cryptic but I think it best to preserve the details until we can speak in person. Suffice to say both my work—and my person—may be in danger, despite the fact that I have already made arrangements for some additional protection. But even with that, I am no longer certain who to trust, even within my own circle.

That is why I am reaching out to you since—if nothing else—I know you can be trusted completely and will receive my plea with all the seriousness that I intend.

If you can come, I believe I can at least arrange a flight to Africa for you on one of my benefactor's private jets. But, to keep your visit under the radar so to speak, it would be unwise for you to reach me here by helicopter, meaning you would have to travel overland for the best part of a day through the jungle. My apologies for that too.

Just do let me know ASAP if you can make it, as the list of those who can help me now is perilously short—so short if fact that I must confess...yours is the only name on it.

Regards,

B.C.

'EVERY DAY ON *MACGYVER* WAS LIKE WAKING UP ON YOUR BIRTHDAY...'

INTRODUCTION BY MIKE GREENBURG

So, it was the spring of 1986 and I was finishing the feature film *Allan Quatermain and the Lost City of Gold.*

Mike Greenburg (Producer) and Richard Dean Anderson

The film was the second of H. Rider Haggard's trilogy. *King Solomon's Mines* was the first. *She* was the third. That never happened. The films were supposed to be spoofs of the action adventure genre that was made popular at the time by *Raiders of the Lost Arc.* Our screenwriter, Gene Quintano, is a brilliant spoof writer (*Police Academy, Loaded Weapon*). The studio heads didn't 'get the spoof thing' and made us rewrite the scripts and play the films as straight action adventure. That note killed the movies. Now, instead of spoofing *Raiders* we were competing with the franchise… Brilliant.

Aside from reading this must read *MacGyver* book, William Goldman's book *Adventures in the Screen Trade* is another must-read for anyone remotely connected to Hollywood. In it, Goldman says: "The first thing you need to know about Hollywood is that no one knows anything."

For some strange reason that line made me feel safe to venture in "the business." This will tie in later. Back to springtime...

I got a call from Mike Schoenbrun, the head of production at Paramount. Mike told me that Steve Downing the Executive Producer of their new series *MacGyver* was going to call me to come in and meet with Henry Winkler and John Rich, the other EPs of the show. They were looking for a producer that could come in and get the show back on track and back on budget. They showed me a couple of 65-page scripts and some finished episodes and asked me what I would do differently. An hour episode is really only 44 minutes of show, the rest being commercials and promos. I told them that I would cut ten pages out of the scripts because in action adventure there is plenty of running time on each page. This edit would also save two days of filming and their direct costs, thereby fixing the over-budget problem as well. I also told the guys that I would lose the wall-to-wall voiceovers where MacGyver tells the audience everything that they were already seeing him do on screen. To me it was like watching a radio show play out. I guess I passed the first test because they sent me to meet Richard Dean Anderson, aka RDA, and aka Rick at the Queen Mary in Long Beach where the crew was filming.

When I met privately with Rick and his dog Whiskey, I asked them what they thought of killing the voiceovers. Rick immediately got up, gave me a hug, told me he hated the voiceovers and the hours in the ADR stage and I got the job. As I was leaving his trailer, he said: "By the way, I walked out of your movie "Quatermain" last night in Westwood." I asked him how long he lasted. He said about twenty minutes max. I told Rick that he got off easy, I had to spend a year and a half watching it. That's the tie-in.

Rick and I became big on *MacGyver* story and back reference tie-ins from that point on.

(Continued on next page)

Schoenbrun said I would be at Paramount for a few months, then I could go back to the spoofs that I was working on with Gene, the next being a Godzilla spoof called *It Ate Cleveland*. This was another hilarious script that those same studio execs didn't 'get' either. Anyway, RDA and I 'got' each other's humor and a few months turned out to be twenty years in production. Every day on *MacGyver* was like waking up on your birthday... A total gift with tons of fun attached.

Lee Zlotoff was our great creator. Obviously none of this would have happened if Lee didn't dream up such a great concept and character. Richard Dean Anderson took the *MacGyver* role and with his voice, tone and sensibility evolved it into the iconic character that the world still quotes and enjoys today. Henry Winkler was the spirit of the cast and crew. Henry has the amazing ability to make everyone he comes in contact with 'happy.' Everyone loved when Henry showed up. Steve Downing was our spitballing story guru and became our final cut guy as well. He rode herd on the writing staff and lived in the editing room. John Rich (of "All in the Family" fame, need I say more) was our mentor. John was a technical camera and editing wizard and made us all better at our jobs whether we liked it or not. I actually enjoyed being summoned to the editing room at night after 12 to 15 hours on the set to be shown what idiots we were. He was always right.

My job was to basically show up everyday with the directors, to make sure all those moving parts went in the right direction staying true to the story and character. We had the best team of alternating core directors. They made my job easy. Charlie Correll, Mike Vejar, Bill Gereghty and Mike Chaffee collectively had thousands of hours of prime television experience, and were great guys to boot. The crews were the best. Hard working and never complained. And, yes, sorry for the cliché, but we were like a family. The recurring characters that also made our jobs easier were *Jack Dalton* played by Bruce MaGill,

Penny Parker played by Teri Hatcher and *Murdoc* played by Michael DesBarres. It's no wonder that these gifted actors would become big stars that would continue to light up the screen whenever they are on.

As you can see, what started out to be one man's, Lee Zlotoff's creative vision in 1985 took a team of hundreds of talented and dedicated professional filmmakers to realize. The end result being an iconic character with strong core values that lives in our dictionaries, encyclopedias, airwaves, streams and more importantly, our hearts. *MacGyver* continues to be a positive force and part of life on this planet. The name or verb *MacGyver* is probably uttered a million times a day around the world whenever anyone uses a Swiss Army knife to fix something or rigs a *MacGyverism* with whatever is at hand to get out of a jam. That alone probably says it all!

Now, have as much fun reading the book as we did in making the show!!

Michael Greenburg (MACGYVER, LEGEND, STARGATE SG-1) and his brother Ross Greenburg (MIRACLE, 61, 51 Emmys and the former President of HBO SPORTS) are currently producing documentaries and the feature film GAME OF SHADOWS, directed by Ron Shelton and based on the New York Times Bestseller.*

Michael was the Executive Producer of Score Productions Inc. (2007-2012), a wholly-owned subsidiary of Score Media Inc. (TSX: SCR). Score Media's main asset is THE SCORE TELEVISION NETWORK, a sports network available across Canada. Score Media also operated THE SCORE RADIO NETWORK available across North America on SIRIUS Satellite Radio, and other interactive assets including theScore.com and SCORE MOBILE.

Prior to his Score deal, Michael and his production partner Richard Dean Anderson, operating under their production company banner GEKKO FILM CORP, together with MGM Worldwide Television, produced their decade-long hit series STARGATE SG-1. STARGATE SG-1 premiered on SHOWTIME during the summer of 1997 and continues to air on the Syfy Network, FOX syndication and in over a hundred countries throughout the world. Michael also produced STARGATE ATLANTIS: RISING, the two-hour premiere spin-off pilot of STARGATE SG-1. The two STARGATE series were the highest rated shows in the history of the Syfy Network.

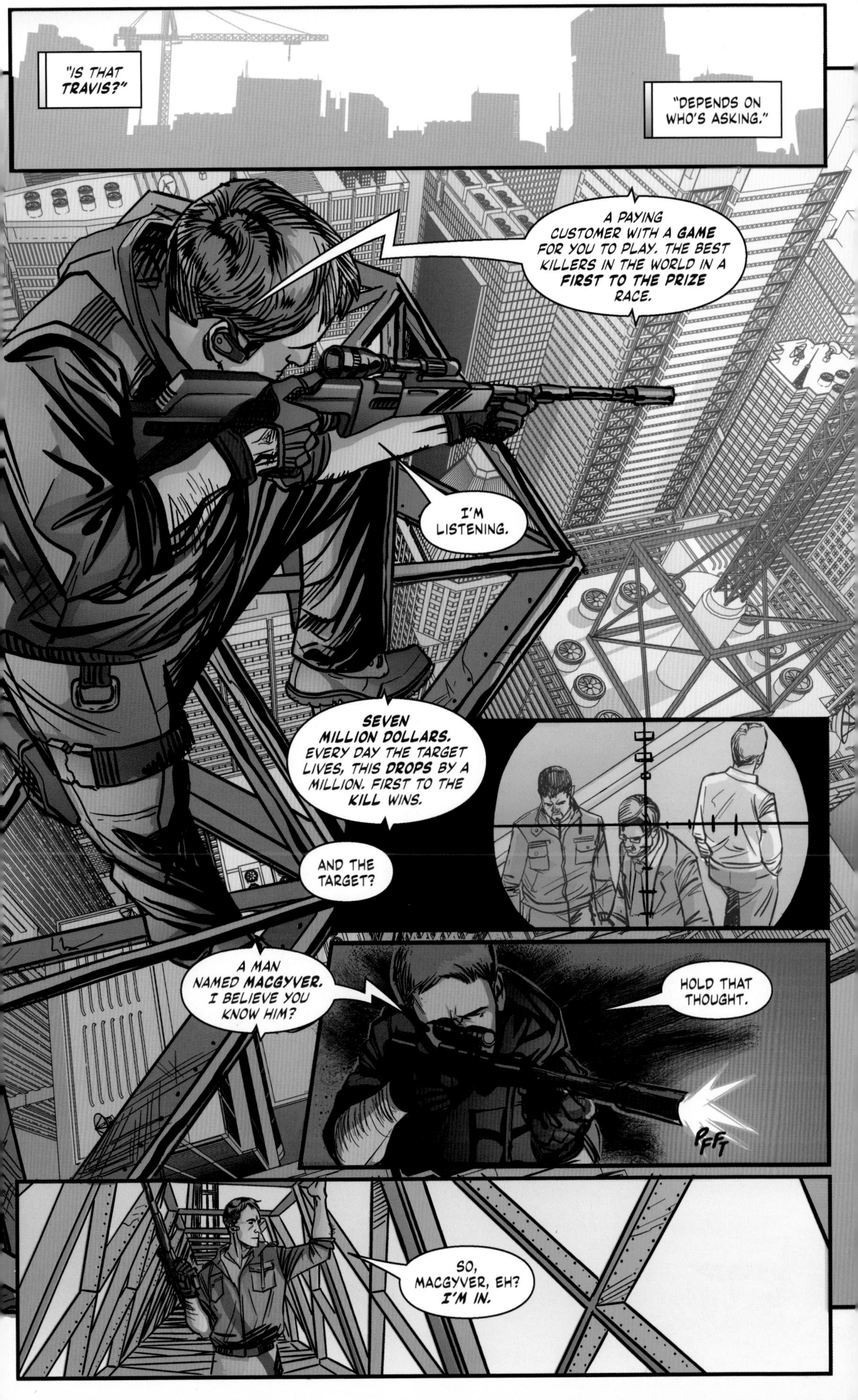
"IS THAT TRAVIS?"
"DEPENDS ON WHO'S ASKING."
A PAYING CUSTOMER WITH A GAME FOR YOU TO PLAY. THE BEST KILLERS IN THE WORLD IN A FIRST TO THE PRIZE RACE.
I'M LISTENING.
SEVEN MILLION DOLLARS. EVERY DAY THE TARGET LIVES, THIS DROPS BY A MILLION. FIRST TO THE KILL WINS.
AND THE TARGET?
A MAN NAMED MACGYVER. I BELIEVE YOU KNOW HIM?
HOLD THAT THOUGHT.
PFFT
SO, MACGYVER, EH? I'M IN.

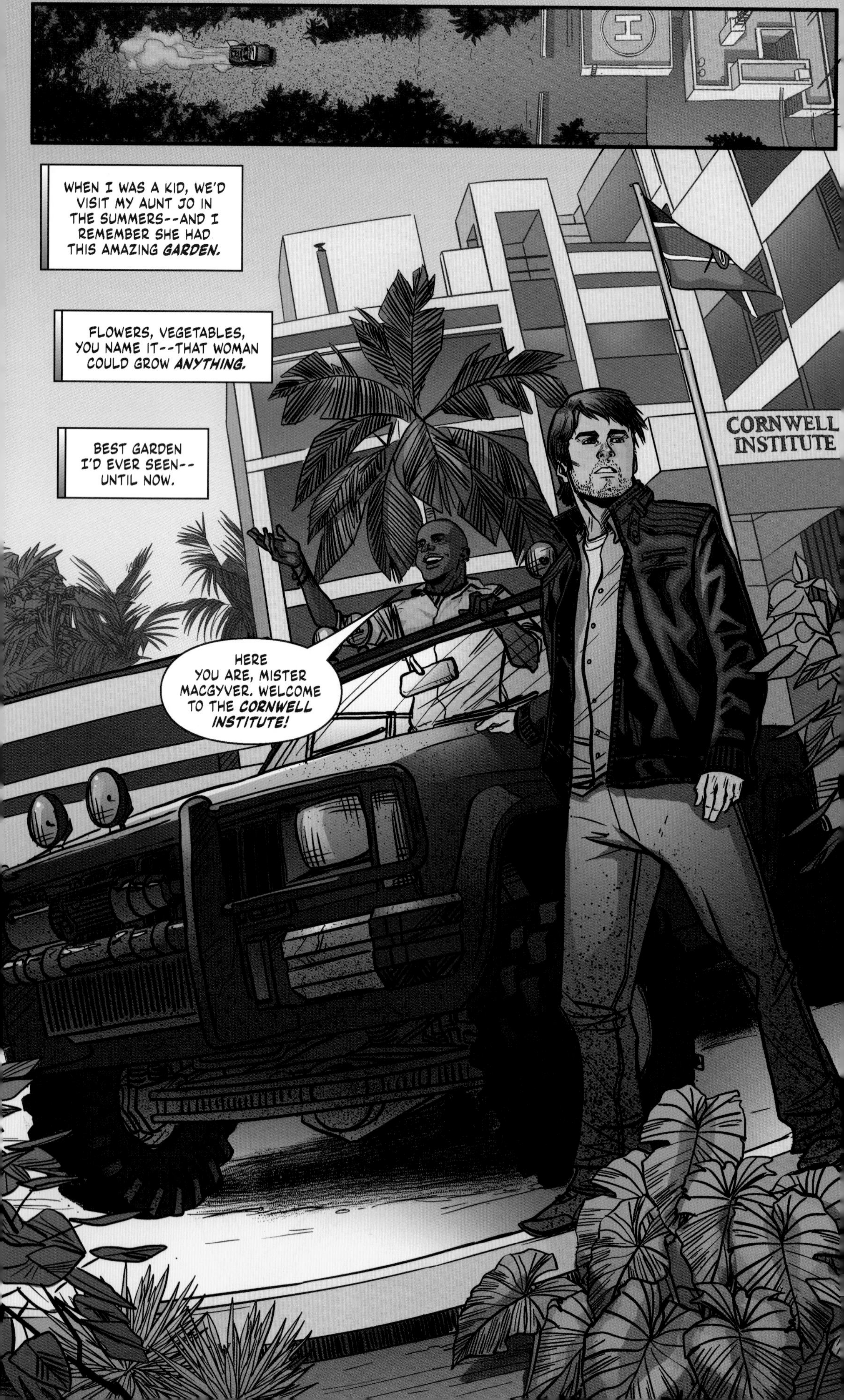
WHEN I WAS A KID, WE'D VISIT MY AUNT JO IN THE SUMMERS--AND I REMEMBER SHE HAD THIS AMAZING GARDEN.
FLOWERS, VEGETABLES, YOU NAME IT--THAT WOMAN COULD GROW ANYTHING.
BEST GARDEN I'D EVER SEEN--UNTIL NOW.
CORNWELL INSTITUTE
HERE YOU ARE, MISTER MACGYVER. WELCOME TO THE CORNWELL INSTITUTE!

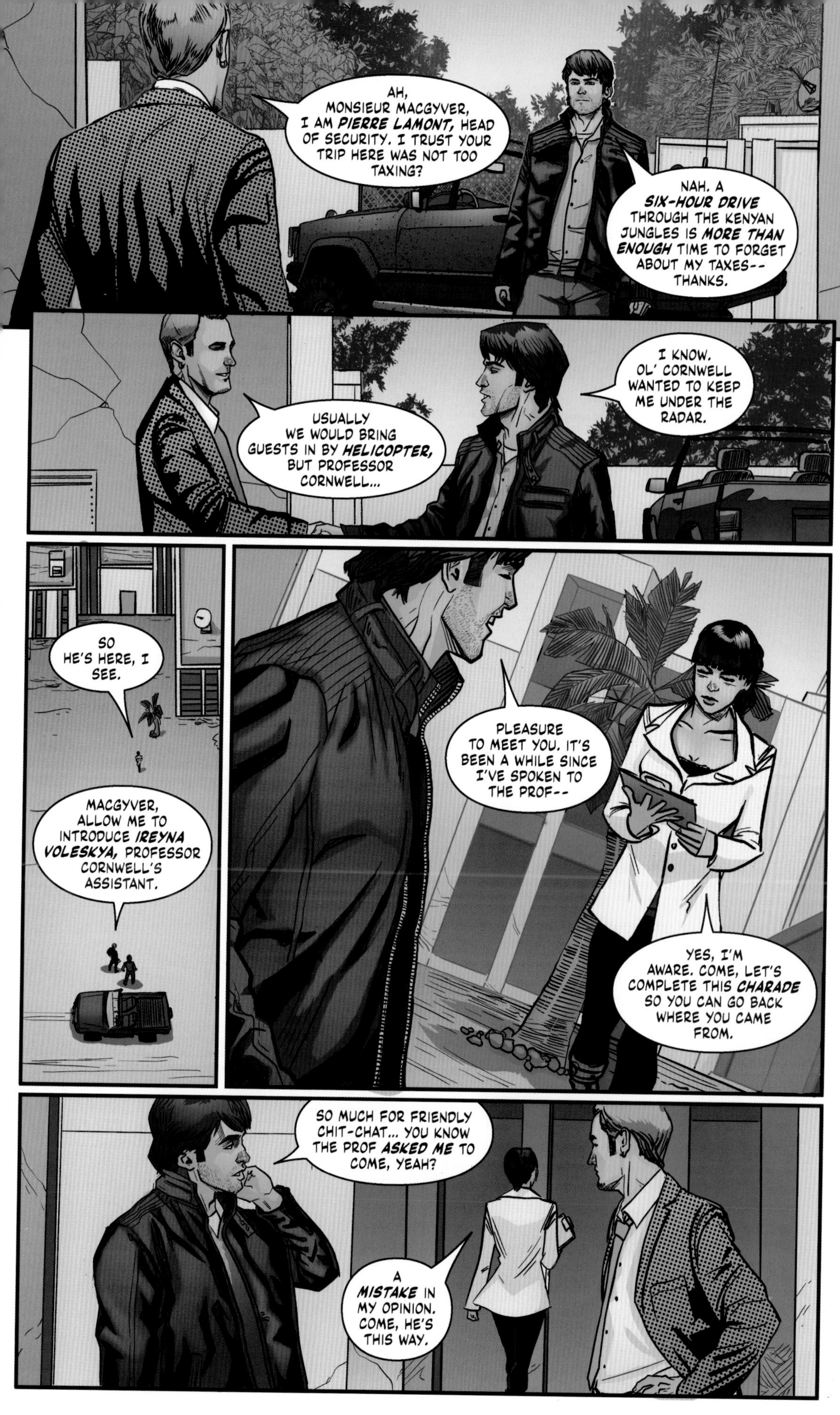
AH, MONSIEUR MACGYVER, I AM PIERRE LAMONT, HEAD OF SECURITY. I TRUST YOUR TRIP HERE WAS NOT TOO TAXING?
NAH. A SIX-HOUR DRIVE THROUGH THE KENYAN JUNGLES IS MORE THAN ENOUGH TIME TO FORGET ABOUT MY TAXES-- THANKS.
USUALLY WE WOULD BRING GUESTS IN BY HELICOPTER, BUT PROFESSOR CORNWELL...
I KNOW. OL' CORNWELL WANTED TO KEEP ME UNDER THE RADAR.
SO HE'S HERE, I SEE.
MACGYVER, ALLOW ME TO INTRODUCE IREYNA VOLESKYA, PROFESSOR CORNWELL'S ASSISTANT.
PLEASURE TO MEET YOU. IT'S BEEN A WHILE SINCE I'VE SPOKEN TO THE PROF--
YES, I'M AWARE. COME, LET'S COMPLETE THIS CHARADE SO YOU CAN GO BACK WHERE YOU CAME FROM.
SO MUCH FOR FRIENDLY CHIT-CHAT... YOU KNOW THE PROF ASKED ME TO COME, YEAH?
A MISTAKE IN MY OPINION. COME, HE'S THIS WAY.

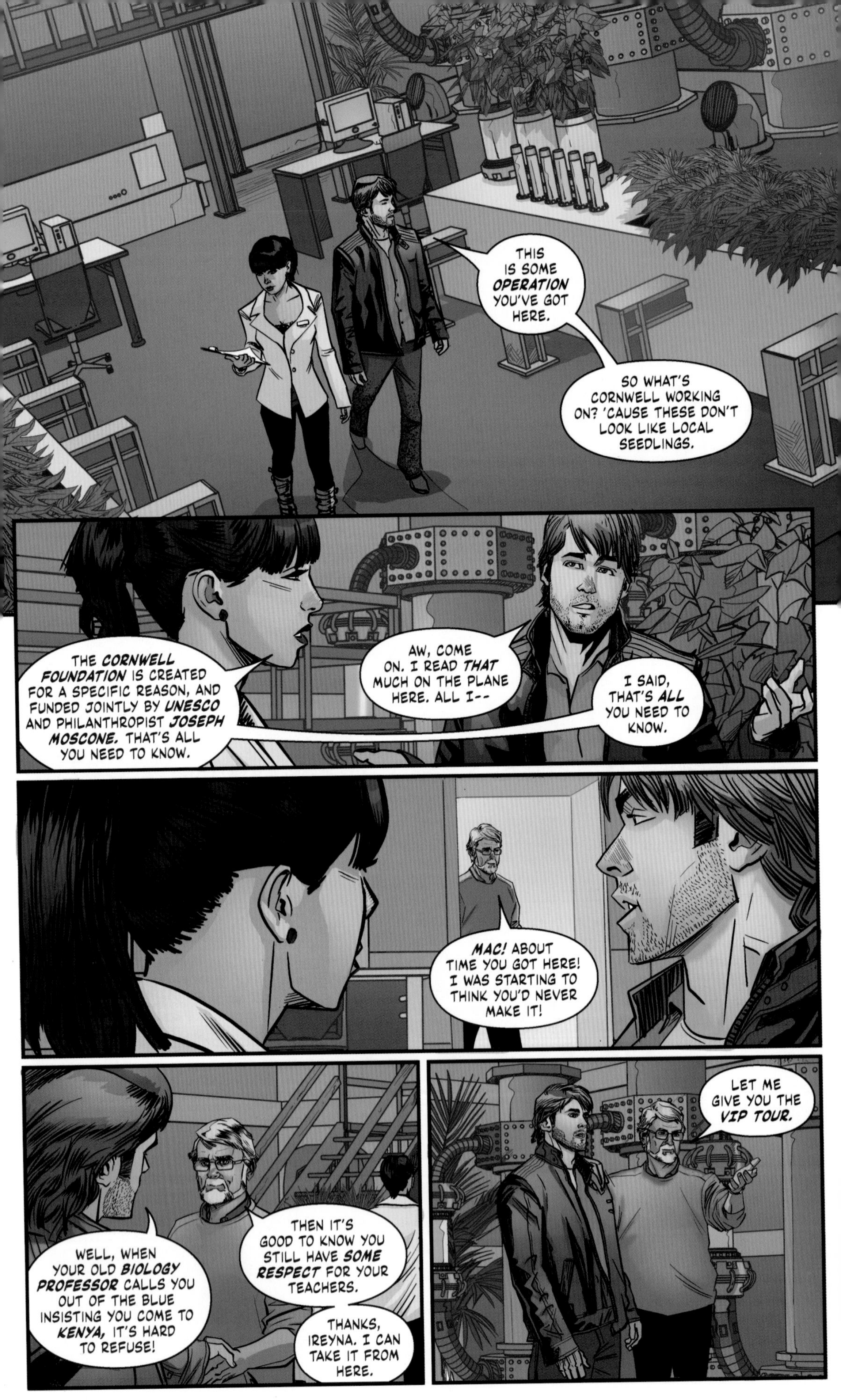
THIS IS SOME OPERATION YOU'VE GOT HERE.
SO WHAT'S CORNWELL WORKING ON? 'CAUSE THESE DON'T LOOK LIKE LOCAL SEEDLINGS.
THE CORNWELL FOUNDATION IS CREATED FOR A SPECIFIC REASON, AND FUNDED JOINTLY BY UNESCO AND PHILANTHROPIST JOSEPH MOSCONE. THAT'S ALL YOU NEED TO KNOW.
AW, COME ON. I READ THAT MUCH ON THE PLANE HERE. ALL I--
I SAID, THAT'S ALL YOU NEED TO KNOW.
MAC! ABOUT TIME YOU GOT HERE! I WAS STARTING TO THINK YOU'D NEVER MAKE IT!
WELL, WHEN YOUR OLD BIOLOGY PROFESSOR CALLS YOU OUT OF THE BLUE INSISTING YOU COME TO KENYA, IT'S HARD TO REFUSE!
THEN IT'S GOOD TO KNOW YOU STILL HAVE SOME RESPECT FOR YOUR TEACHERS.
THANKS, IREYNA. I CAN TAKE IT FROM HERE.
LET ME GIVE YOU THE VIP TOUR.

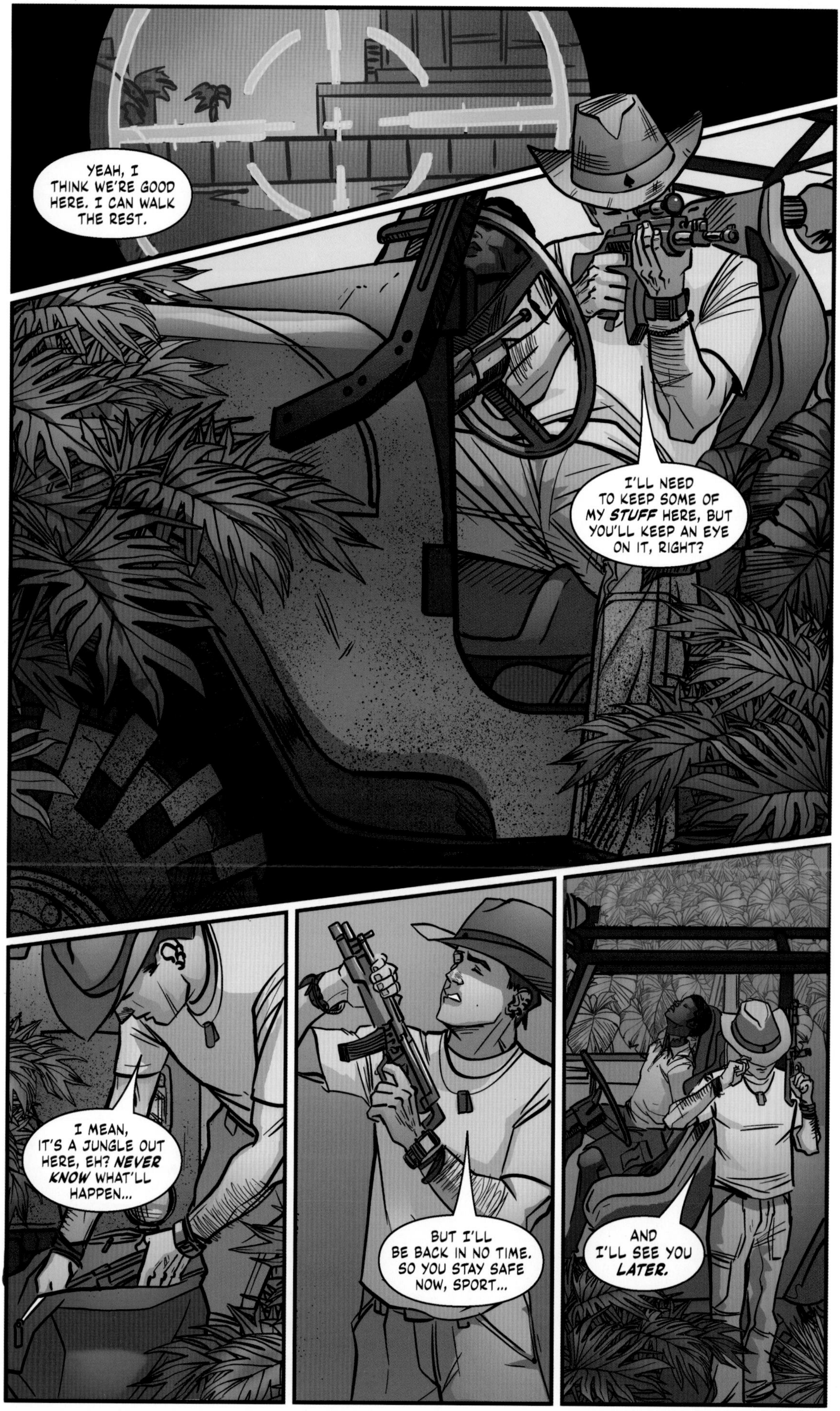
YEAH, I THINK WE'RE GOOD HERE. I CAN WALK THE REST.
I'LL NEED TO KEEP SOME OF MY STUFF HERE, BUT YOU'LL KEEP AN EYE ON IT, RIGHT?
I MEAN, IT'S A JUNGLE OUT HERE, EH? NEVER KNOW WHAT'LL HAPPEN...
BUT I'LL BE BACK IN NO TIME. SO YOU STAY SAFE NOW, SPORT...
AND I'LL SEE YOU LATER.

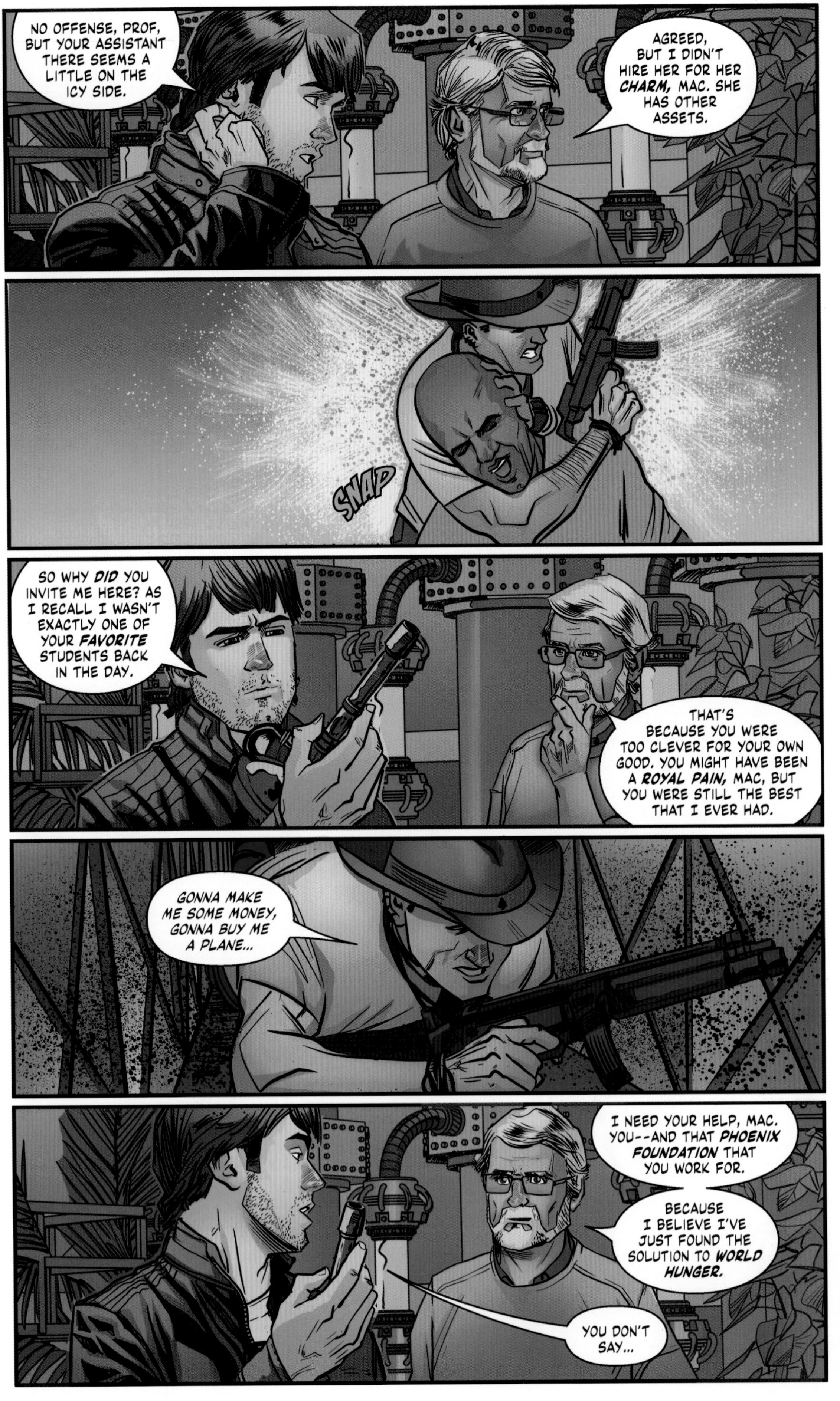
NO OFFENSE, PROF, BUT YOUR ASSISTANT THERE SEEMS A LITTLE ON THE ICY SIDE.
AGREED, BUT I DIDN'T HIRE HER FOR HER *CHARM,* MAC. SHE HAS OTHER ASSETS.
SNAP
SO WHY *DID* YOU INVITE ME HERE? AS I RECALL I WASN'T EXACTLY ONE OF YOUR *FAVORITE* STUDENTS BACK IN THE DAY.
THAT'S BECAUSE YOU WERE TOO CLEVER FOR YOUR OWN GOOD. YOU MIGHT HAVE BEEN A *ROYAL PAIN,* MAC, BUT YOU WERE STILL THE BEST THAT I EVER HAD.
GONNA MAKE ME SOME MONEY, GONNA BUY ME A PLANE...
I NEED YOUR HELP, MAC. YOU--AND THAT *PHOENIX FOUNDATION* THAT YOU WORK FOR.
BECAUSE I BELIEVE I'VE JUST FOUND THE SOLUTION TO *WORLD HUNGER.*
YOU DON'T SAY...

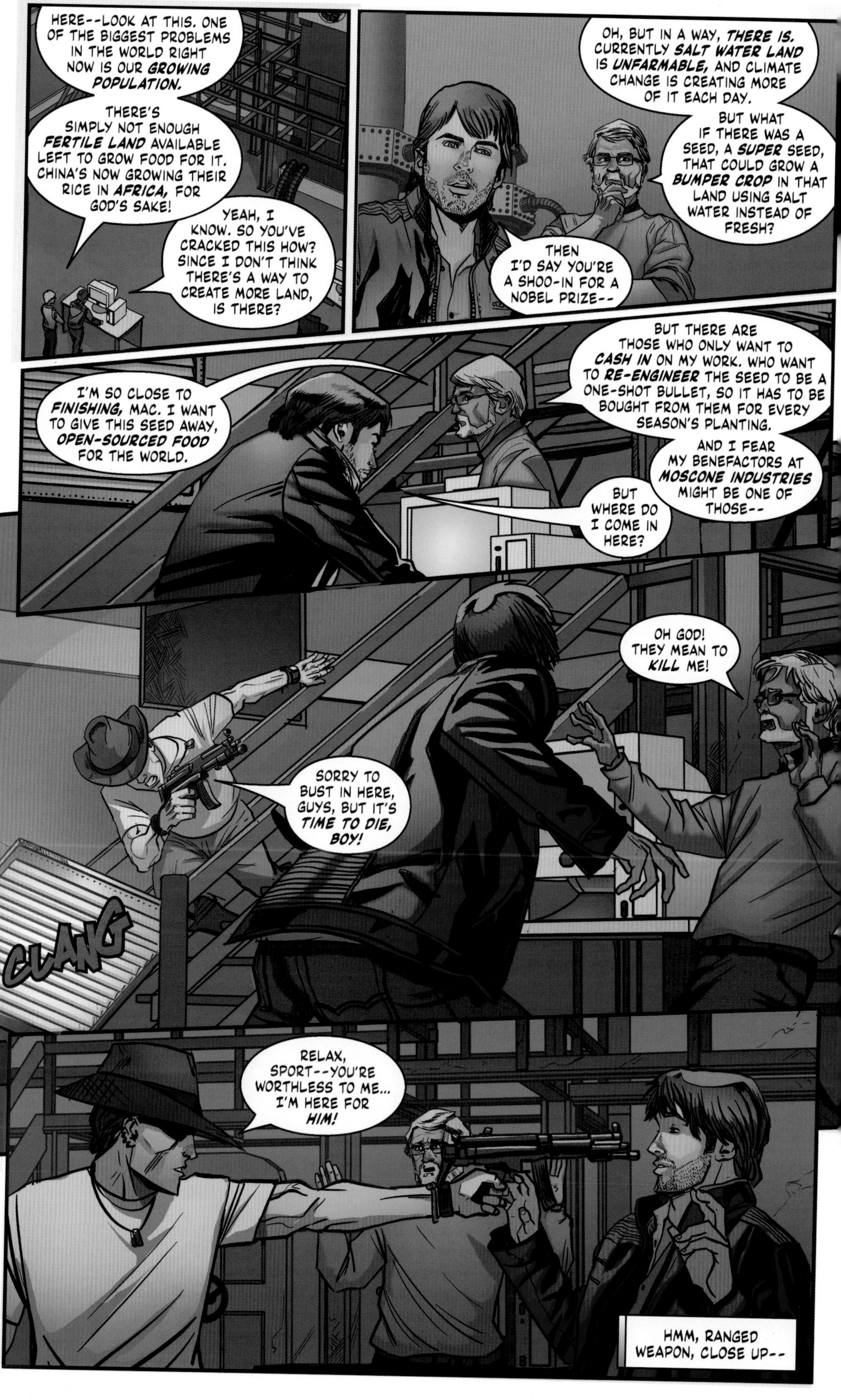
HERE--LOOK AT THIS. ONE OF THE BIGGEST PROBLEMS IN THE WORLD RIGHT NOW IS OUR GROWING POPULATION.
THERE'S SIMPLY NOT ENOUGH FERTILE LAND AVAILABLE LEFT TO GROW FOOD FOR IT. CHINA'S NOW GROWING THEIR RICE IN AFRICA, FOR GOD'S SAKE!
YEAH, I KNOW. SO YOU'VE CRACKED THIS HOW? SINCE I DON'T THINK THERE'S A WAY TO CREATE MORE LAND, IS THERE?
OH, BUT IN A WAY, THERE IS. CURRENTLY SALT WATER LAND IS UNFARMABLE, AND CLIMATE CHANGE IS CREATING MORE OF IT EACH DAY.
BUT WHAT IF THERE WAS A SEED, A SUPER SEED, THAT COULD GROW A BUMPER CROP IN THAT LAND USING SALT WATER INSTEAD OF FRESH?
THEN I'D SAY YOU'RE A SHOO-IN FOR A NOBEL PRIZE--
I'M SO CLOSE TO FINISHING, MAC. I WANT TO GIVE THIS SEED AWAY, OPEN-SOURCED FOOD FOR THE WORLD.
BUT THERE ARE THOSE WHO ONLY WANT TO CASH IN ON MY WORK. WHO WANT TO RE-ENGINEER THE SEED TO BE A ONE-SHOT BULLET, SO IT HAS TO BE BOUGHT FROM THEM FOR EVERY SEASON'S PLANTING.
AND I FEAR MY BENEFACTORS AT MOSCONE INDUSTRIES MIGHT BE ONE OF THOSE--
BUT WHERE DO I COME IN HERE?
OH GOD! THEY MEAN TO KILL ME!
SORRY TO BUST IN HERE, GUYS, BUT IT'S TIME TO DIE, BOY!
CLANG
RELAX, SPORT--YOU'RE WORTHLESS TO ME... I'M HERE FOR HIM!
HMM, RANGED WEAPON, CLOSE UP--

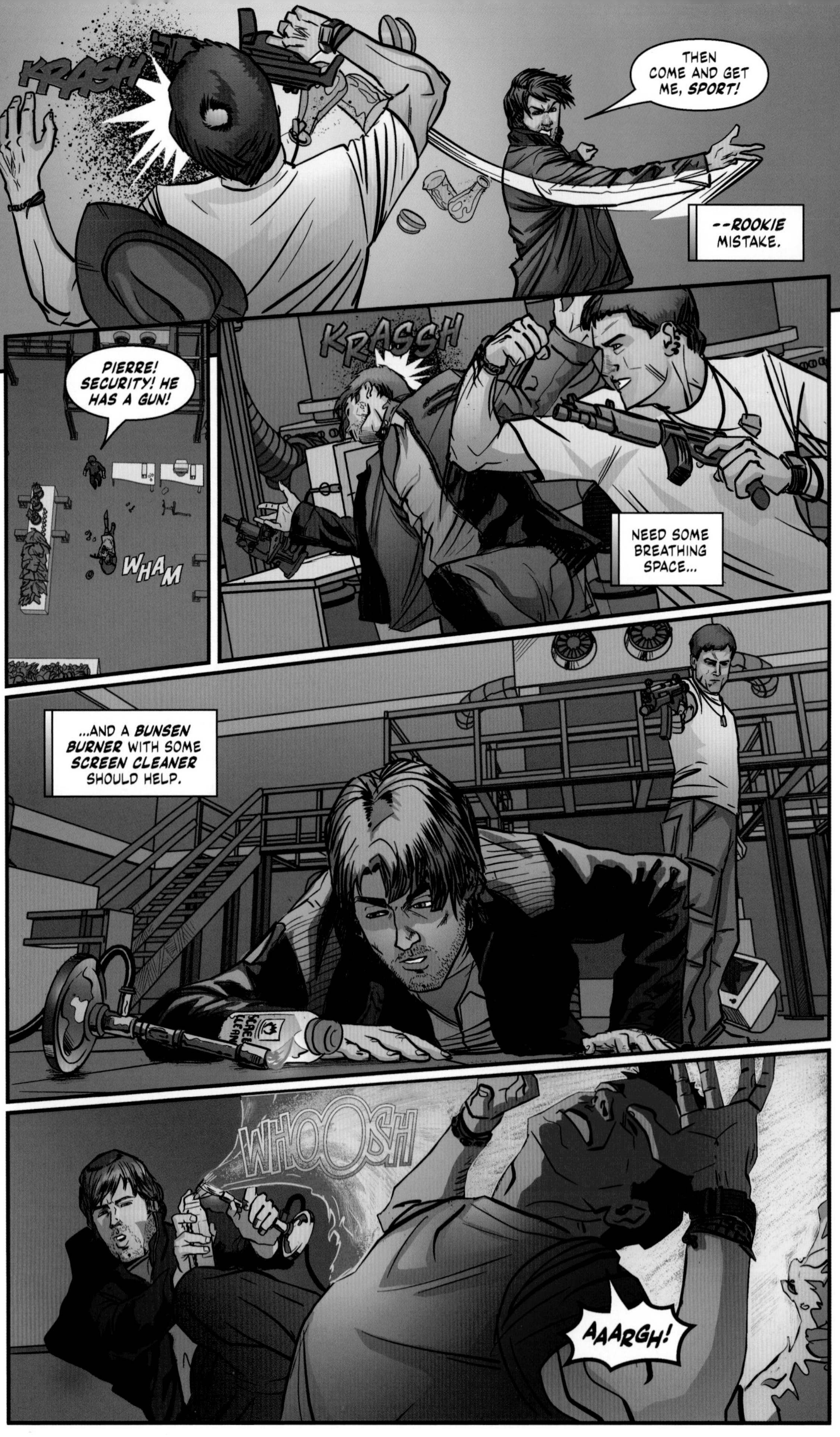
KRASH
THEN COME AND GET ME, SPORT!
--ROOKIE MISTAKE.
PIERRE! SECURITY! HE HAS A GUN!
WHAM
KRASSH
NEED SOME BREATHING SPACE...
...AND A BUNSEN BURNER WITH SOME SCREEN CLEANER SHOULD HELP.
WHOOOSH
AAARGH!

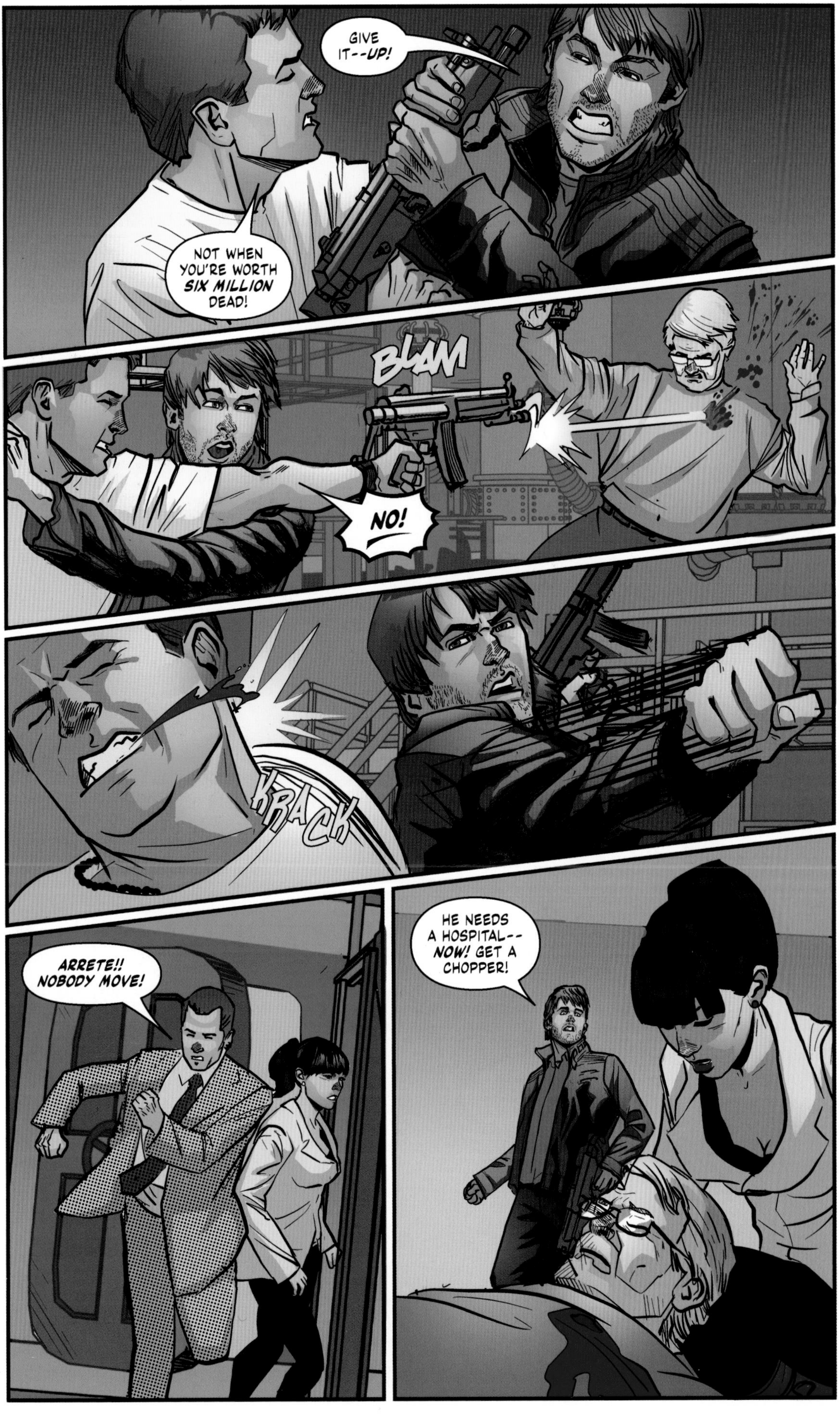
GIVE IT--UP!
NOT WHEN YOU'RE WORTH SIX MILLION DEAD!
BLAM
NO!
KRACK
ARRETE!! NOBODY MOVE!
HE NEEDS A HOSPITAL-- NOW! GET A CHOPPER!

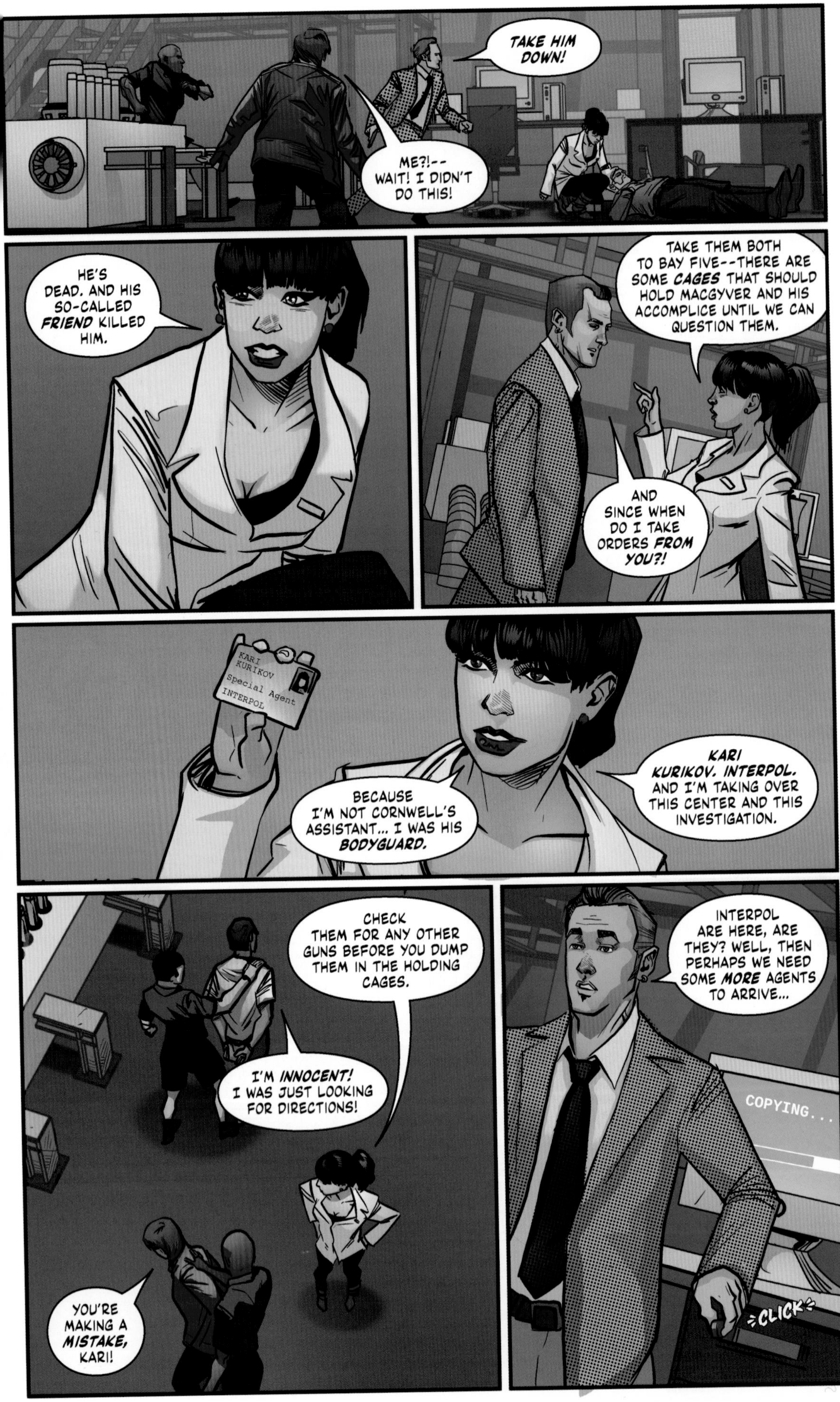
TAKE HIM DOWN!
ME?!-- WAIT! I DIDN'T DO THIS!
HE'S DEAD. AND HIS SO-CALLED FRIEND KILLED HIM.
TAKE THEM BOTH TO BAY FIVE--THERE ARE SOME CAGES THAT SHOULD HOLD MACGYVER AND HIS ACCOMPLICE UNTIL WE CAN QUESTION THEM.
AND SINCE WHEN DO I TAKE ORDERS FROM YOU?!
KARI KURIKOV Special Agent INTERPOL
BECAUSE I'M NOT CORNWELL'S ASSISTANT... I WAS HIS BODYGUARD.
KARI KURIKOV. INTERPOL. AND I'M TAKING OVER THIS CENTER AND THIS INVESTIGATION.
CHECK THEM FOR ANY OTHER GUNS BEFORE YOU DUMP THEM IN THE HOLDING CAGES.
I'M INNOCENT! I WAS JUST LOOKING FOR DIRECTIONS!
YOU'RE MAKING A MISTAKE, KARI!
INTERPOL ARE HERE, ARE THEY? WELL, THEN PERHAPS WE NEED SOME MORE AGENTS TO ARRIVE...
COPYING...
CLICK

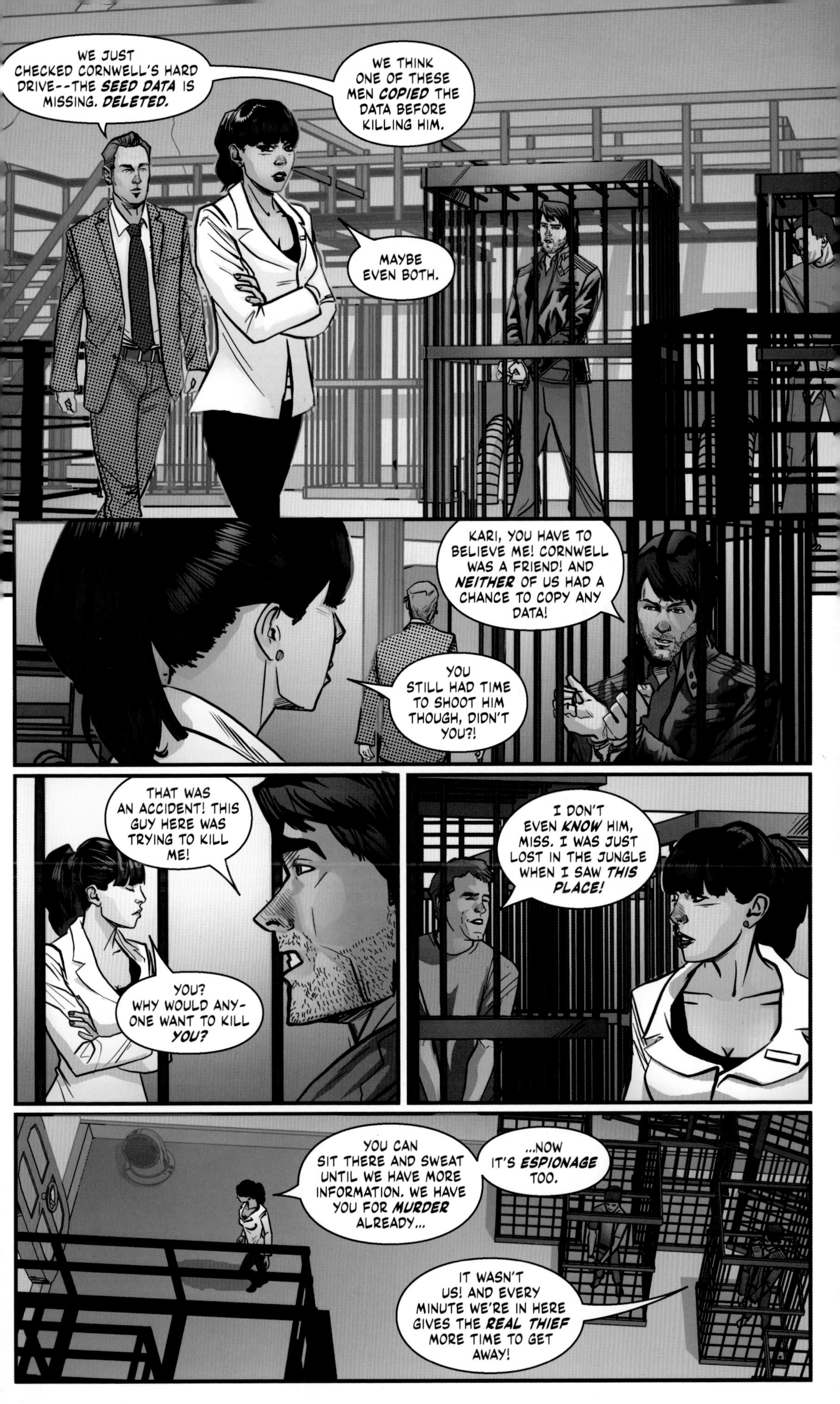
WE JUST CHECKED CORNWELL'S HARD DRIVE--THE **SEED DATA** IS MISSING. **DELETED.**
WE THINK ONE OF THESE MEN **COPIED** THE DATA BEFORE KILLING HIM.
MAYBE EVEN BOTH.
KARI, YOU HAVE TO BELIEVE ME! CORNWELL WAS A FRIEND! AND **NEITHER** OF US HAD A CHANCE TO COPY ANY DATA!
YOU STILL HAD TIME TO SHOOT HIM THOUGH, DIDN'T YOU?!
THAT WAS AN ACCIDENT! THIS GUY HERE WAS TRYING TO KILL ME!
YOU? WHY WOULD ANY-ONE WANT TO KILL **YOU?**
I DON'T EVEN **KNOW** HIM, MISS. I WAS JUST LOST IN THE JUNGLE WHEN I SAW **THIS PLACE!**
YOU CAN SIT THERE AND SWEAT UNTIL WE HAVE MORE INFORMATION. WE HAVE YOU FOR **MURDER** ALREADY...
...NOW IT'S **ESPIONAGE** TOO.
IT WASN'T US! AND EVERY MINUTE WE'RE IN HERE GIVES THE **REAL THIEF** MORE TIME TO GET AWAY!

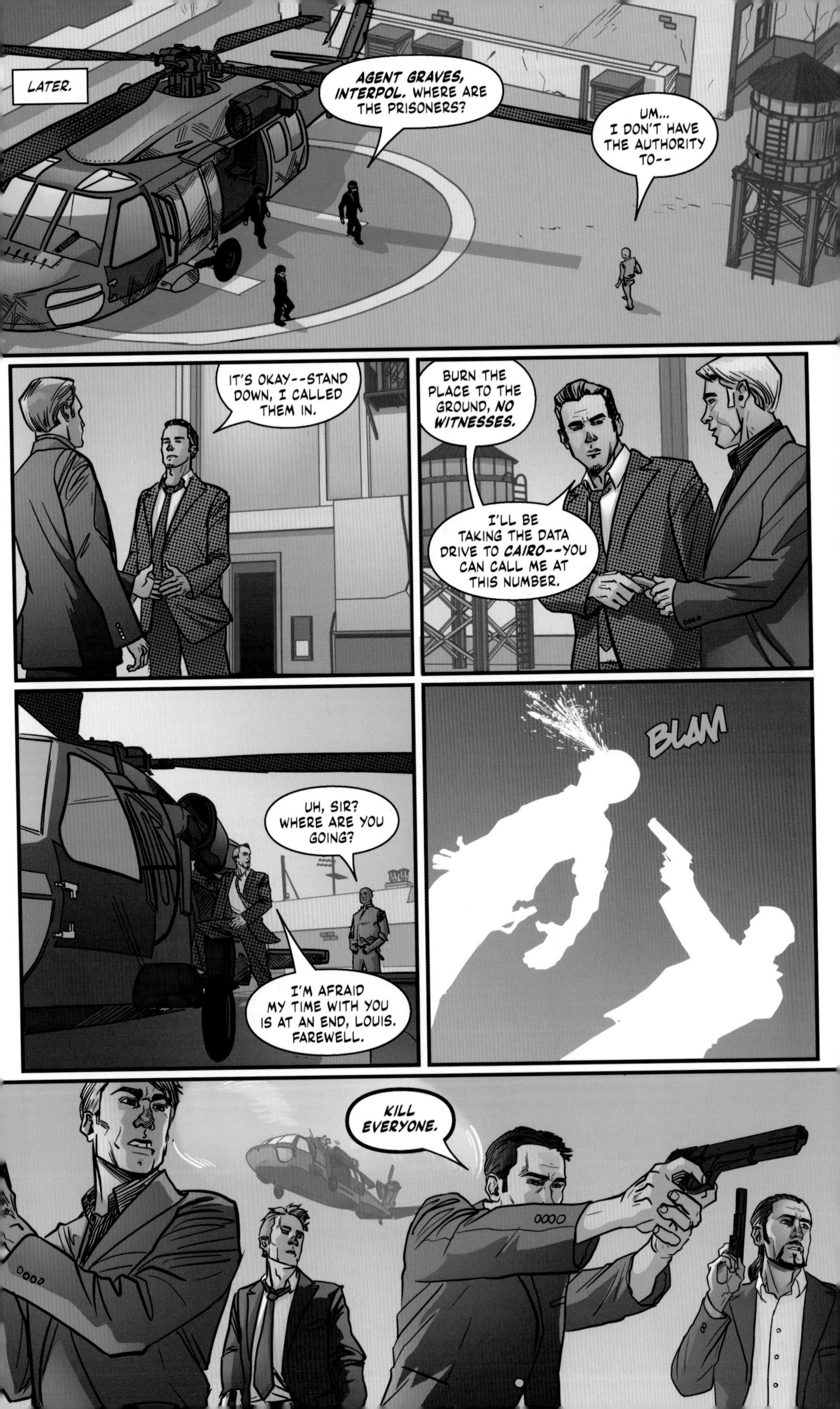
LATER.
AGENT GRAVES, INTERPOL. WHERE ARE THE PRISONERS?
UM... I DON'T HAVE THE AUTHORITY TO--
IT'S OKAY--STAND DOWN, I CALLED THEM IN.
BURN THE PLACE TO THE GROUND, NO WITNESSES.
I'LL BE TAKING THE DATA DRIVE TO CAIRO--YOU CAN CALL ME AT THIS NUMBER.
UH, SIR? WHERE ARE YOU GOING?
I'M AFRAID MY TIME WITH YOU IS AT AN END, LOUIS. FAREWELL.
BLAM
KILL EVERYONE.

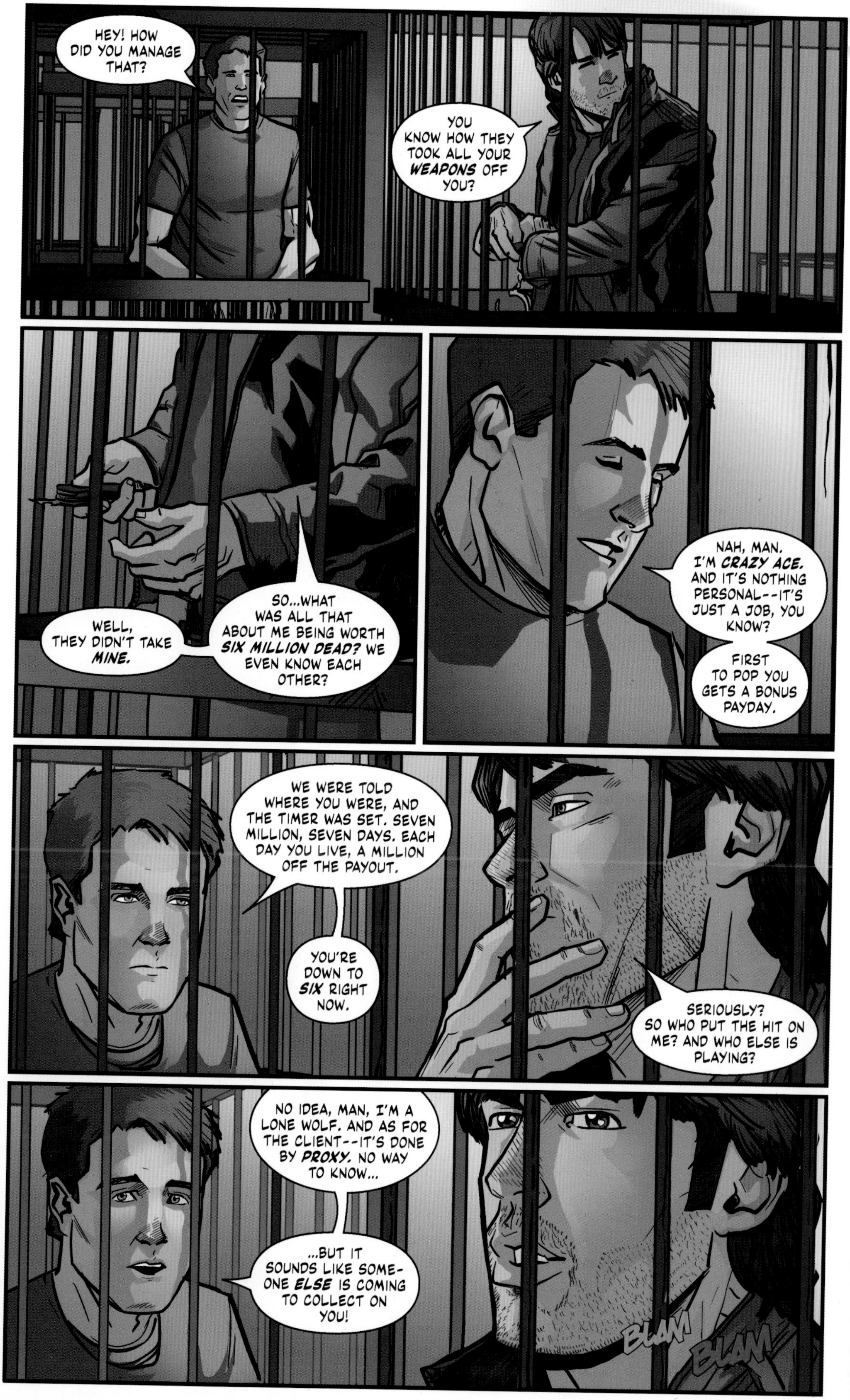
HEY! HOW DID YOU MANAGE THAT?
YOU KNOW HOW THEY TOOK ALL YOUR WEAPONS OFF YOU?
WELL, THEY DIDN'T TAKE MINE.
SO...WHAT WAS ALL THAT ABOUT ME BEING WORTH SIX MILLION DEAD? WE EVEN KNOW EACH OTHER?
NAH, MAN. I'M CRAZY ACE. AND IT'S NOTHING PERSONAL--IT'S JUST A JOB, YOU KNOW?
FIRST TO POP YOU GETS A BONUS PAYDAY.
WE WERE TOLD WHERE YOU WERE, AND THE TIMER WAS SET. SEVEN MILLION, SEVEN DAYS. EACH DAY YOU LIVE, A MILLION OFF THE PAYOUT.
YOU'RE DOWN TO SIX RIGHT NOW.
SERIOUSLY? SO WHO PUT THE HIT ON ME? AND WHO ELSE IS PLAYING?
NO IDEA, MAN, I'M A LONE WOLF. AND AS FOR THE CLIENT--IT'S DONE BY PROXY. NO WAY TO KNOW...
...BUT IT SOUNDS LIKE SOME-ONE ELSE IS COMING TO COLLECT ON YOU!
BLAM
BLAM

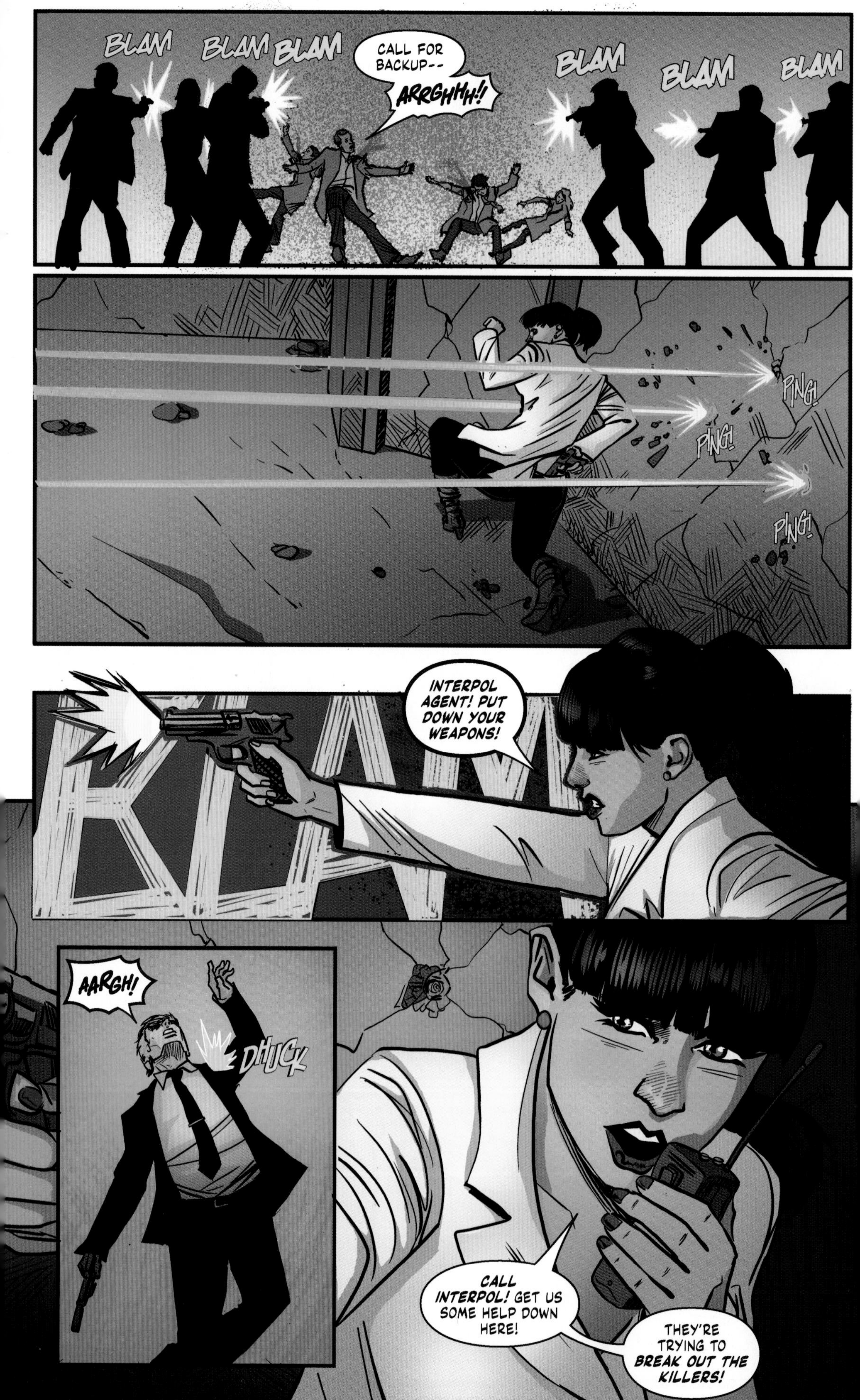
BLAM
BLAM
BLAM
CALL FOR BACKUP-- ARRGHHH!!
BLAM
BLAM
BLAM
PING!
PING!
PING!
INTERPOL AGENT! PUT DOWN YOUR WEAPONS!
AARGH!
DHUCK
CALL INTERPOL! GET US SOME HELP DOWN HERE!
THEY'RE TRYING TO BREAK OUT THE KILLERS!

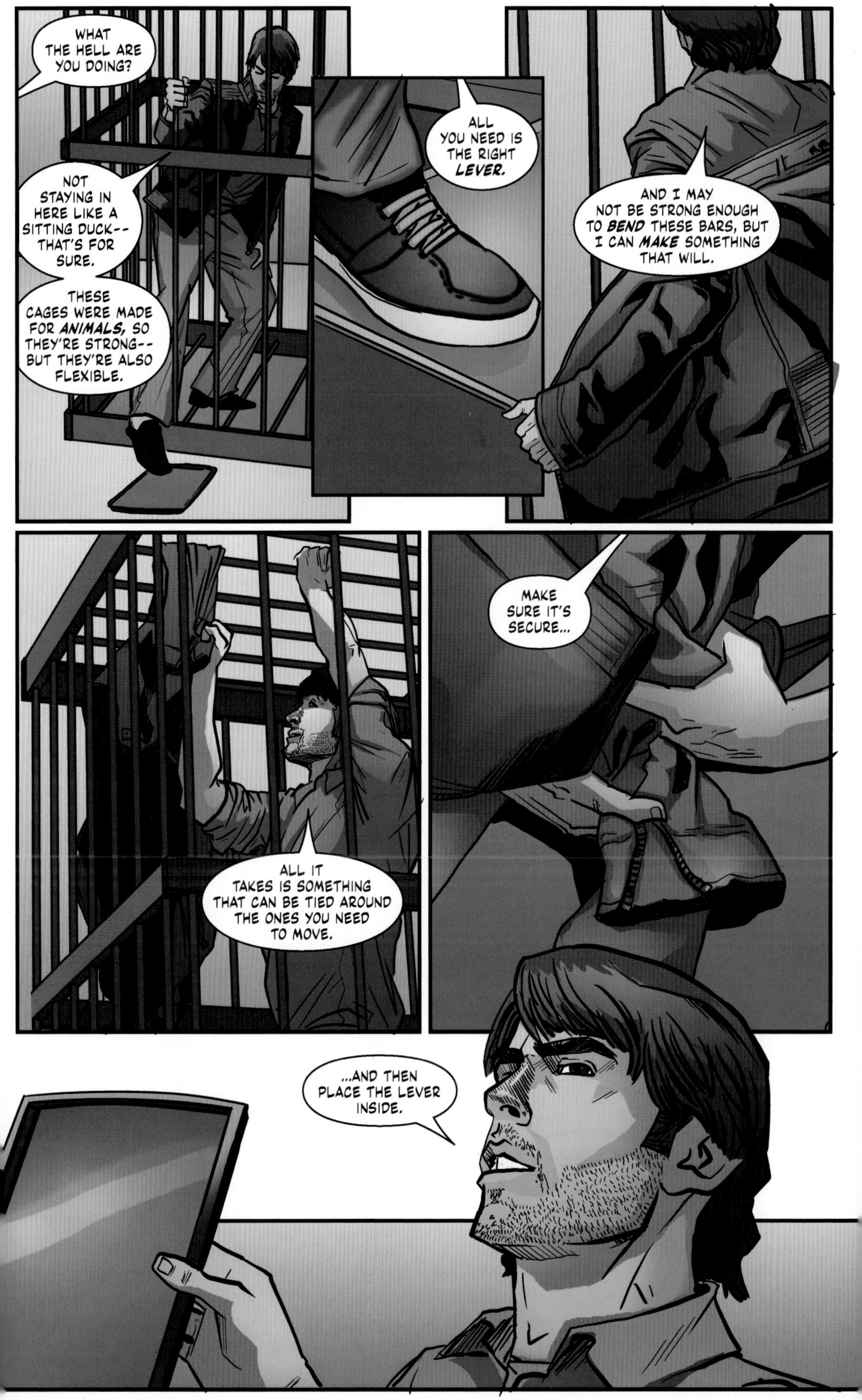

WHAT THE HELL ARE YOU DOING?
NOT STAYING IN HERE LIKE A SITTING DUCK-- THAT'S FOR SURE.
THESE CAGES WERE MADE FOR *ANIMALS,* SO THEY'RE STRONG-- BUT THEY'RE ALSO FLEXIBLE.
ALL YOU NEED IS THE RIGHT *LEVER.*
AND I MAY NOT BE STRONG ENOUGH TO *BEND* THESE BARS, BUT I CAN *MAKE* SOMETHING THAT WILL.
ALL IT TAKES IS SOMETHING THAT CAN BE TIED AROUND THE ONES YOU NEED TO MOVE.
MAKE SURE IT'S SECURE...
...AND THEN PLACE THE LEVER INSIDE.

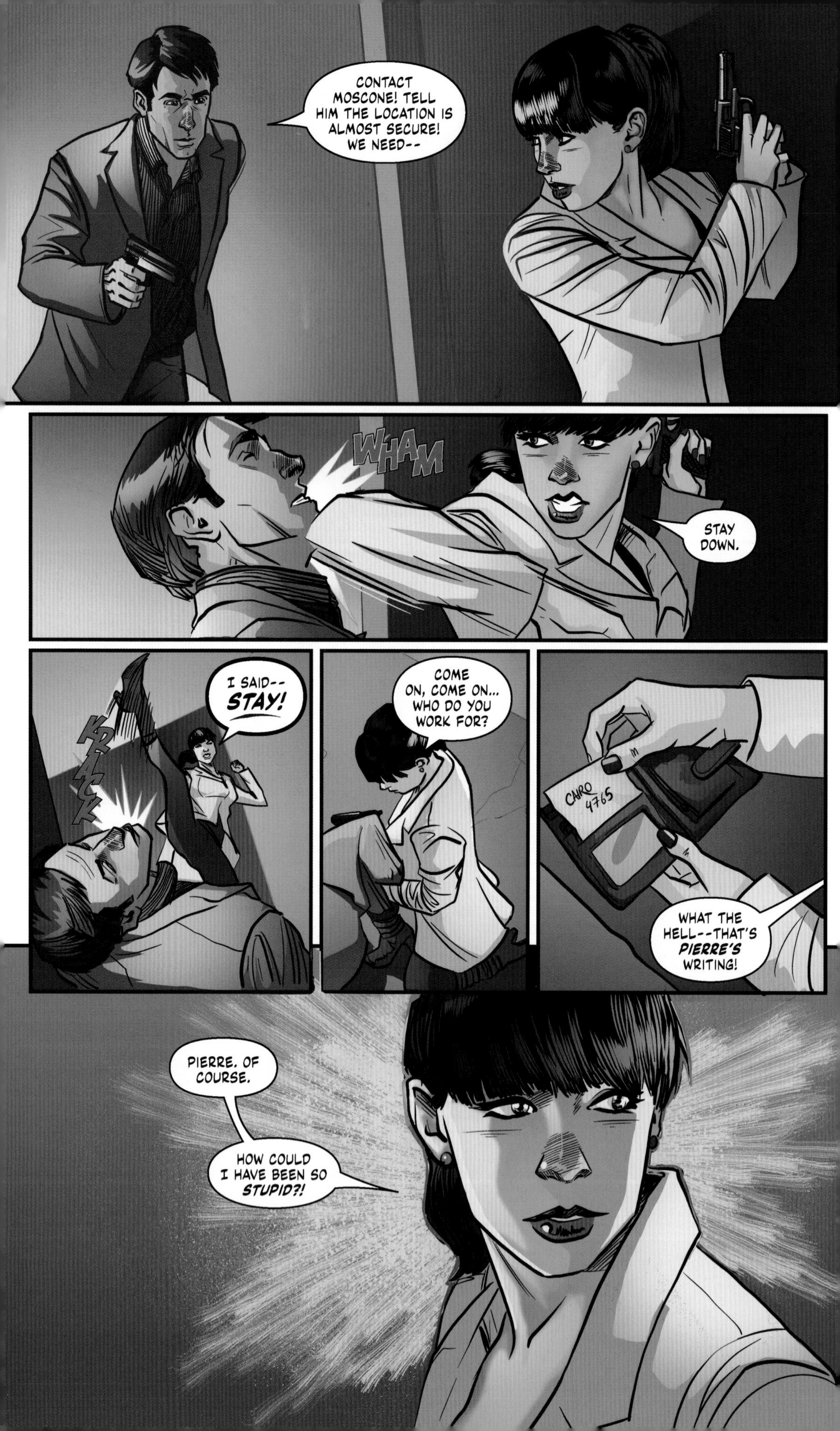
CONTACT MOSCONE! TELL HIM THE LOCATION IS ALMOST SECURE! WE NEED--
WHAM
STAY DOWN.
KRACK
I SAID-- STAY!
COME ON, COME ON... WHO DO YOU WORK FOR?
CAIRO 4765
WHAT THE HELL--THAT'S PIERRE'S WRITING!
PIERRE. OF COURSE.
HOW COULD I HAVE BEEN SO STUPID?!

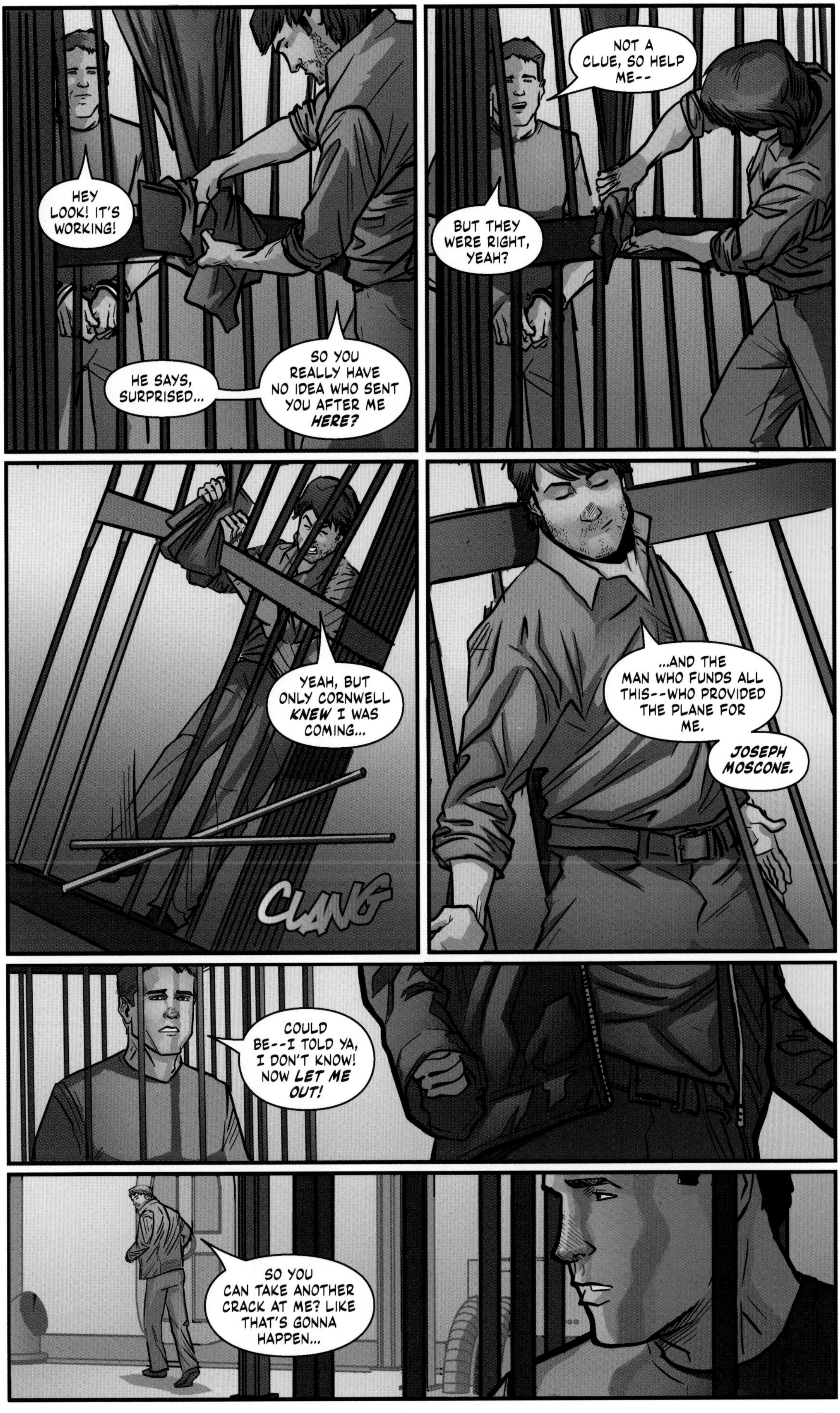
HEY LOOK! IT'S WORKING!
HE SAYS, SURPRISED...
SO YOU REALLY HAVE NO IDEA WHO SENT YOU AFTER ME *HERE?*
NOT A CLUE, SO HELP ME--
BUT THEY WERE RIGHT, YEAH?
YEAH, BUT ONLY CORNWELL *KNEW* I WAS COMING...
CLANG
...AND THE MAN WHO FUNDS ALL THIS--WHO PROVIDED THE PLANE FOR ME.
JOSEPH MOSCONE.
COULD BE--I TOLD YA, I DON'T KNOW! NOW *LET ME OUT!*
SO YOU CAN TAKE ANOTHER CRACK AT ME? LIKE THAT'S GONNA HAPPEN...

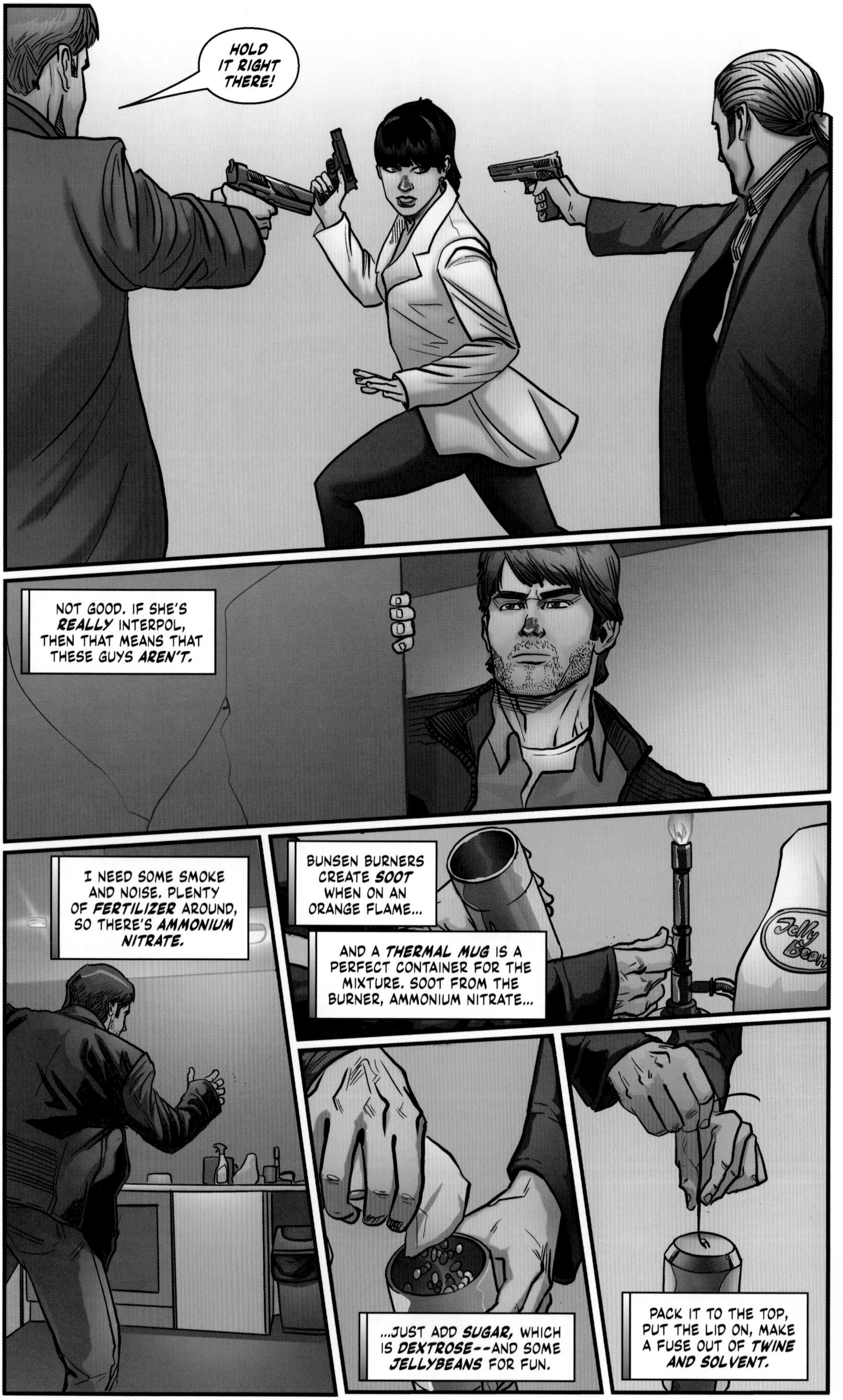
HOLD IT RIGHT THERE!
NOT GOOD. IF SHE'S REALLY INTERPOL, THEN THAT MEANS THAT THESE GUYS AREN'T.
I NEED SOME SMOKE AND NOISE. PLENTY OF FERTILIZER AROUND, SO THERE'S AMMONIUM NITRATE.
BUNSEN BURNERS CREATE SOOT WHEN ON AN ORANGE FLAME...
AND A THERMAL MUG IS A PERFECT CONTAINER FOR THE MIXTURE. SOOT FROM THE BURNER, AMMONIUM NITRATE...
...JUST ADD SUGAR, WHICH IS DEXTROSE--AND SOME JELLYBEANS FOR FUN.
PACK IT TO THE TOP, PUT THE LID ON, MAKE A FUSE OUT OF TWINE AND SOLVENT.

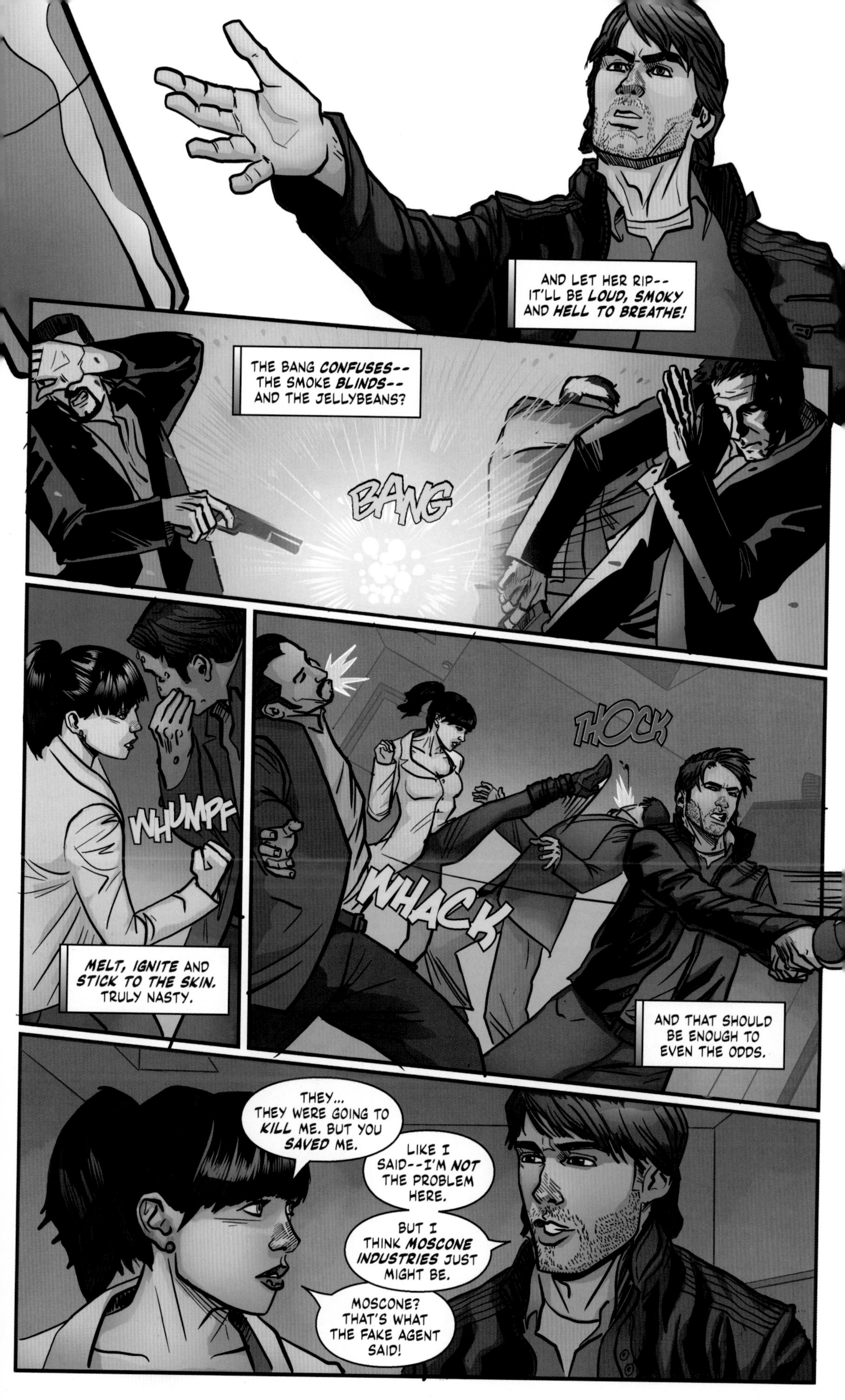
AND LET HER RIP--
IT'LL BE LOUD, SMOKY
AND HELL TO BREATHE!
THE BANG CONFUSES--
THE SMOKE BLINDS--
AND THE JELLYBEANS?
BANG
WHUMPF
MELT, IGNITE AND
STICK TO THE SKIN.
TRULY NASTY.
THOCK
WHACK
AND THAT SHOULD
BE ENOUGH TO
EVEN THE ODDS.
THEY... THEY WERE GOING TO KILL ME. BUT YOU SAVED ME.
LIKE I SAID--I'M NOT THE PROBLEM HERE.
BUT I THINK MOSCONE INDUSTRIES JUST MIGHT BE.
MOSCONE? THAT'S WHAT THE FAKE AGENT SAID!

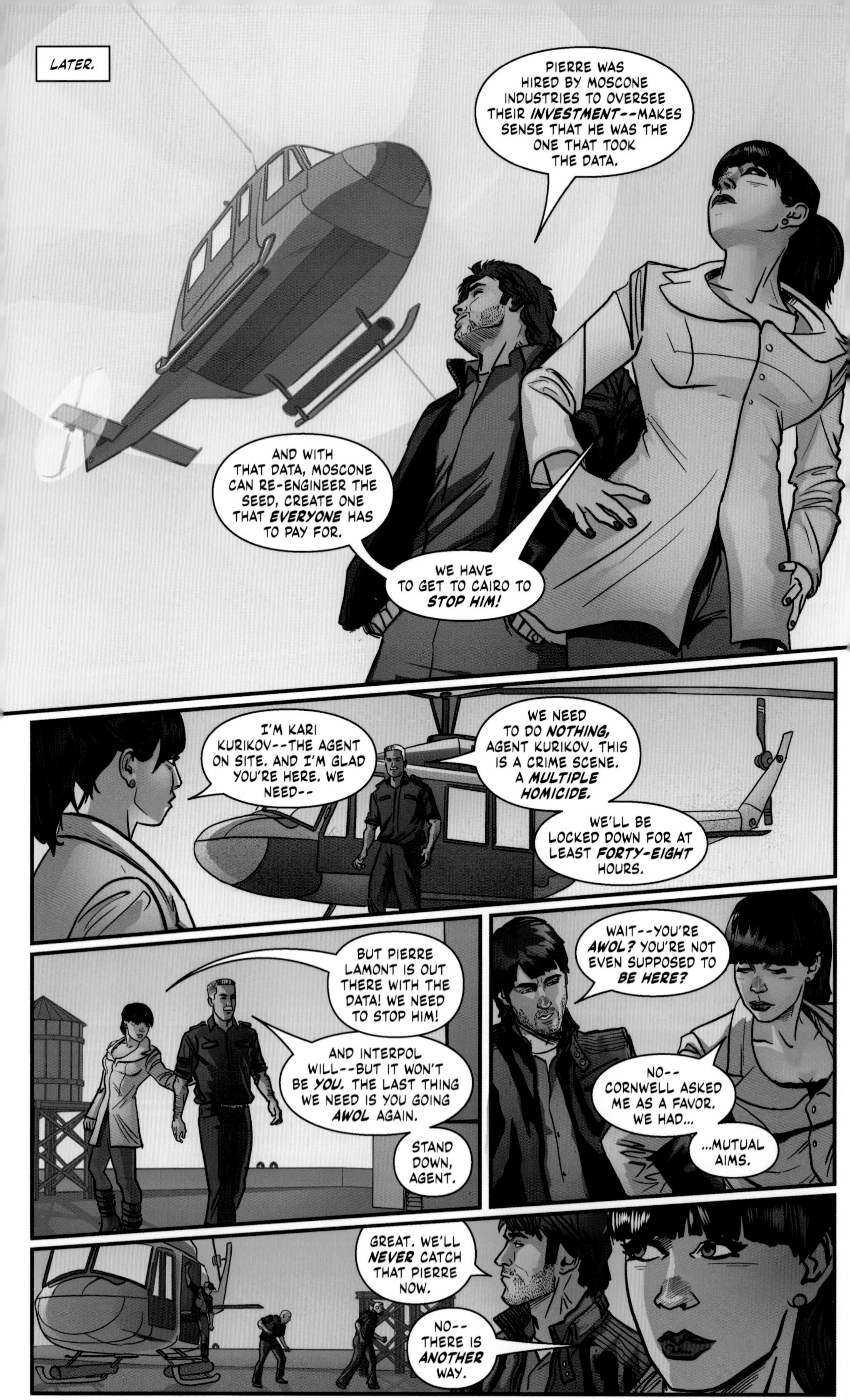
LATER.
PIERRE WAS HIRED BY MOSCONE INDUSTRIES TO OVERSEE THEIR INVESTMENT--MAKES SENSE THAT HE WAS THE ONE THAT TOOK THE DATA.
AND WITH THAT DATA, MOSCONE CAN RE-ENGINEER THE SEED, CREATE ONE THAT EVERYONE HAS TO PAY FOR.
WE HAVE TO GET TO CAIRO TO STOP HIM!
I'M KARI KURIKOV--THE AGENT ON SITE. AND I'M GLAD YOU'RE HERE. WE NEED--
WE NEED TO DO NOTHING, AGENT KURIKOV. THIS IS A CRIME SCENE. A MULTIPLE HOMICIDE.
WE'LL BE LOCKED DOWN FOR AT LEAST FORTY-EIGHT HOURS.
BUT PIERRE LAMONT IS OUT THERE WITH THE DATA! WE NEED TO STOP HIM!
AND INTERPOL WILL--BUT IT WON'T BE YOU. THE LAST THING WE NEED IS YOU GOING AWOL AGAIN.
STAND DOWN, AGENT.
WAIT--YOU'RE AWOL? YOU'RE NOT EVEN SUPPOSED TO BE HERE?
NO-- CORNWELL ASKED ME AS A FAVOR. WE HAD...
...MUTUAL AIMS.
GREAT. WE'LL NEVER CATCH THAT PIERRE NOW.
NO-- THERE IS ANOTHER WAY.

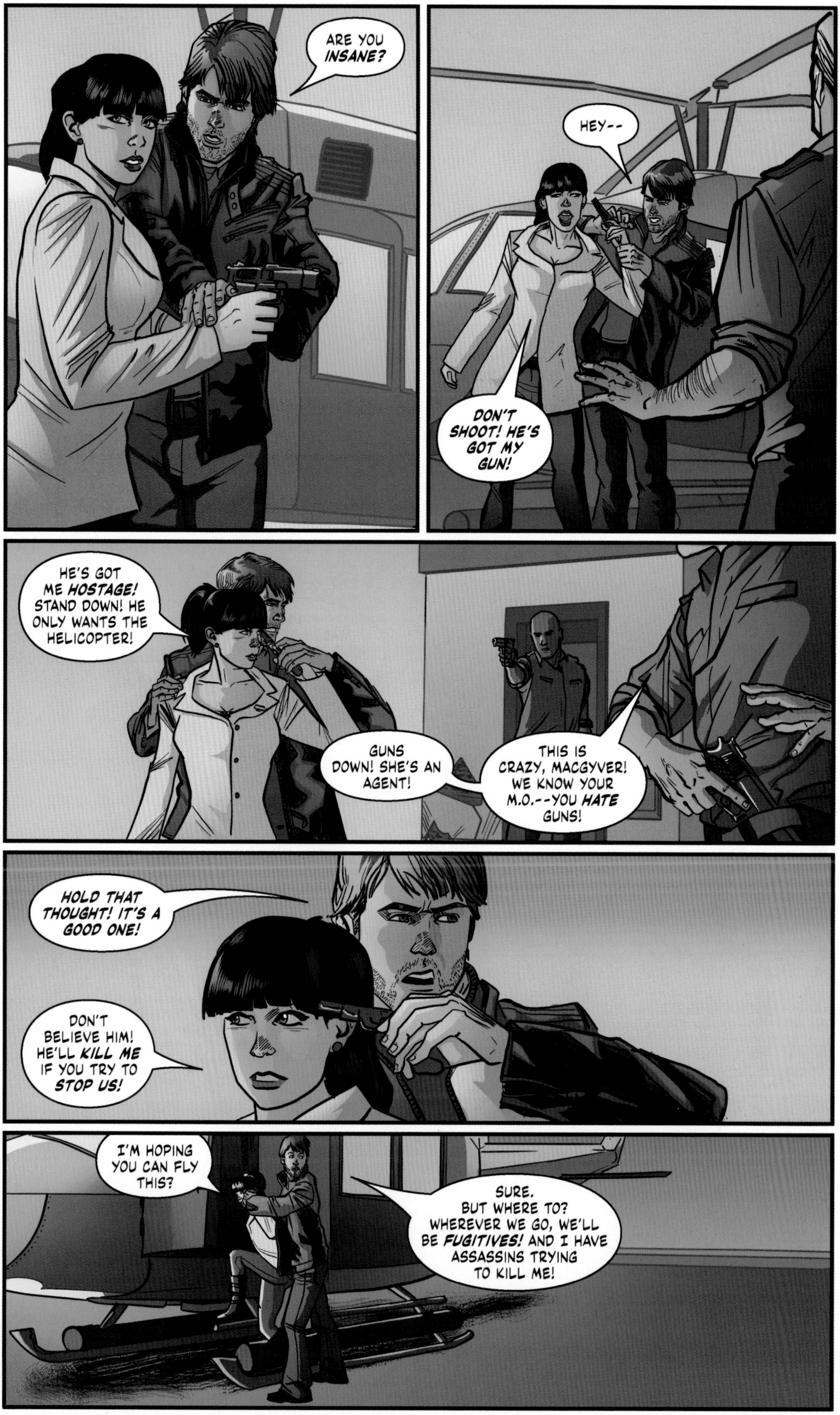
ARE YOU *INSANE?*
HEY--
DON'T SHOOT! HE'S GOT MY GUN!
HE'S GOT ME *HOSTAGE!* STAND DOWN! HE ONLY WANTS THE HELICOPTER!
GUNS DOWN! SHE'S AN AGENT!
THIS IS CRAZY, MACGYVER! WE KNOW YOUR M.O.--YOU *HATE* GUNS!
HOLD THAT THOUGHT! IT'S A GOOD ONE!
DON'T BELIEVE HIM! HE'LL *KILL ME* IF YOU TRY TO *STOP US!*
I'M HOPING YOU CAN FLY THIS?
SURE. BUT WHERE TO? WHEREVER WE GO, WE'LL BE *FUGITIVES!* AND I HAVE ASSASSINS TRYING TO KILL ME!

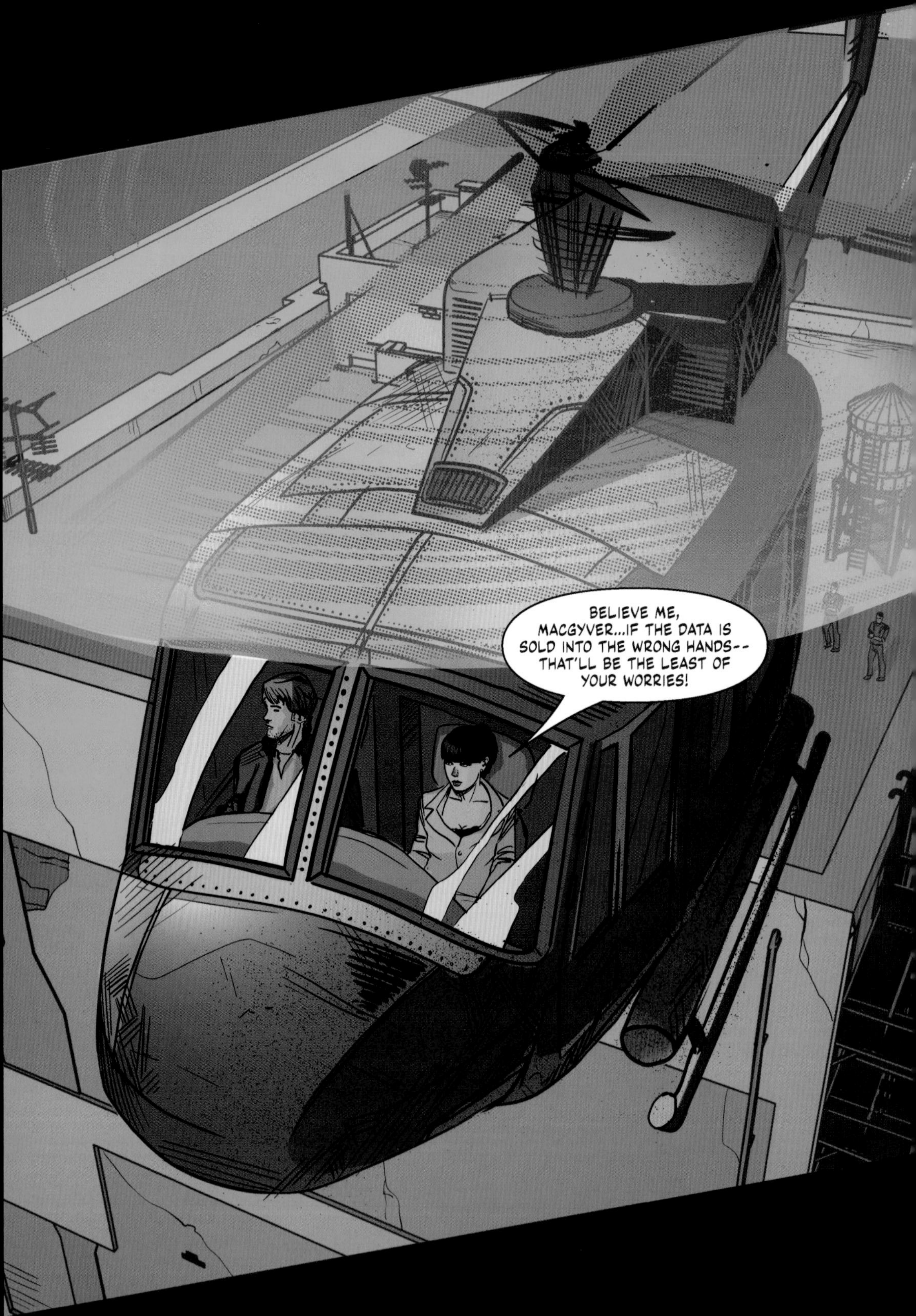
BELIEVE ME, MACGYVER...IF THE DATA IS SOLD INTO THE WRONG HANDS-- THAT'LL BE THE LEAST OF YOUR WORRIES!

END OF PART ONE.

CHINESE EMBASSY.
CAIRO.

<SO WHAT DO WE HAVE FOR ME TODAY, LAU?>*

* TRANSLATED FROM THE CHINESE.

<THERE IS A VISIT FROM THE GREEK AMBASSADOR THIS MORNING, YOUR EXCELLENCY. AND THE RUSSIAN AMBASSADOR WISHES TO SEE YOU THIS AFTERNOON-->

<ME? OR DO YOU MEAN OUR AMBASSADOR HERE?>

<MANY APOLOGIES--SOMETIMES I FORGET THAT, AS HEAD OF SECURITY, YOU ARE NOT TRULY IN COMMAND.>

<SUCH IS THE BURDEN I MUST BEAR, LAU.>

<WAIT-- THIS CAME IN TODAY? THIS MAN IS ALREADY IN CAIRO?>

<NOT OFFICIALLY, BUT IT IS BELIEVED SO, EXCELLENCY. YOU KNOW OF HIM?>

多次性高潮的
勝利你認為你
些告訴來自地
的天堂你以
可以告訴
裏你交易
雄鬼熱
色的

MACGYVER...

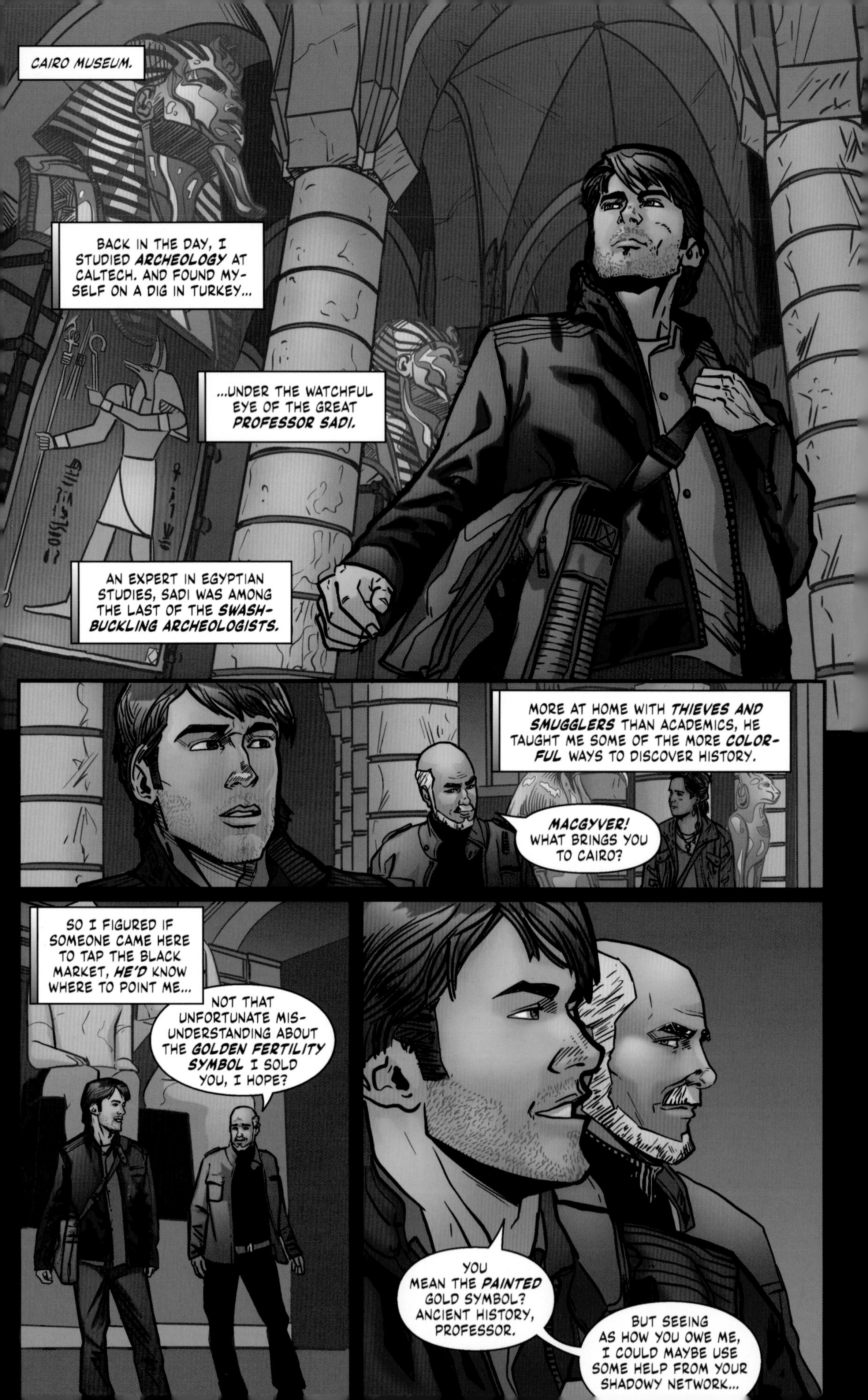
CAIRO MUSEUM.
BACK IN THE DAY, I STUDIED ARCHEOLOGY AT CALTECH. AND FOUND MY-SELF ON A DIG IN TURKEY...
...UNDER THE WATCHFUL EYE OF THE GREAT PROFESSOR SADI.
AN EXPERT IN EGYPTIAN STUDIES, SADI WAS AMONG THE LAST OF THE SWASH-BUCKLING ARCHEOLOGISTS.
MORE AT HOME WITH THIEVES AND SMUGGLERS THAN ACADEMICS, HE TAUGHT ME SOME OF THE MORE COLOR-FUL WAYS TO DISCOVER HISTORY.
MACGYVER! WHAT BRINGS YOU TO CAIRO?
SO I FIGURED IF SOMEONE CAME HERE TO TAP THE BLACK MARKET, HE'D KNOW WHERE TO POINT ME...
NOT THAT UNFORTUNATE MIS-UNDERSTANDING ABOUT THE GOLDEN FERTILITY SYMBOL I SOLD YOU, I HOPE?
YOU MEAN THE PAINTED GOLD SYMBOL? ANCIENT HISTORY, PROFESSOR.
BUT SEEING AS HOW YOU OWE ME, I COULD MAYBE USE SOME HELP FROM YOUR SHADOWY NETWORK...

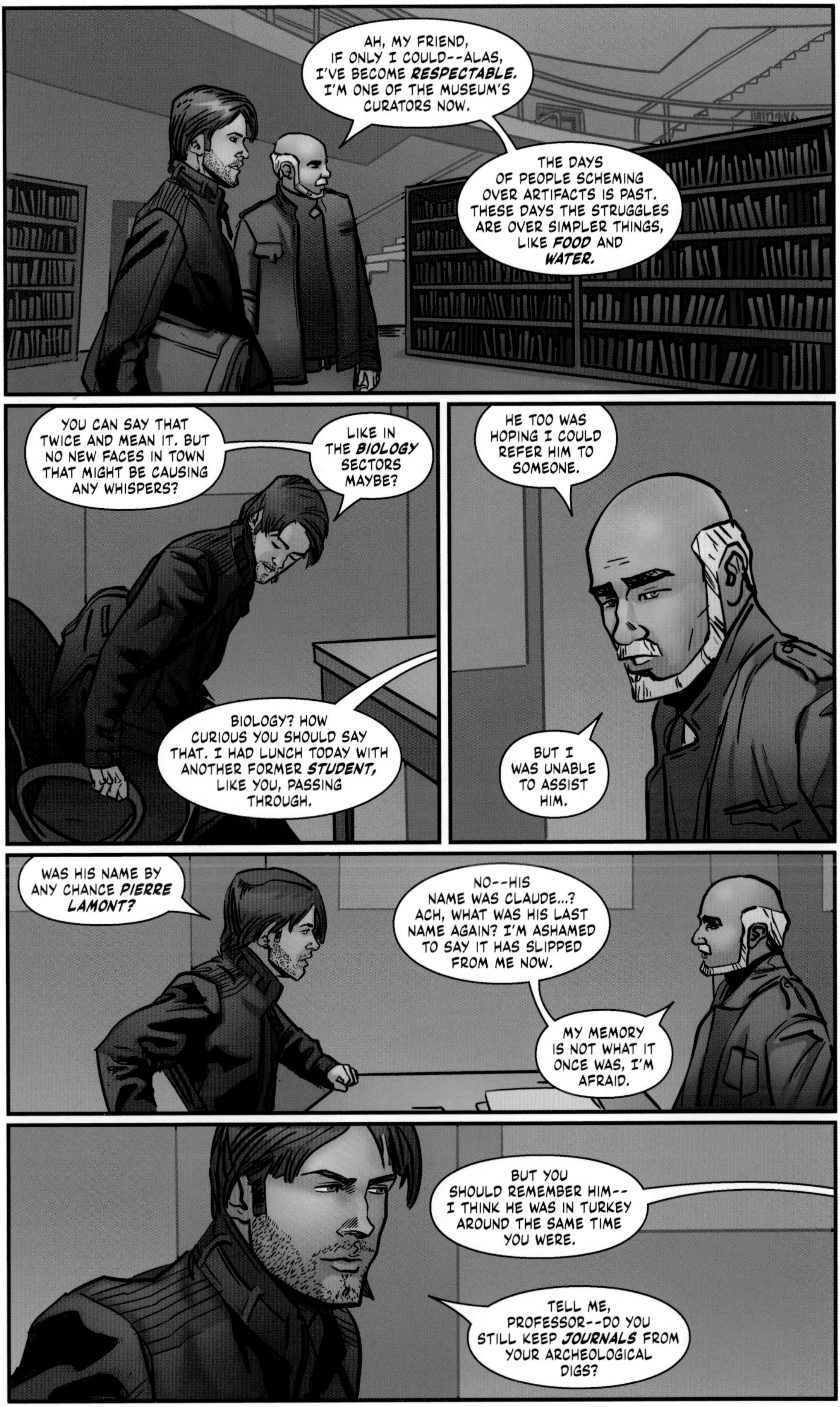
AH, MY FRIEND, IF ONLY I COULD--ALAS, I'VE BECOME ***RESPECTABLE.*** I'M ONE OF THE MUSEUM'S CURATORS NOW.
THE DAYS OF PEOPLE SCHEMING OVER ARTIFACTS IS PAST. THESE DAYS THE STRUGGLES ARE OVER SIMPLER THINGS, LIKE ***FOOD*** AND ***WATER.***
YOU CAN SAY THAT TWICE AND MEAN IT. BUT NO NEW FACES IN TOWN THAT MIGHT BE CAUSING ANY WHISPERS?
LIKE IN THE ***BIOLOGY*** SECTORS MAYBE?
BIOLOGY? HOW CURIOUS YOU SHOULD SAY THAT. I HAD LUNCH TODAY WITH ANOTHER FORMER ***STUDENT,*** LIKE YOU, PASSING THROUGH.
HE TOO WAS HOPING I COULD REFER HIM TO SOMEONE.
BUT I WAS UNABLE TO ASSIST HIM.
WAS HIS NAME BY ANY CHANCE ***PIERRE LAMONT?***
NO--HIS NAME WAS CLAUDE...? ACH, WHAT WAS HIS LAST NAME AGAIN? I'M ASHAMED TO SAY IT HAS SLIPPED FROM ME NOW.
MY MEMORY IS NOT WHAT IT ONCE WAS, I'M AFRAID.
BUT YOU SHOULD REMEMBER HIM-- I THINK HE WAS IN TURKEY AROUND THE SAME TIME YOU WERE.
TELL ME, PROFESSOR--DO YOU STILL KEEP ***JOURNALS*** FROM YOUR ARCHEOLOGICAL DIGS?

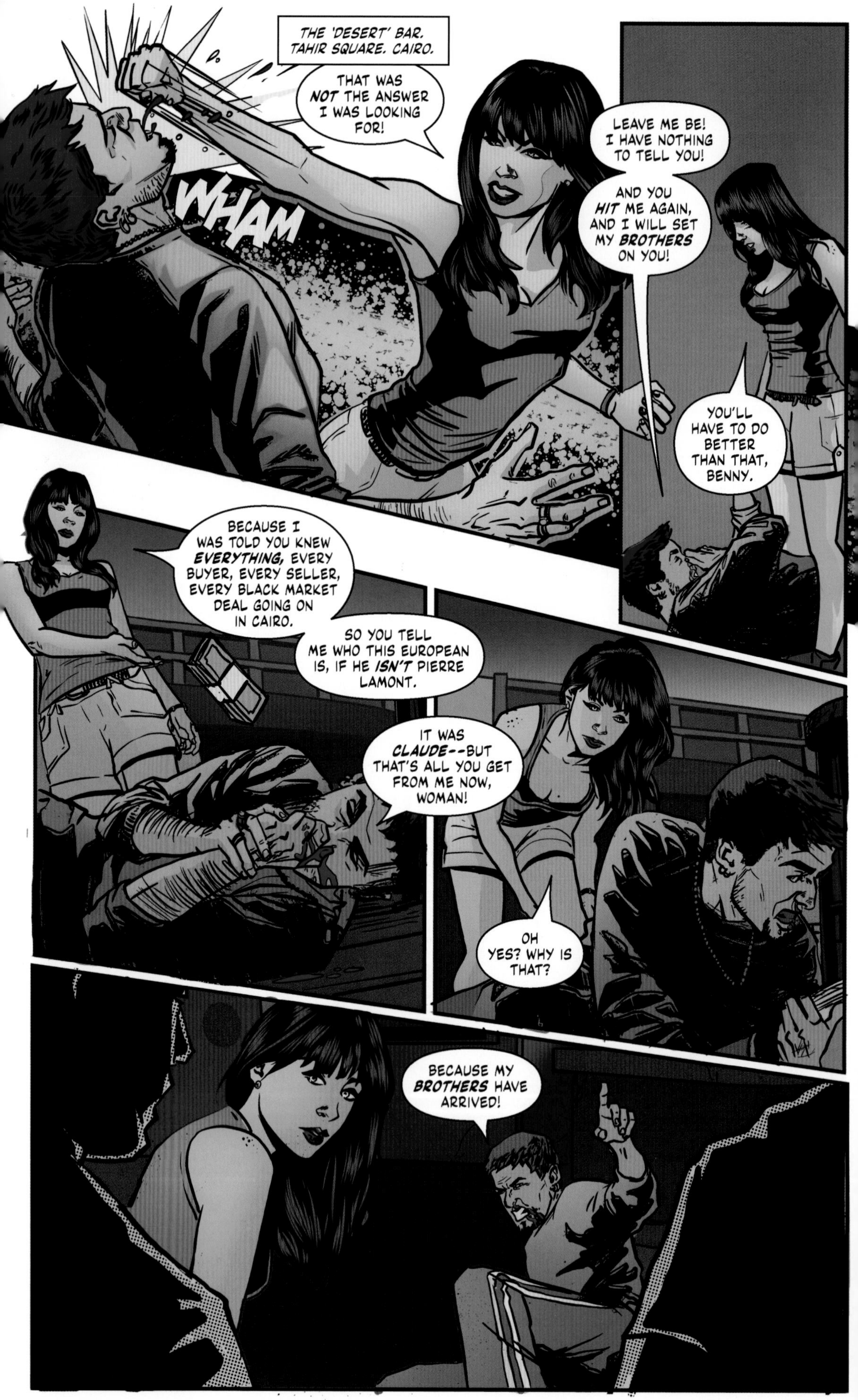
THE 'DESERT' BAR. TAHIR SQUARE. CAIRO.
THAT WAS NOT THE ANSWER I WAS LOOKING FOR!
WHAM
LEAVE ME BE! I HAVE NOTHING TO TELL YOU!
AND YOU HIT ME AGAIN, AND I WILL SET MY BROTHERS ON YOU!
YOU'LL HAVE TO DO BETTER THAN THAT, BENNY.
BECAUSE I WAS TOLD YOU KNEW EVERYTHING, EVERY BUYER, EVERY SELLER, EVERY BLACK MARKET DEAL GOING ON IN CAIRO.
SO YOU TELL ME WHO THIS EUROPEAN IS, IF HE ISN'T PIERRE LAMONT.
IT WAS CLAUDE--BUT THAT'S ALL YOU GET FROM ME NOW, WOMAN!
OH YES? WHY IS THAT?
BECAUSE MY BROTHERS HAVE ARRIVED!

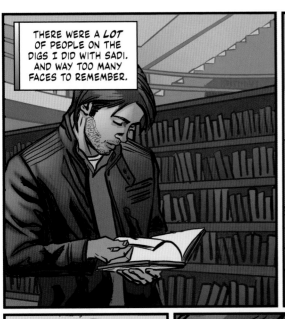

THERE WERE A *LOT* OF PEOPLE ON THE DIGS I DID WITH SADI. AND WAY TOO MANY FACES TO REMEMBER.

MAC

RHODEY

CLAUDE

PENNY

SADI

LUCKILY, SADI JUST *LOVED* THAT CHEAP CAMERA OF HIS.

SO WHERE ARE YOU, *CLAUDE* OR *PIERRE* OR WHATEVER YOU CALL YOURSELF? 'CAUSE IF YOU WERE THERE THEN...

...THEN YOU'VE GOTTA BE ON A *LIST*.

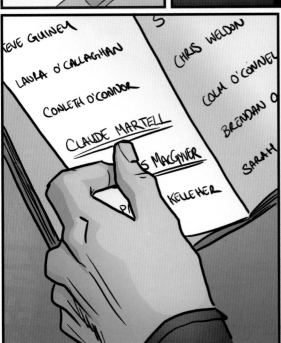

EVE GUINEY

LAURA O'CALLAGHAN

CONLETH O'CONNOR

CLAUDE MARTELL

S MACGYVER

KELLEHER

CHRIS WELDON

COLM O'CONNEL

BRENDAN O

SARAH

AND THERE YOU ARE, *CLAUDE MARTELL*.

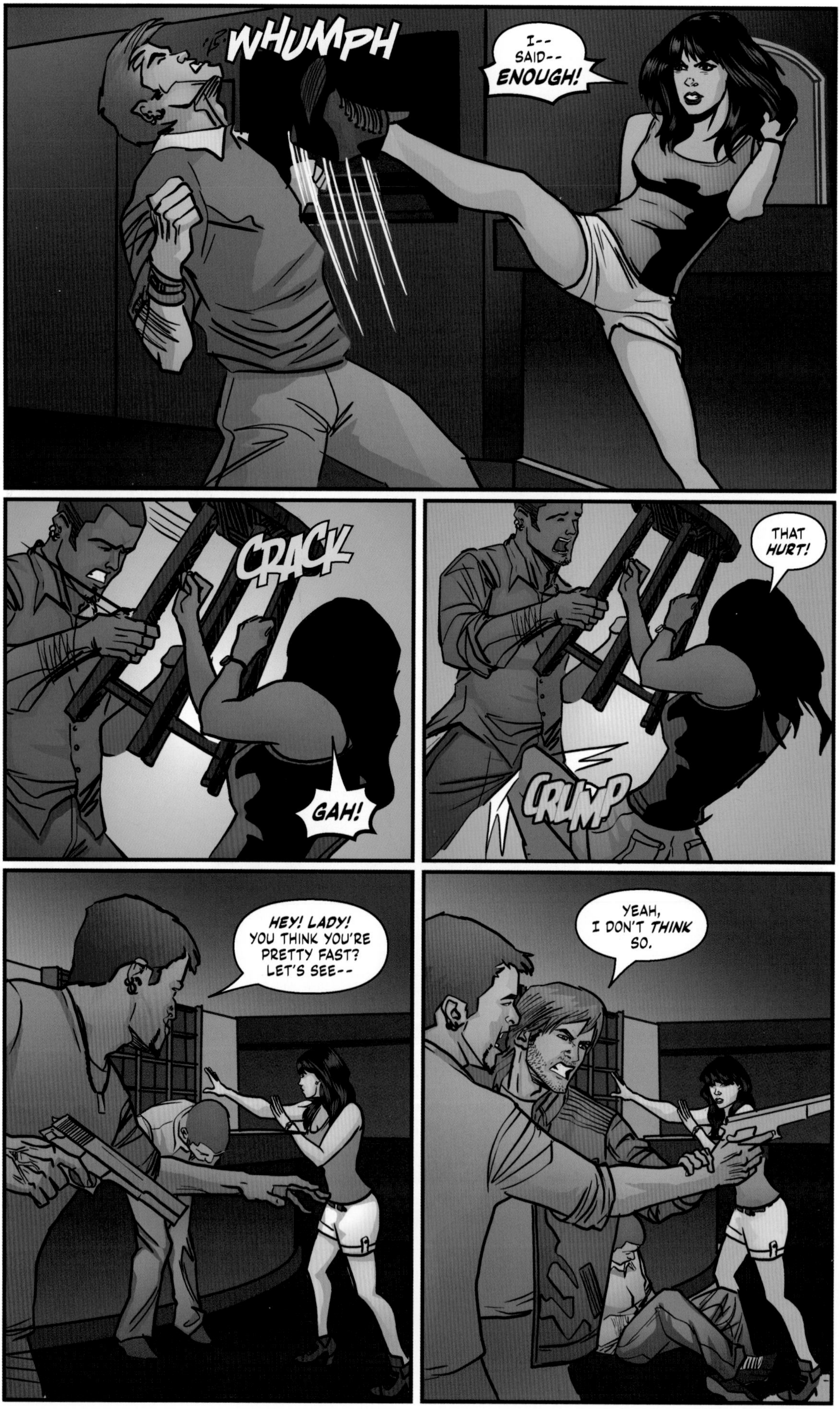

WHUMPH
I-- SAID-- ENOUGH!
CRACK
GAH!
THAT HURT!
CRUMP
HEY! LADY! YOU THINK YOU'RE PRETTY FAST? LET'S SEE--
YEAH, I DON'T THINK SO.

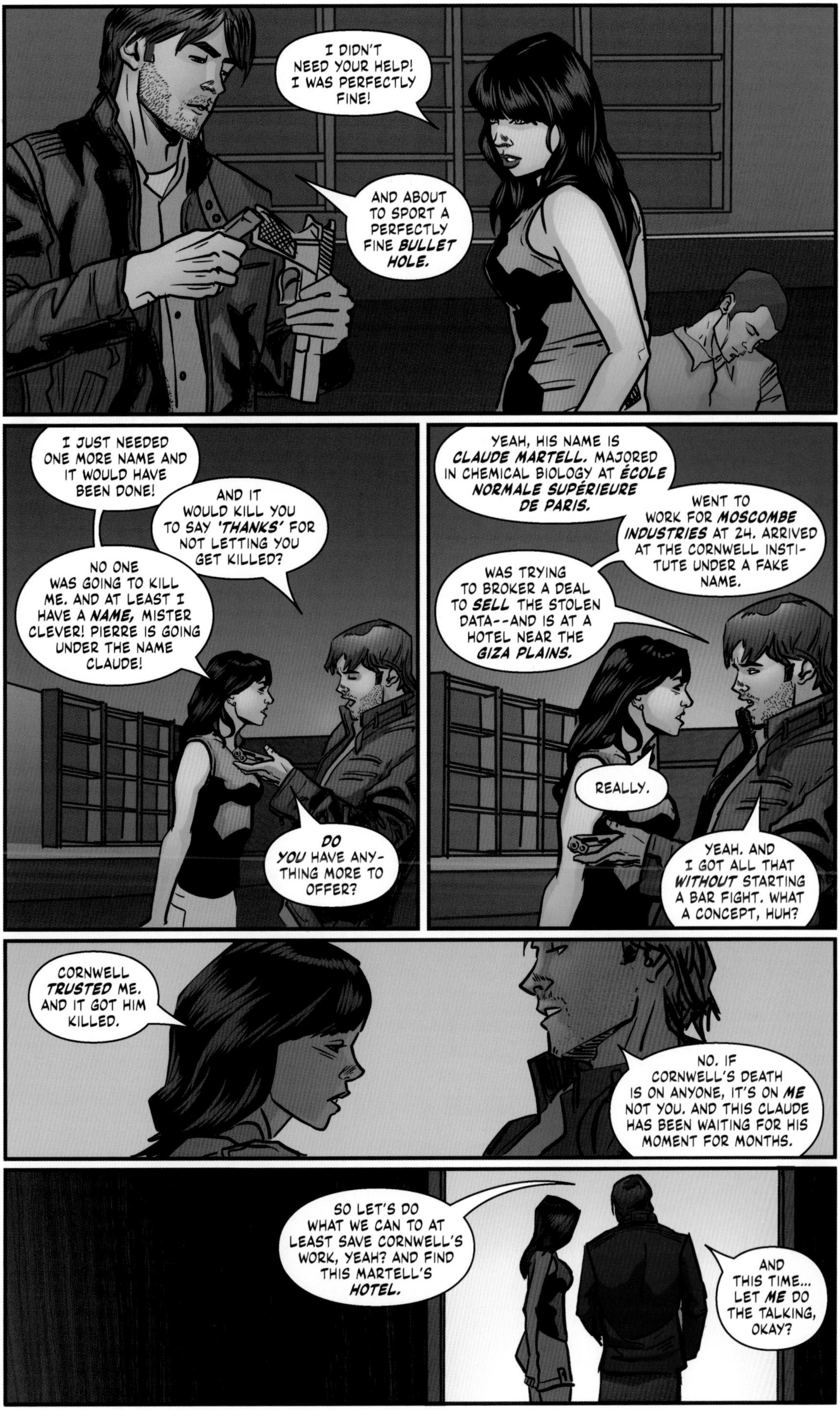
I DIDN'T NEED YOUR HELP! I WAS PERFECTLY FINE!
AND ABOUT TO SPORT A PERFECTLY FINE *BULLET HOLE.*
I JUST NEEDED ONE MORE NAME AND IT WOULD HAVE BEEN DONE!
AND IT WOULD KILL YOU TO SAY *'THANKS'* FOR NOT LETTING YOU GET KILLED?
NO ONE WAS GOING TO KILL ME. AND AT LEAST I HAVE A *NAME,* MISTER CLEVER! PIERRE IS GOING UNDER THE NAME CLAUDE!
DO YOU HAVE ANY-THING MORE TO OFFER?
YEAH, HIS NAME IS *CLAUDE MARTELL.* MAJORED IN CHEMICAL BIOLOGY AT *ÉCOLE NORMALE SUPÉRIEURE DE PARIS.*
WENT TO WORK FOR *MOSCOMBE INDUSTRIES* AT 24. ARRIVED AT THE CORNWELL INSTI-TUTE UNDER A FAKE NAME.
WAS TRYING TO BROKER A DEAL TO *SELL* THE STOLEN DATA--AND IS AT A HOTEL NEAR THE *GIZA PLAINS.*
REALLY.
YEAH. AND I GOT ALL THAT *WITHOUT* STARTING A BAR FIGHT. WHAT A CONCEPT, HUH?
CORNWELL *TRUSTED* ME. AND IT GOT HIM KILLED.
NO. IF CORNWELL'S DEATH IS ON ANYONE, IT'S ON *ME* NOT YOU. AND THIS CLAUDE HAS BEEN WAITING FOR HIS MOMENT FOR MONTHS.
SO LET'S DO WHAT WE CAN TO AT LEAST SAVE CORNWELL'S WORK, YEAH? AND FIND THIS MARTELL'S *HOTEL.*
AND THIS TIME... LET *ME* DO THE TALKING, OKAY?

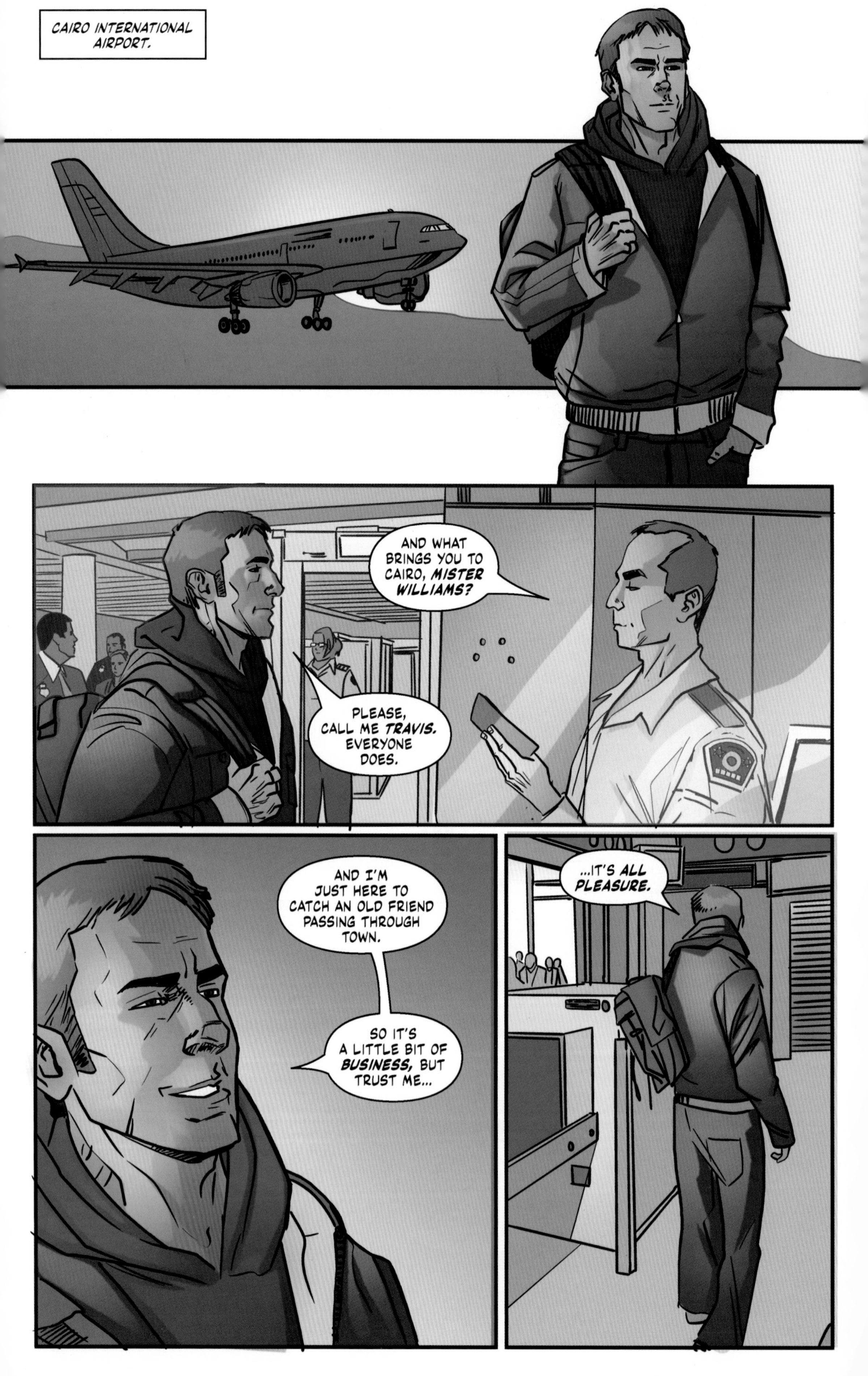
CAIRO INTERNATIONAL AIRPORT.
AND WHAT BRINGS YOU TO CAIRO, MISTER WILLIAMS?
PLEASE, CALL ME TRAVIS. EVERYONE DOES.
AND I'M JUST HERE TO CATCH AN OLD FRIEND PASSING THROUGH TOWN.
SO IT'S A LITTLE BIT OF BUSINESS, BUT TRUST ME...
...IT'S ALL PLEASURE.

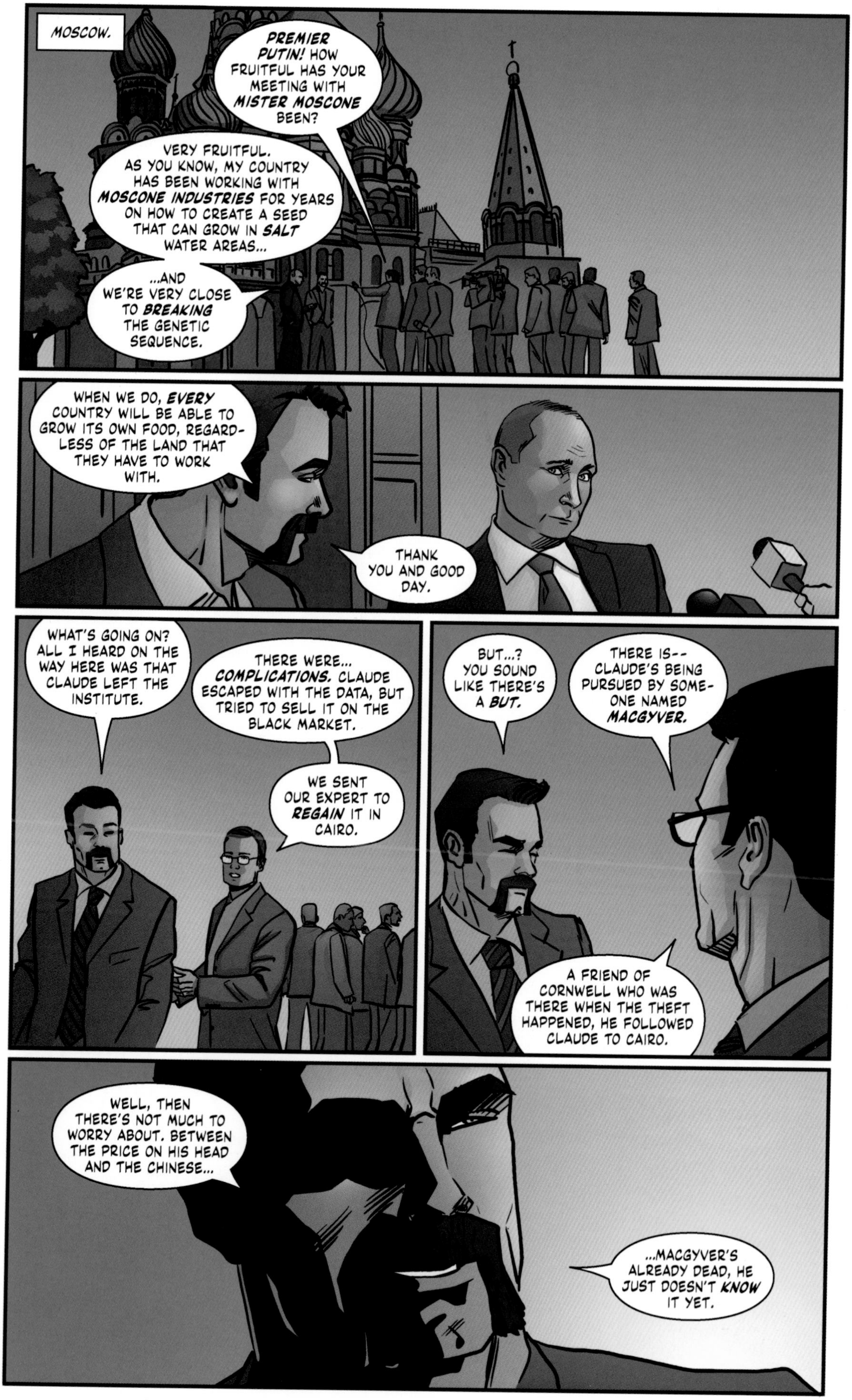
MOSCOW.
PREMIER PUTIN! HOW FRUITFUL HAS YOUR MEETING WITH MISTER MOSCONE BEEN?
VERY FRUITFUL. AS YOU KNOW, MY COUNTRY HAS BEEN WORKING WITH MOSCONE INDUSTRIES FOR YEARS ON HOW TO CREATE A SEED THAT CAN GROW IN SALT WATER AREAS...
...AND WE'RE VERY CLOSE TO BREAKING THE GENETIC SEQUENCE.
WHEN WE DO, EVERY COUNTRY WILL BE ABLE TO GROW ITS OWN FOOD, REGARDLESS OF THE LAND THAT THEY HAVE TO WORK WITH.
THANK YOU AND GOOD DAY.
WHAT'S GOING ON? ALL I HEARD ON THE WAY HERE WAS THAT CLAUDE LEFT THE INSTITUTE.
THERE WERE... COMPLICATIONS. CLAUDE ESCAPED WITH THE DATA, BUT TRIED TO SELL IT ON THE BLACK MARKET.
WE SENT OUR EXPERT TO REGAIN IT IN CAIRO.
BUT...? YOU SOUND LIKE THERE'S A BUT.
THERE IS-- CLAUDE'S BEING PURSUED BY SOMEONE NAMED MACGYVER.
A FRIEND OF CORNWELL WHO WAS THERE WHEN THE THEFT HAPPENED, HE FOLLOWED CLAUDE TO CAIRO.
WELL, THEN THERE'S NOT MUCH TO WORRY ABOUT. BETWEEN THE PRICE ON HIS HEAD AND THE CHINESE...
...MACGYVER'S ALREADY DEAD, HE JUST DOESN'T KNOW IT YET.

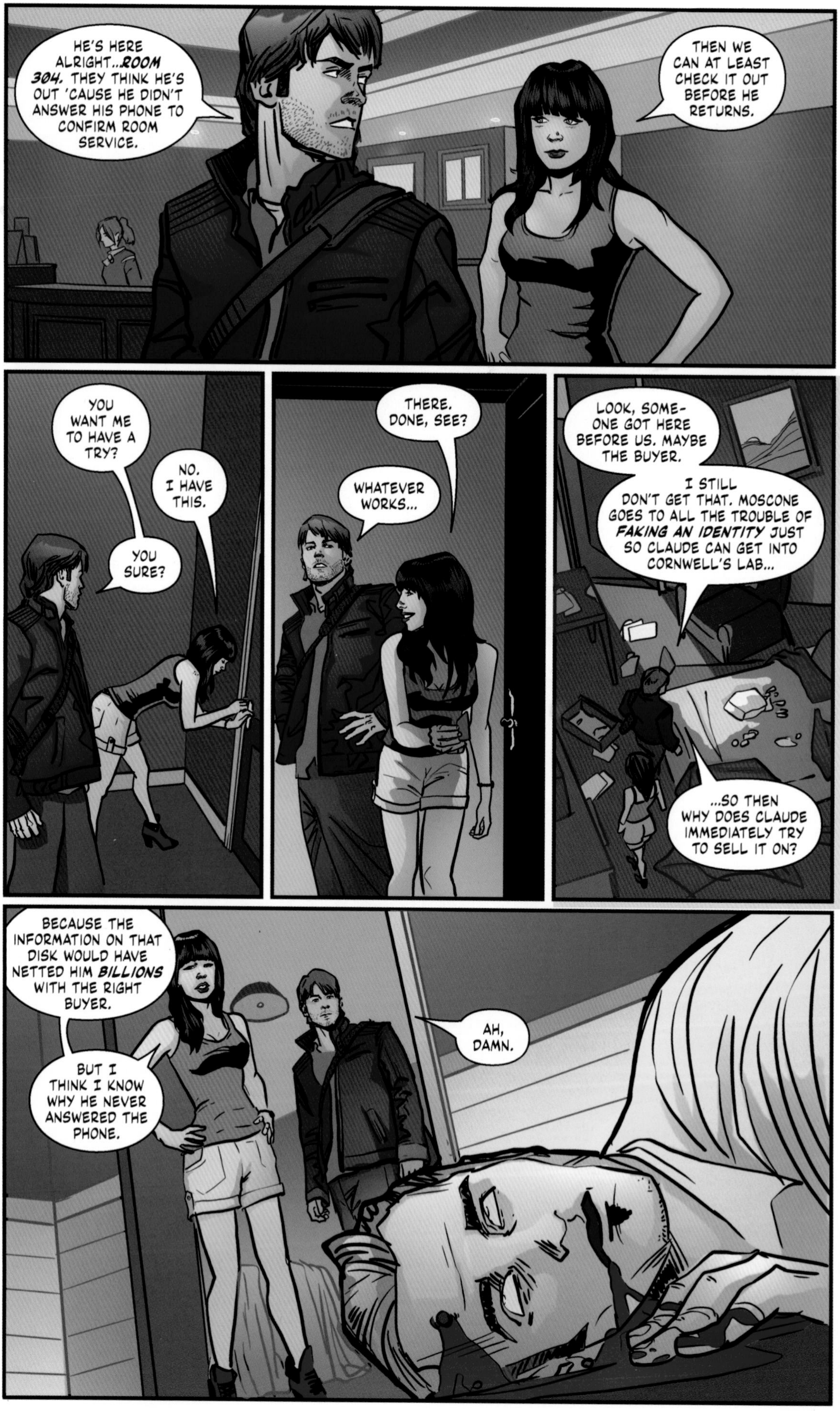
HE'S HERE ALRIGHT...ROOM 304. THEY THINK HE'S OUT 'CAUSE HE DIDN'T ANSWER HIS PHONE TO CONFIRM ROOM SERVICE.
THEN WE CAN AT LEAST CHECK IT OUT BEFORE HE RETURNS.
YOU WANT ME TO HAVE A TRY?
NO. I HAVE THIS.
YOU SURE?
THERE. DONE, SEE?
WHATEVER WORKS...
LOOK, SOME-ONE GOT HERE BEFORE US. MAYBE THE BUYER.
I STILL DON'T GET THAT. MOSCONE GOES TO ALL THE TROUBLE OF FAKING AN IDENTITY JUST SO CLAUDE CAN GET INTO CORNWELL'S LAB...
...SO THEN WHY DOES CLAUDE IMMEDIATELY TRY TO SELL IT ON?
BECAUSE THE INFORMATION ON THAT DISK WOULD HAVE NETTED HIM BILLIONS WITH THE RIGHT BUYER.
BUT I THINK I KNOW WHY HE NEVER ANSWERED THE PHONE.
AH, DAMN.

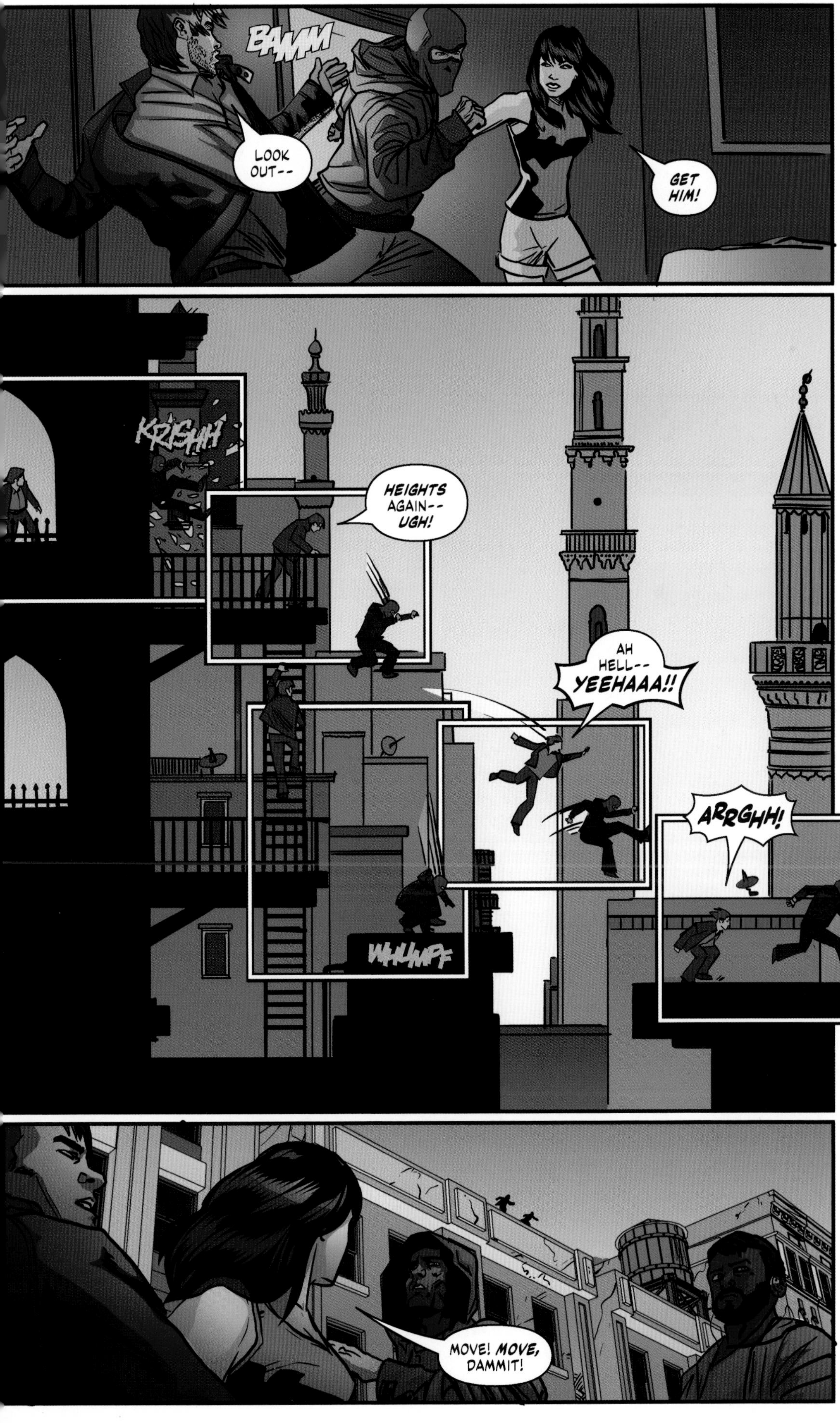
BAMM
LOOK OUT--
GET HIM!
KRISHH
HEIGHTS AGAIN-- UGH!
AH HELL-- YEEHAAA!!
WHUMPF
ARRGHH!
MOVE! MOVE, DAMMIT!

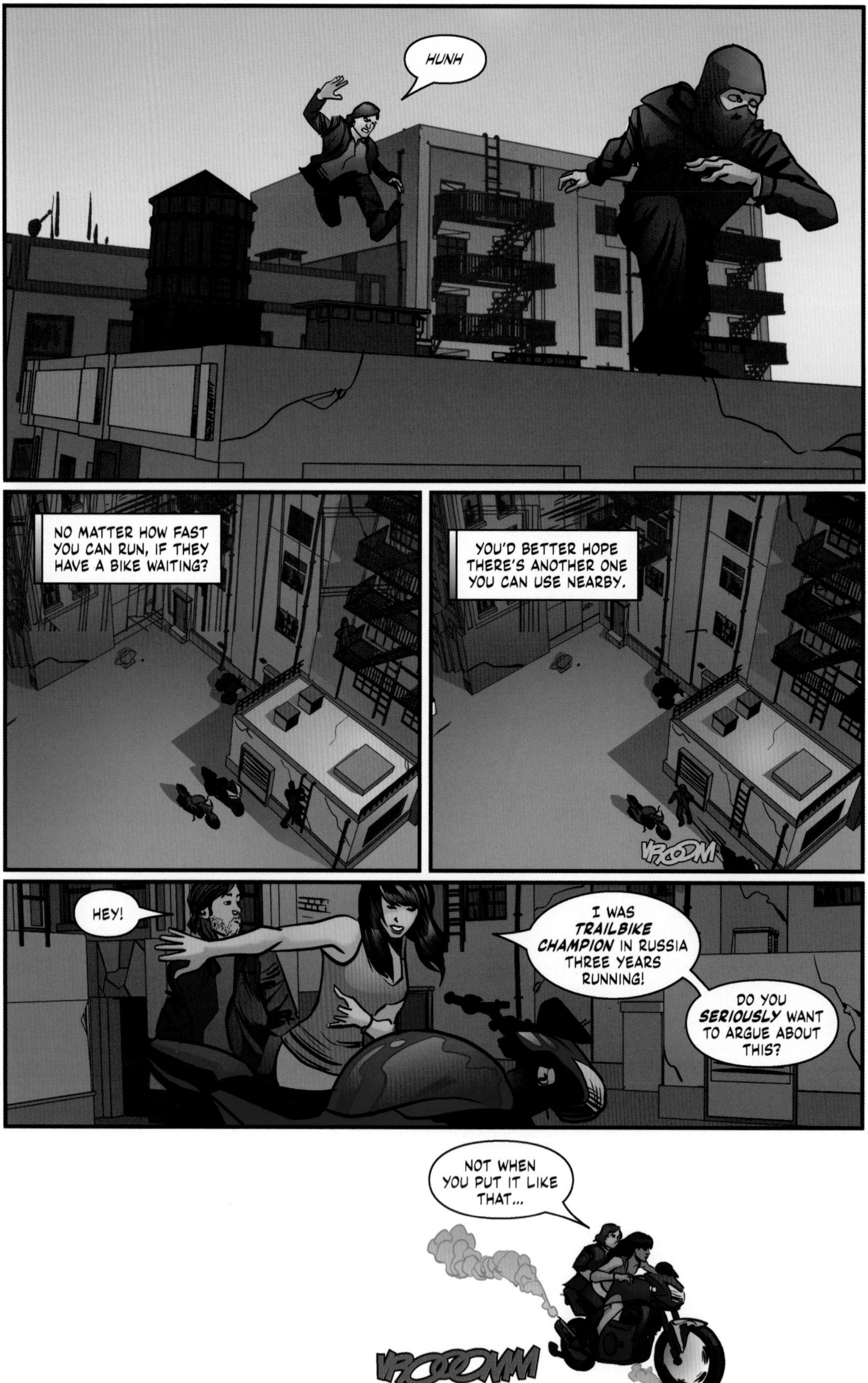
HUNH
NO MATTER HOW FAST YOU CAN RUN, IF THEY HAVE A BIKE WAITING?
YOU'D BETTER HOPE THERE'S ANOTHER ONE YOU CAN USE NEARBY.
VROOM
HEY!
I WAS TRAILBIKE CHAMPION IN RUSSIA THREE YEARS RUNNING!
DO YOU SERIOUSLY WANT TO ARGUE ABOUT THIS?
NOT WHEN YOU PUT IT LIKE THAT...
VROOOMM

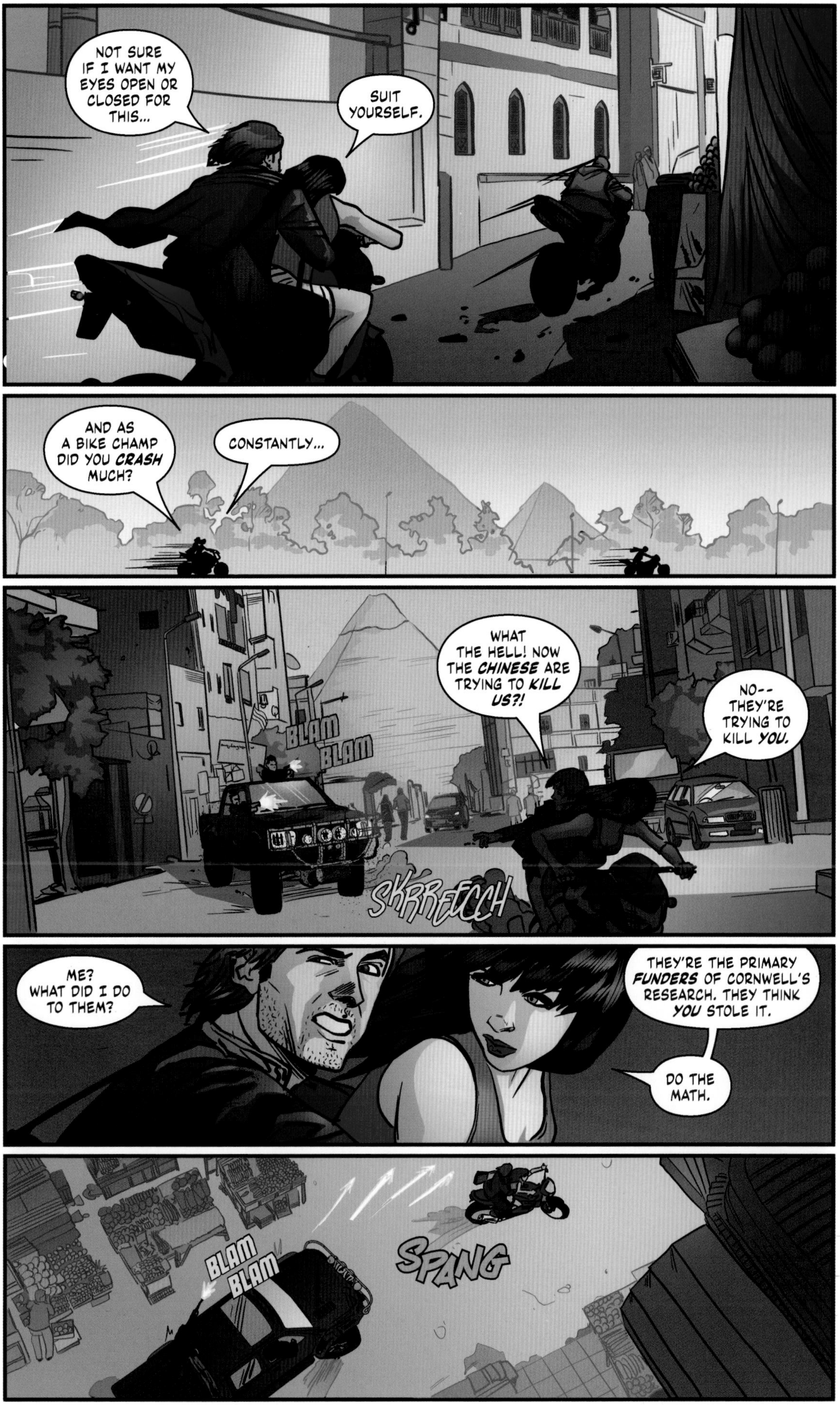
NOT SURE IF I WANT MY EYES OPEN OR CLOSED FOR THIS...
SUIT YOURSELF.
AND AS A BIKE CHAMP DID YOU CRASH MUCH?
CONSTANTLY...
BLAM
BLAM
WHAT THE HELL! NOW THE CHINESE ARE TRYING TO KILL US?!
NO-- THEY'RE TRYING TO KILL YOU.
SKRREECCH
ME? WHAT DID I DO TO THEM?
THEY'RE THE PRIMARY FUNDERS OF CORNWELL'S RESEARCH. THEY THINK YOU STOLE IT.
DO THE MATH.
BLAM
BLAM
SPANG

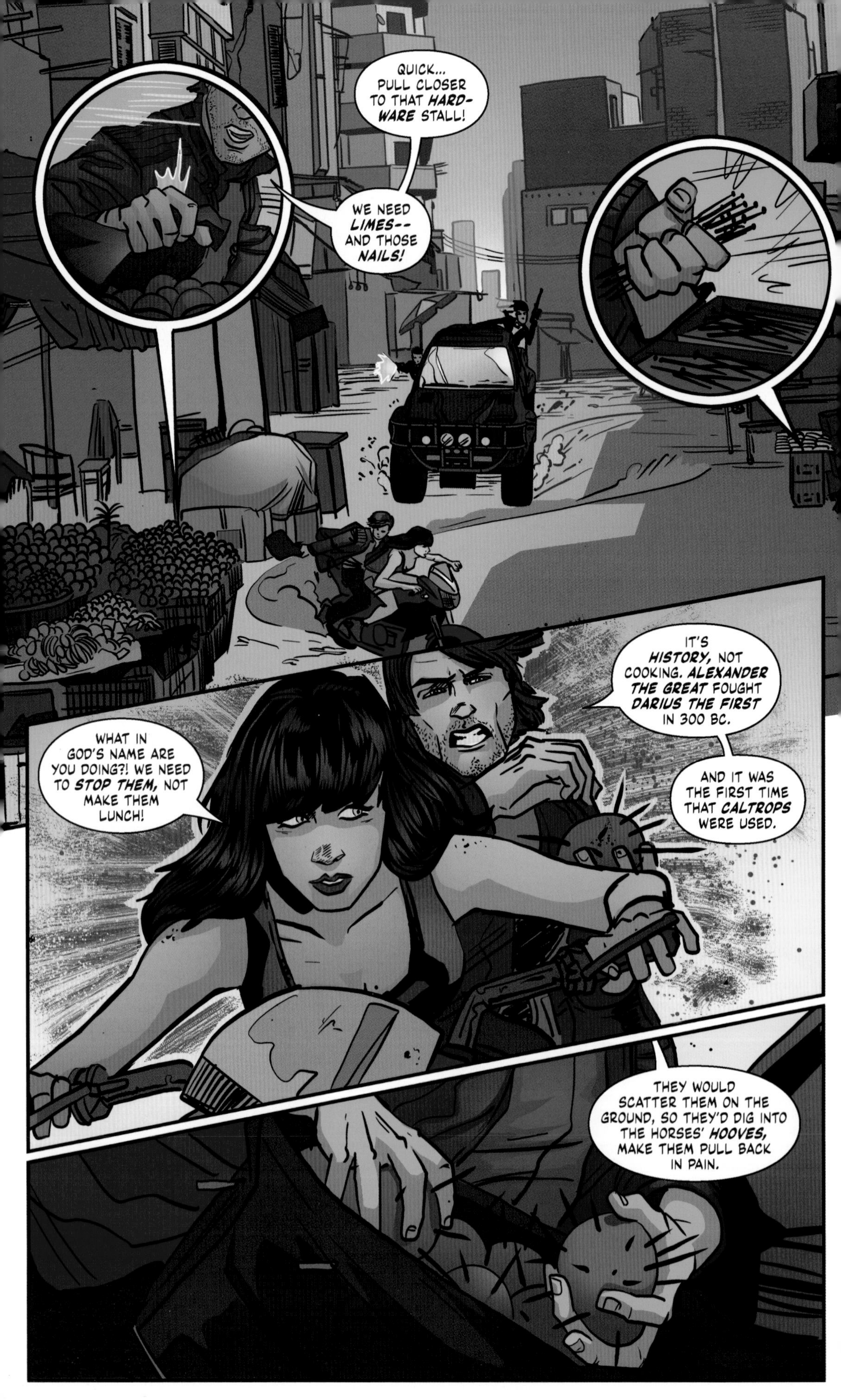
QUICK... PULL CLOSER TO THAT HARD-WARE STALL!
WE NEED LIMES-- AND THOSE NAILS!
WHAT IN GOD'S NAME ARE YOU DOING?! WE NEED TO STOP THEM, NOT MAKE THEM LUNCH!
IT'S HISTORY, NOT COOKING. ALEXANDER THE GREAT FOUGHT DARIUS THE FIRST IN 300 BC.
AND IT WAS THE FIRST TIME THAT CALTROPS WERE USED.
THEY WOULD SCATTER THEM ON THE GROUND, SO THEY'D DIG INTO THE HORSES' HOOVES, MAKE THEM PULL BACK IN PAIN.

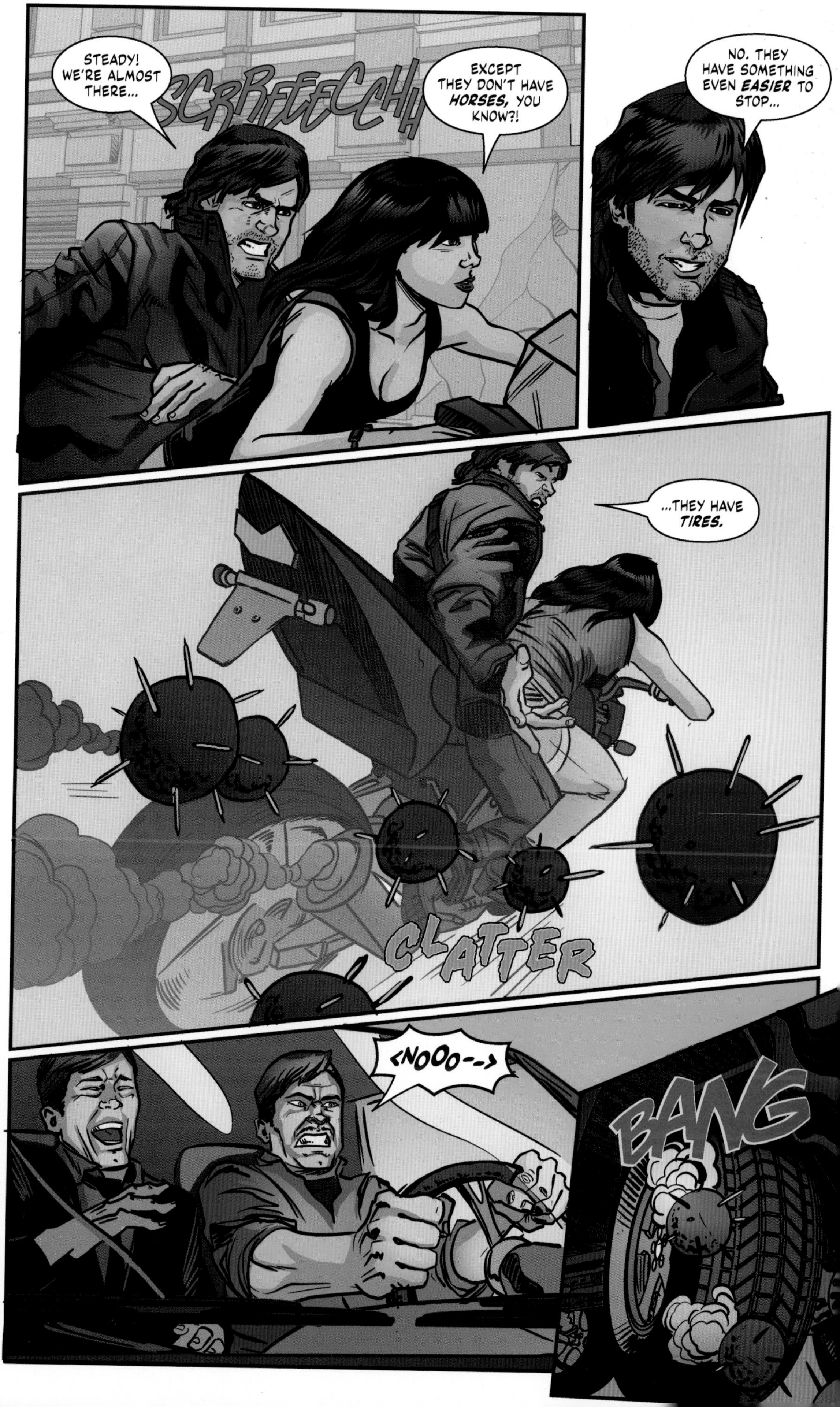
STEADY! WE'RE ALMOST THERE...
SCRREEECCHH
EXCEPT THEY DON'T HAVE HORSES, YOU KNOW?!
NO. THEY HAVE SOMETHING EVEN EASIER TO STOP...
...THEY HAVE TIRES.
CLATTER
<NOOO-->
BANG

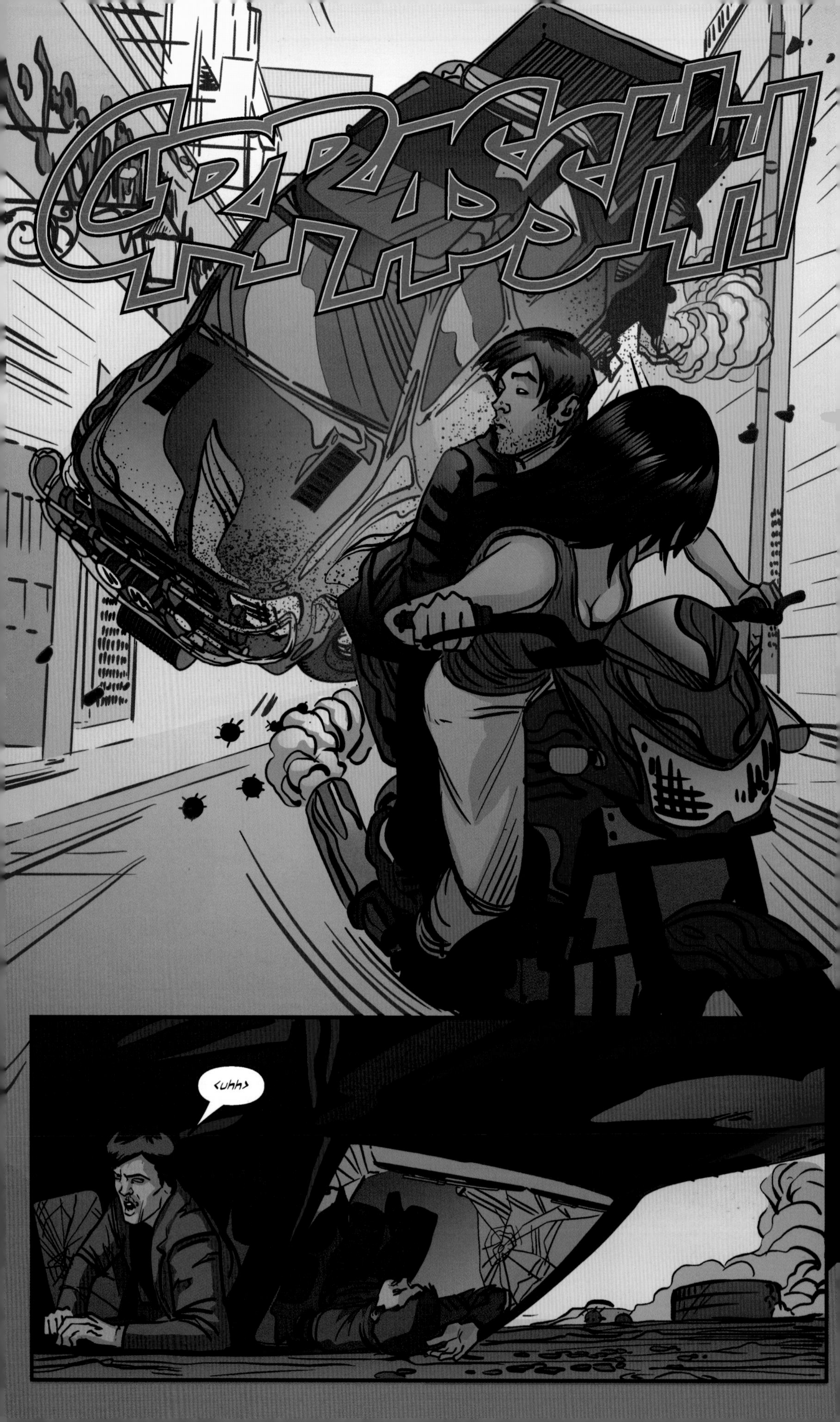
CRASHH
<uhh>

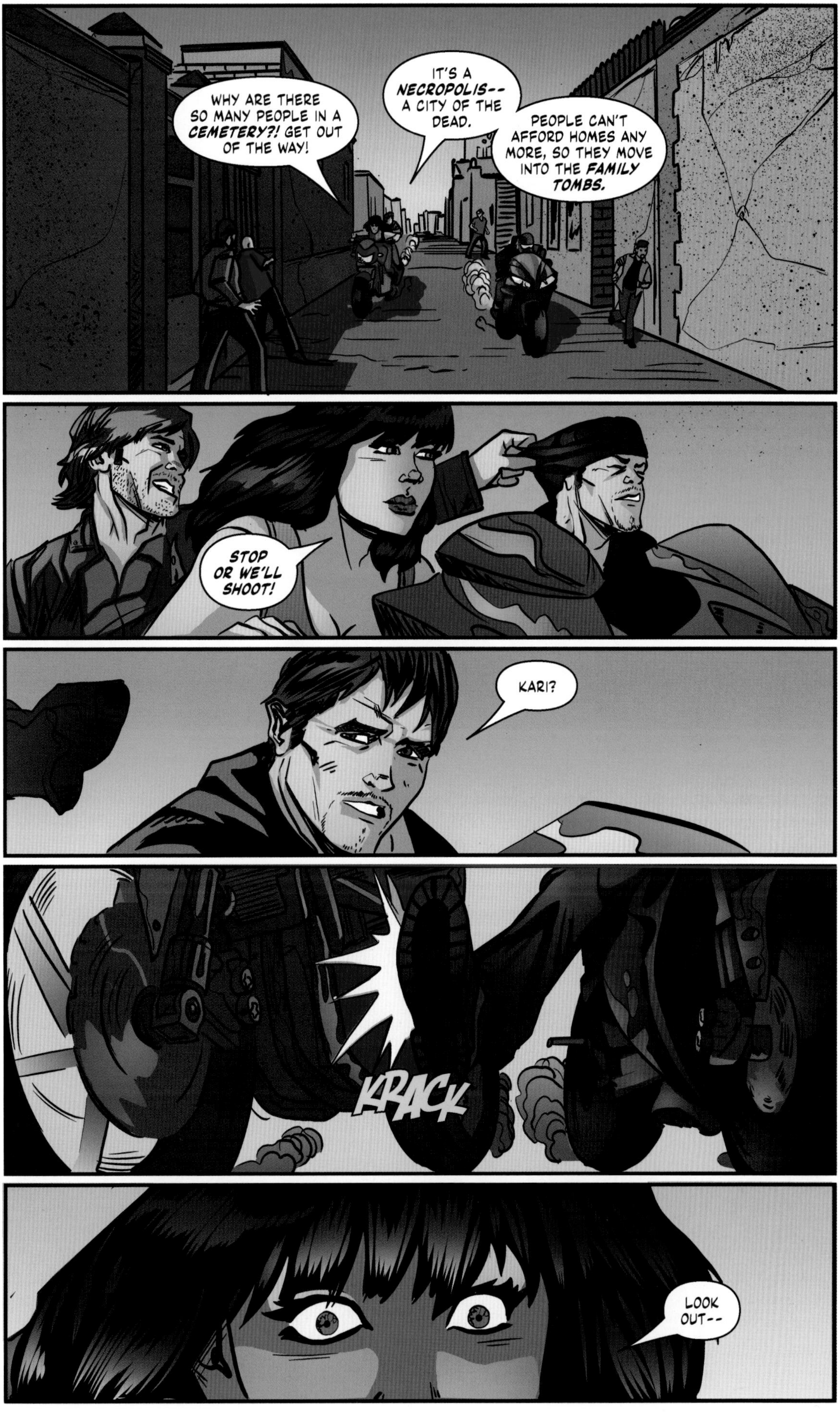
WHY ARE THERE SO MANY PEOPLE IN A CEMETERY?! GET OUT OF THE WAY!
IT'S A NECROPOLIS-- A CITY OF THE DEAD.
PEOPLE CAN'T AFFORD HOMES ANY MORE, SO THEY MOVE INTO THE FAMILY TOMBS.
STOP OR WE'LL SHOOT!
KARI?
KRACK
LOOK OUT--

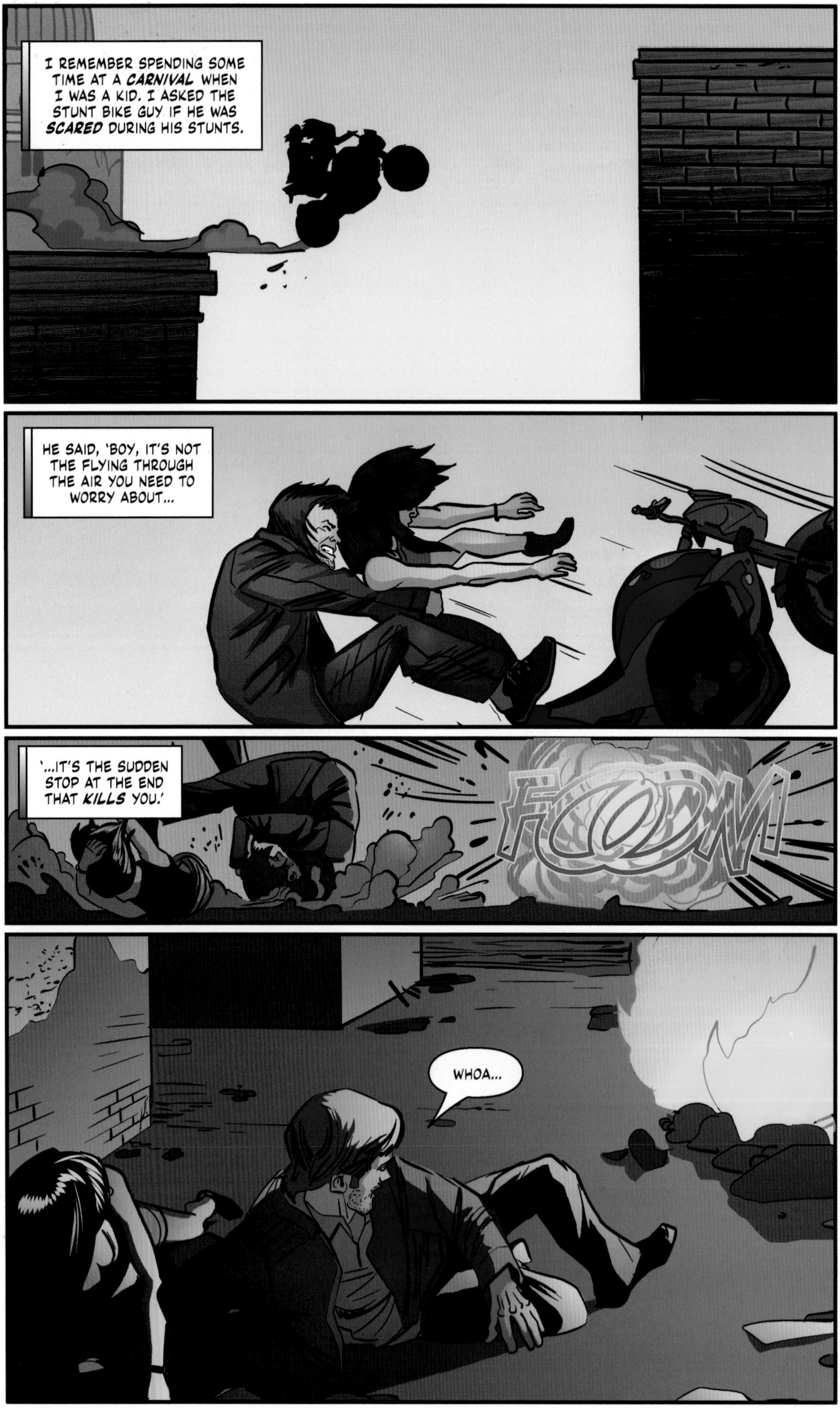
I REMEMBER SPENDING SOME TIME AT A *CARNIVAL* WHEN I WAS A KID. I ASKED THE STUNT BIKE GUY IF HE WAS *SCARED* DURING HIS STUNTS.
HE SAID, 'BOY, IT'S NOT THE FLYING THROUGH THE AIR YOU NEED TO WORRY ABOUT...
'...IT'S THE SUDDEN STOP AT THE END THAT *KILLS* YOU.'
FOOM
WHOA...

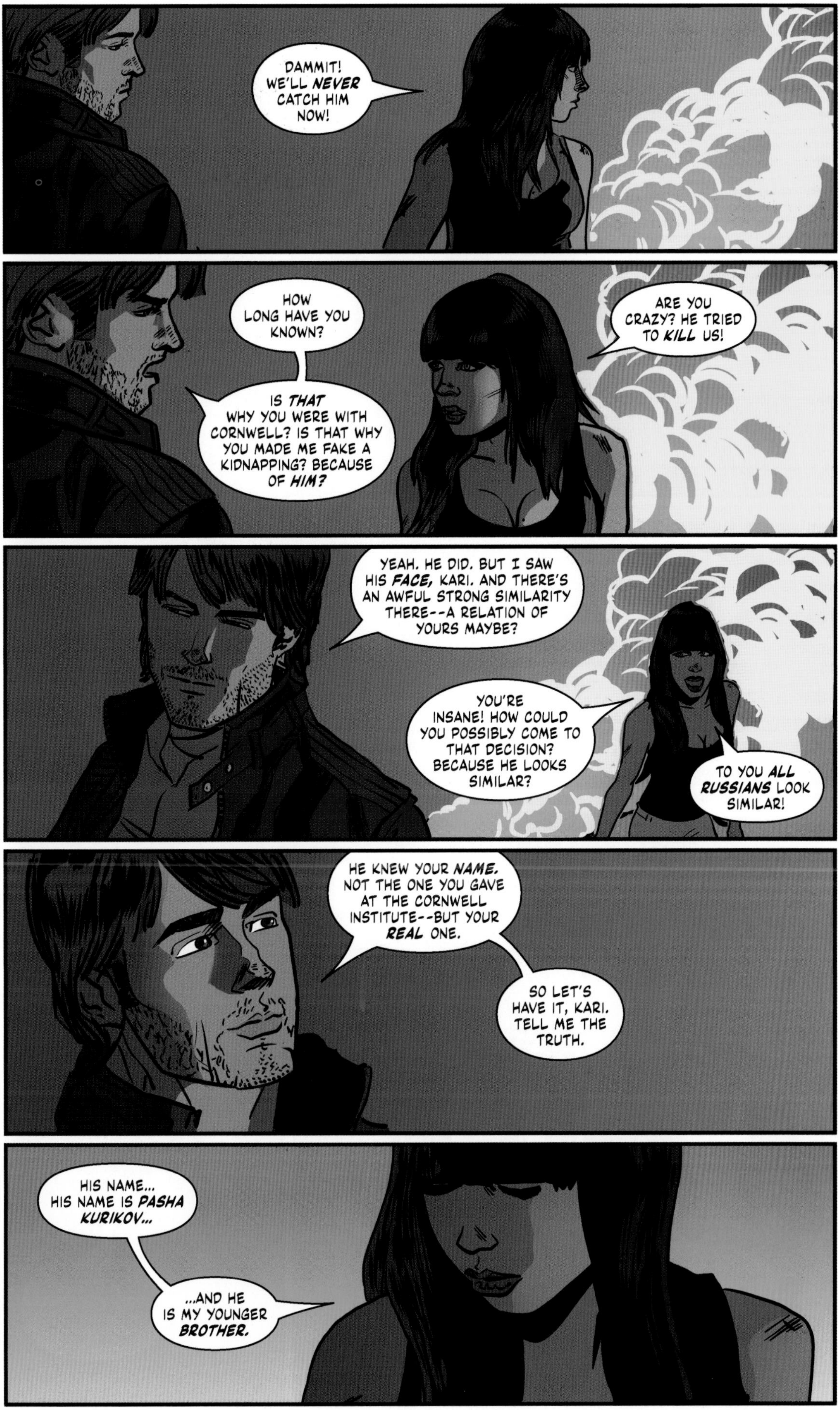
DAMMIT! WE'LL NEVER CATCH HIM NOW!
HOW LONG HAVE YOU KNOWN?
IS THAT WHY YOU WERE WITH CORNWELL? IS THAT WHY YOU MADE ME FAKE A KIDNAPPING? BECAUSE OF HIM?
ARE YOU CRAZY? HE TRIED TO KILL US!
YEAH. HE DID. BUT I SAW HIS FACE, KARI. AND THERE'S AN AWFUL STRONG SIMILARITY THERE--A RELATION OF YOURS MAYBE?
YOU'RE INSANE! HOW COULD YOU POSSIBLY COME TO THAT DECISION? BECAUSE HE LOOKS SIMILAR?
TO YOU ALL RUSSIANS LOOK SIMILAR!
HE KNEW YOUR NAME. NOT THE ONE YOU GAVE AT THE CORNWELL INSTITUTE--BUT YOUR REAL ONE.
SO LET'S HAVE IT, KARI. TELL ME THE TRUTH.
HIS NAME... HIS NAME IS PASHA KURIKOV...
...AND HE IS MY YOUNGER BROTHER.

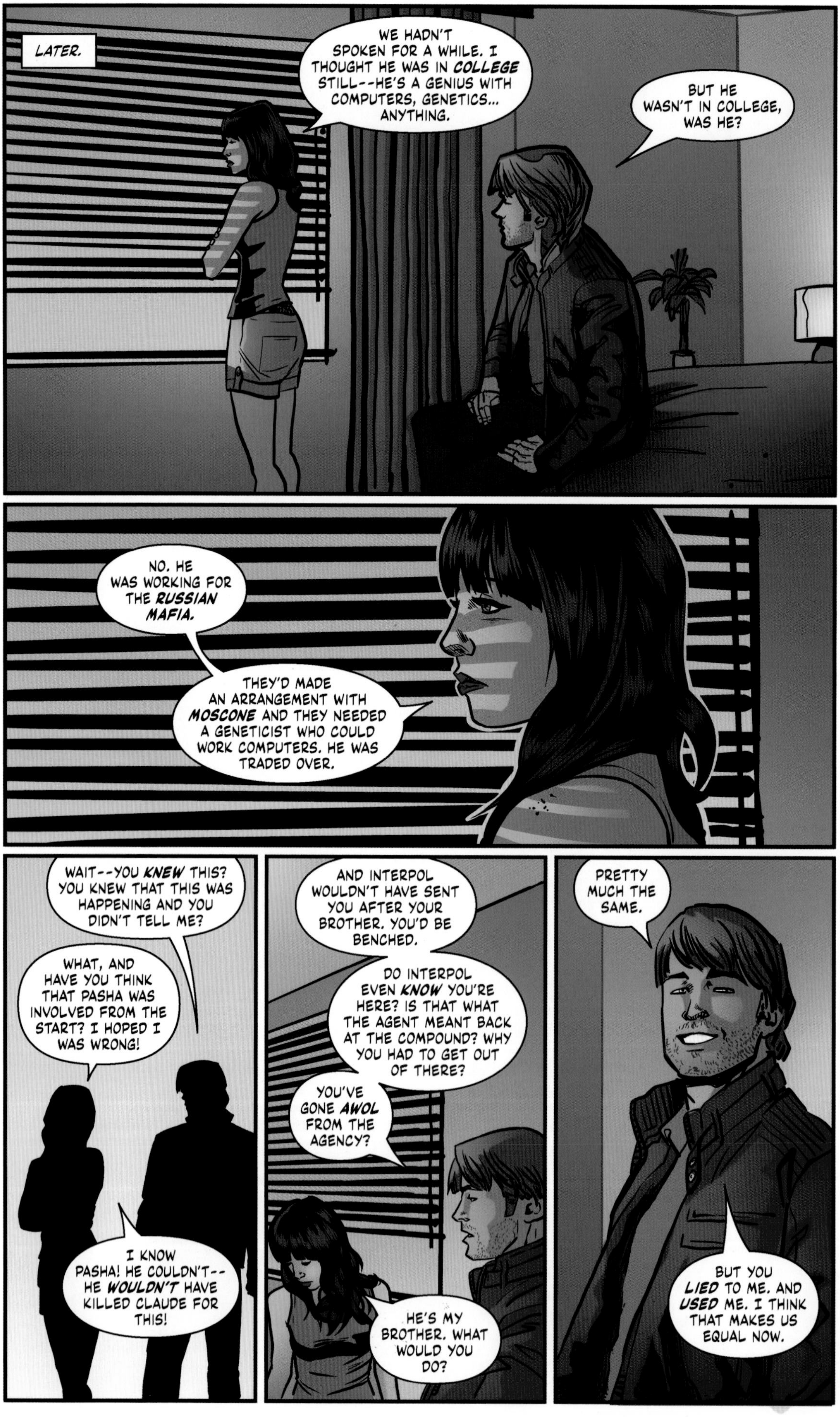
LATER.
WE HADN'T SPOKEN FOR A WHILE. I THOUGHT HE WAS IN COLLEGE STILL--HE'S A GENIUS WITH COMPUTERS, GENETICS... ANYTHING.
BUT HE WASN'T IN COLLEGE, WAS HE?
NO. HE WAS WORKING FOR THE RUSSIAN MAFIA.
THEY'D MADE AN ARRANGEMENT WITH MOSCONE AND THEY NEEDED A GENETICIST WHO COULD WORK COMPUTERS. HE WAS TRADED OVER.
WAIT--YOU KNEW THIS? YOU KNEW THAT THIS WAS HAPPENING AND YOU DIDN'T TELL ME?
WHAT, AND HAVE YOU THINK THAT PASHA WAS INVOLVED FROM THE START? I HOPED I WAS WRONG!
I KNOW PASHA! HE COULDN'T--HE WOULDN'T HAVE KILLED CLAUDE FOR THIS!
AND INTERPOL WOULDN'T HAVE SENT YOU AFTER YOUR BROTHER. YOU'D BE BENCHED.
DO INTERPOL EVEN KNOW YOU'RE HERE? IS THAT WHAT THE AGENT MEANT BACK AT THE COMPOUND? WHY YOU HAD TO GET OUT OF THERE?
YOU'VE GONE AWOL FROM THE AGENCY?
HE'S MY BROTHER. WHAT WOULD YOU DO?
PRETTY MUCH THE SAME.
BUT YOU LIED TO ME. AND USED ME. I THINK THAT MAKES US EQUAL NOW.

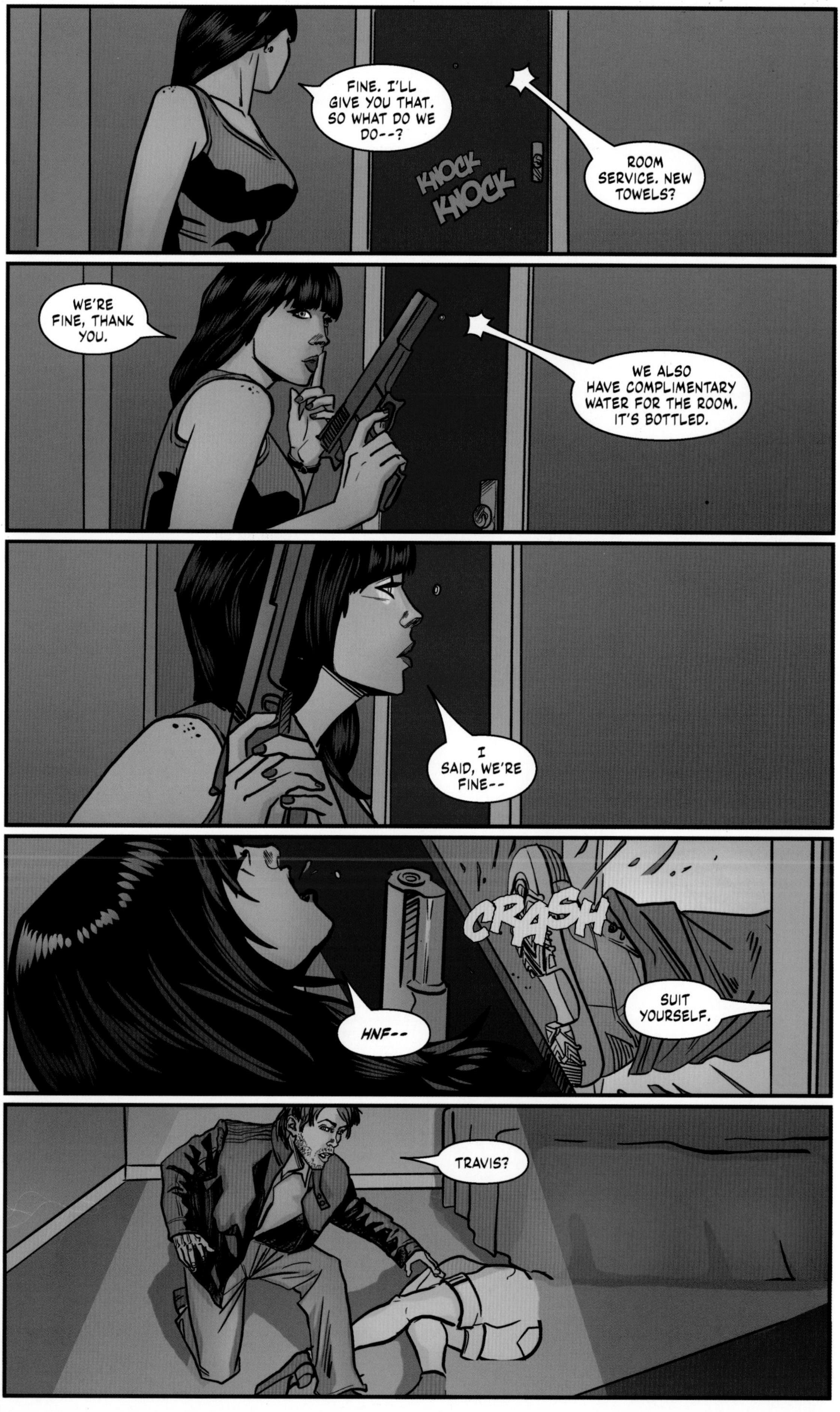
FINE. I'LL GIVE YOU THAT. SO WHAT DO WE DO--?
KNOCK KNOCK
ROOM SERVICE. NEW TOWELS?
WE'RE FINE, THANK YOU.
WE ALSO HAVE COMPLIMENTARY WATER FOR THE ROOM. IT'S BOTTLED.
I SAID, WE'RE FINE--
CRASH
HNF--
SUIT YOURSELF.
TRAVIS?

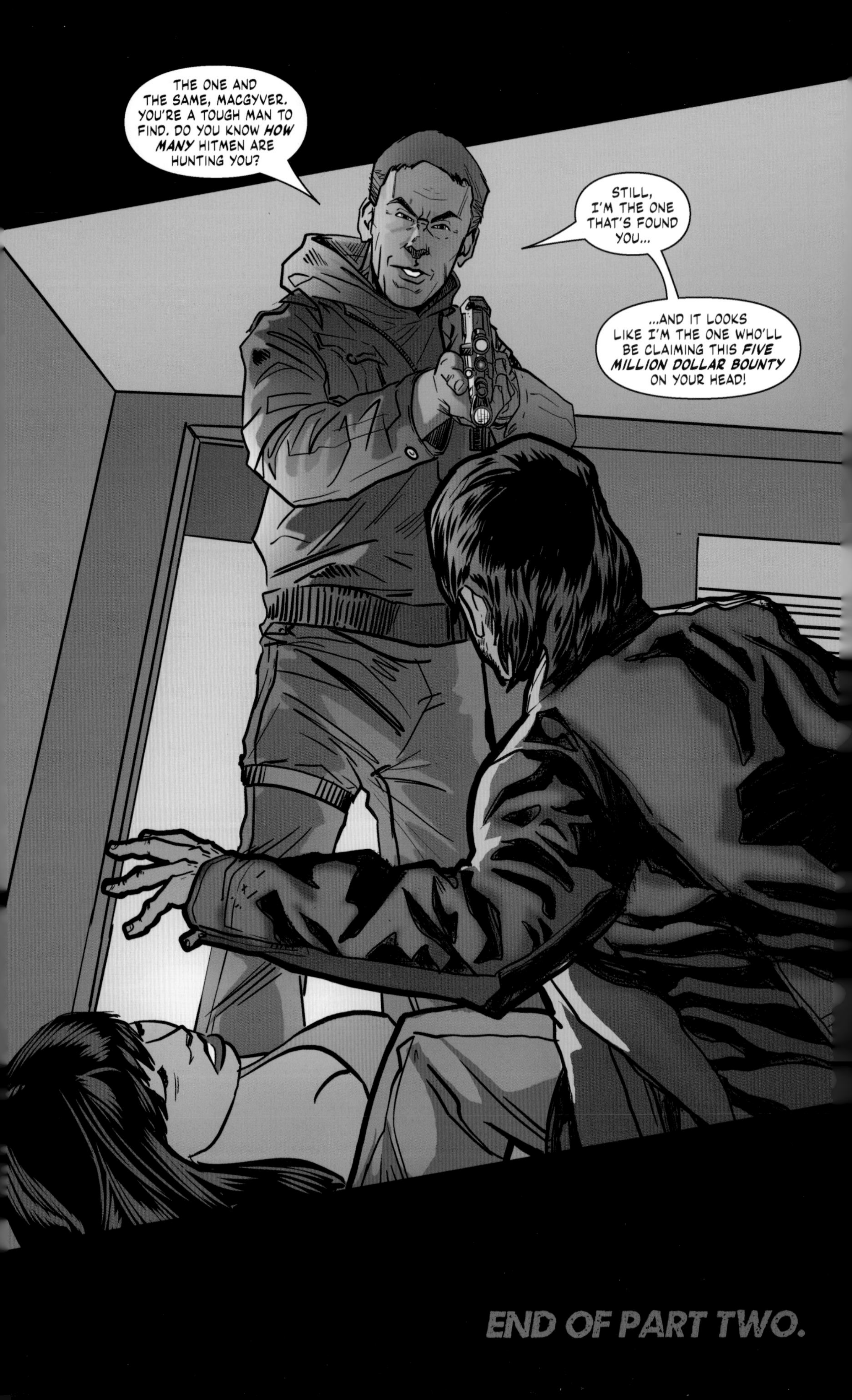
THE ONE AND THE SAME, MACGYVER. YOU'RE A TOUGH MAN TO FIND. DO YOU KNOW *HOW MANY* HITMEN ARE HUNTING YOU?
STILL, I'M THE ONE THAT'S FOUND YOU...
...AND IT LOOKS LIKE I'M THE ONE WHO'LL BE CLAIMING THIS *FIVE MILLION DOLLAR BOUNTY* ON YOUR HEAD!
END OF PART TWO.

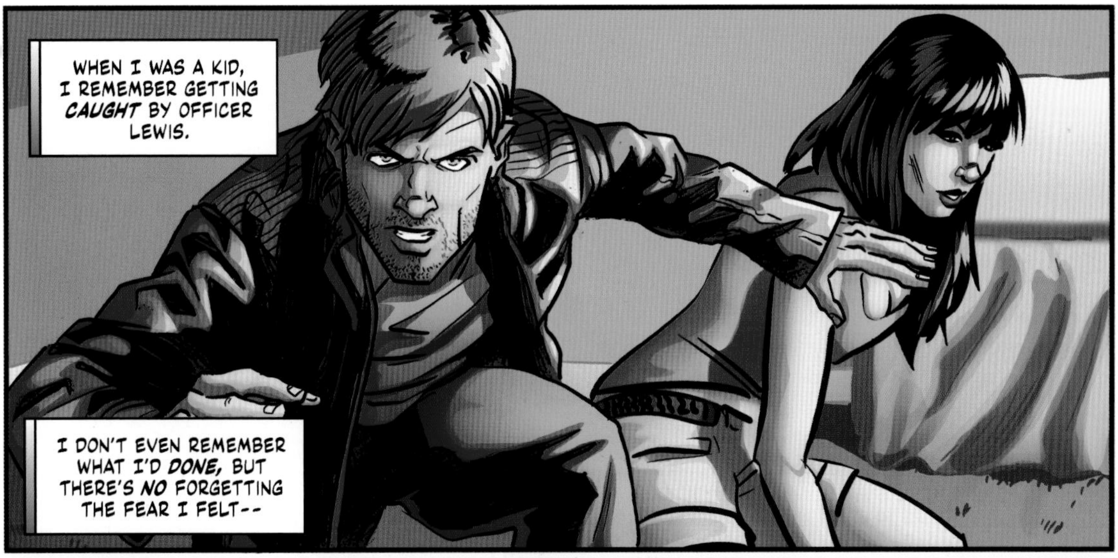
WHEN I WAS A KID, I REMEMBER GETTING CAUGHT BY OFFICER LEWIS.
I DON'T EVEN REMEMBER WHAT I'D DONE, BUT THERE'S NO FORGETTING THE FEAR I FELT--

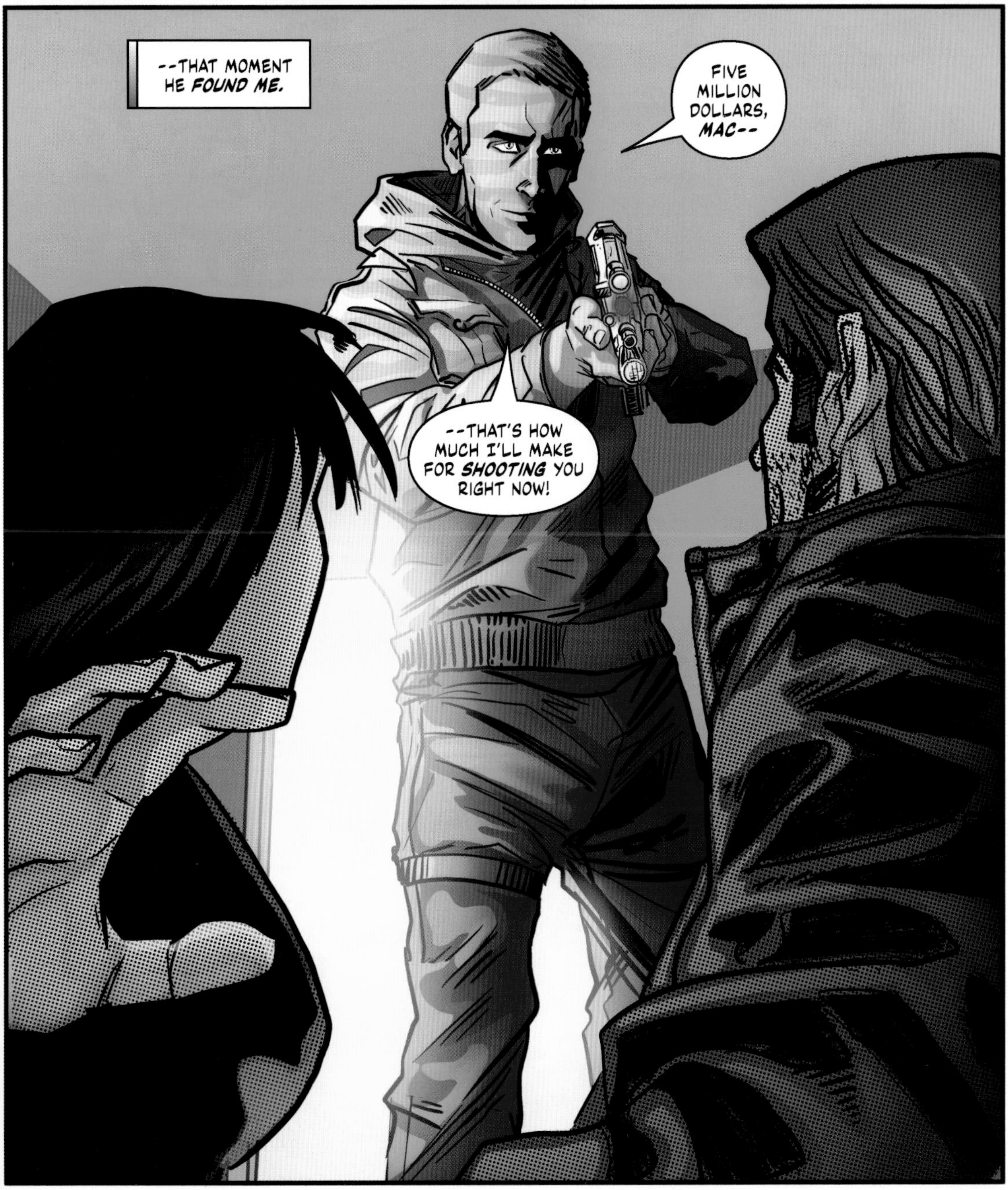
--THAT MOMENT HE FOUND ME.
FIVE MILLION DOLLARS, MAC--
--THAT'S HOW MUCH I'LL MAKE FOR SHOOTING YOU RIGHT NOW!

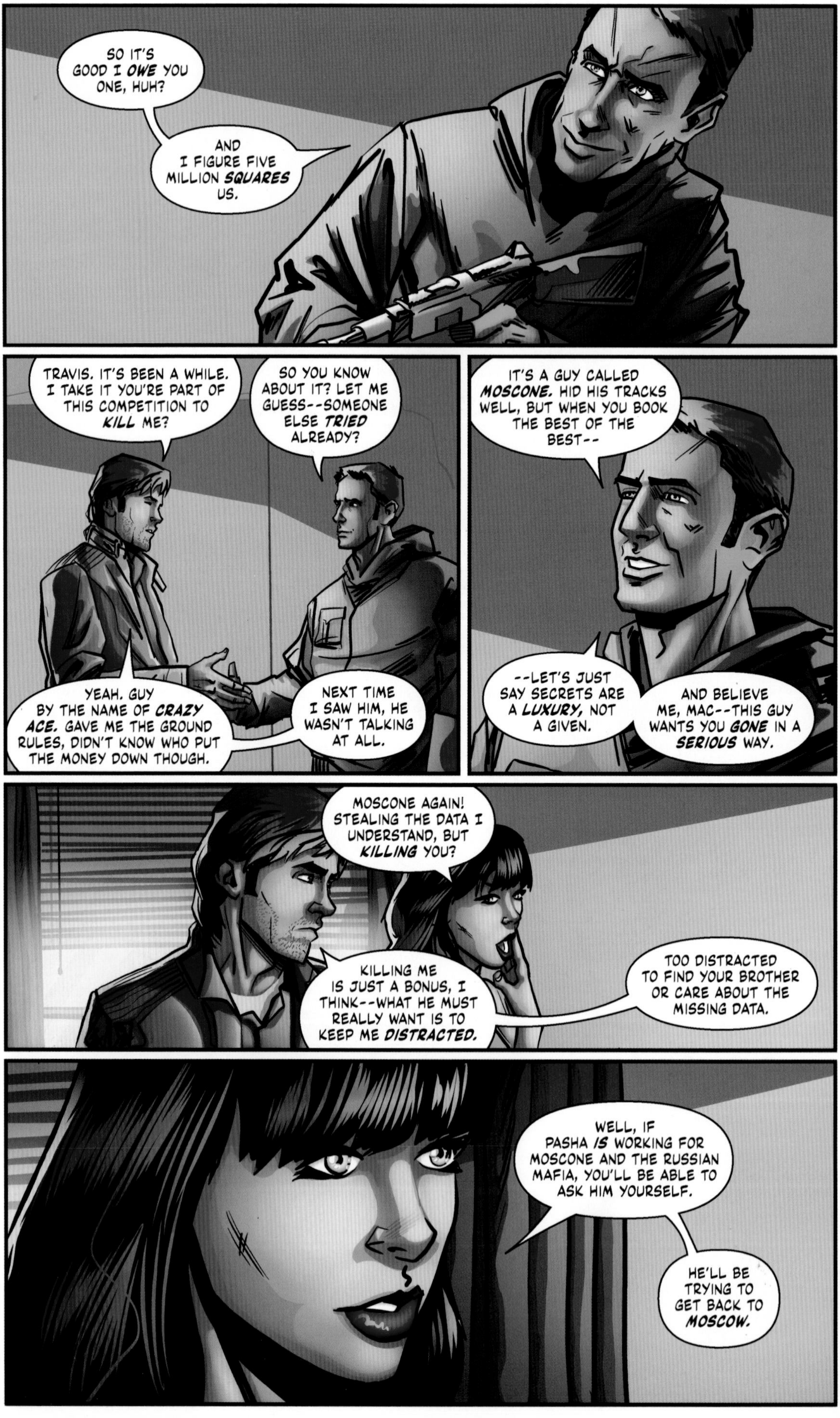
SO IT'S GOOD I OWE YOU ONE, HUH?
AND I FIGURE FIVE MILLION SQUARES US.
TRAVIS. IT'S BEEN A WHILE. I TAKE IT YOU'RE PART OF THIS COMPETITION TO KILL ME?
SO YOU KNOW ABOUT IT? LET ME GUESS--SOMEONE ELSE TRIED ALREADY?
YEAH. GUY BY THE NAME OF CRAZY ACE. GAVE ME THE GROUND RULES, DIDN'T KNOW WHO PUT THE MONEY DOWN THOUGH.
NEXT TIME I SAW HIM, HE WASN'T TALKING AT ALL.
IT'S A GUY CALLED MOSCONE. HID HIS TRACKS WELL, BUT WHEN YOU BOOK THE BEST OF THE BEST--
--LET'S JUST SAY SECRETS ARE A LUXURY, NOT A GIVEN.
AND BELIEVE ME, MAC--THIS GUY WANTS YOU GONE IN A SERIOUS WAY.
MOSCONE AGAIN! STEALING THE DATA I UNDERSTAND, BUT KILLING YOU?
KILLING ME IS JUST A BONUS, I THINK--WHAT HE MUST REALLY WANT IS TO KEEP ME DISTRACTED.
TOO DISTRACTED TO FIND YOUR BROTHER OR CARE ABOUT THE MISSING DATA.
WELL, IF PASHA IS WORKING FOR MOSCONE AND THE RUSSIAN MAFIA, YOU'LL BE ABLE TO ASK HIM YOURSELF.
HE'LL BE TRYING TO GET BACK TO MOSCOW.

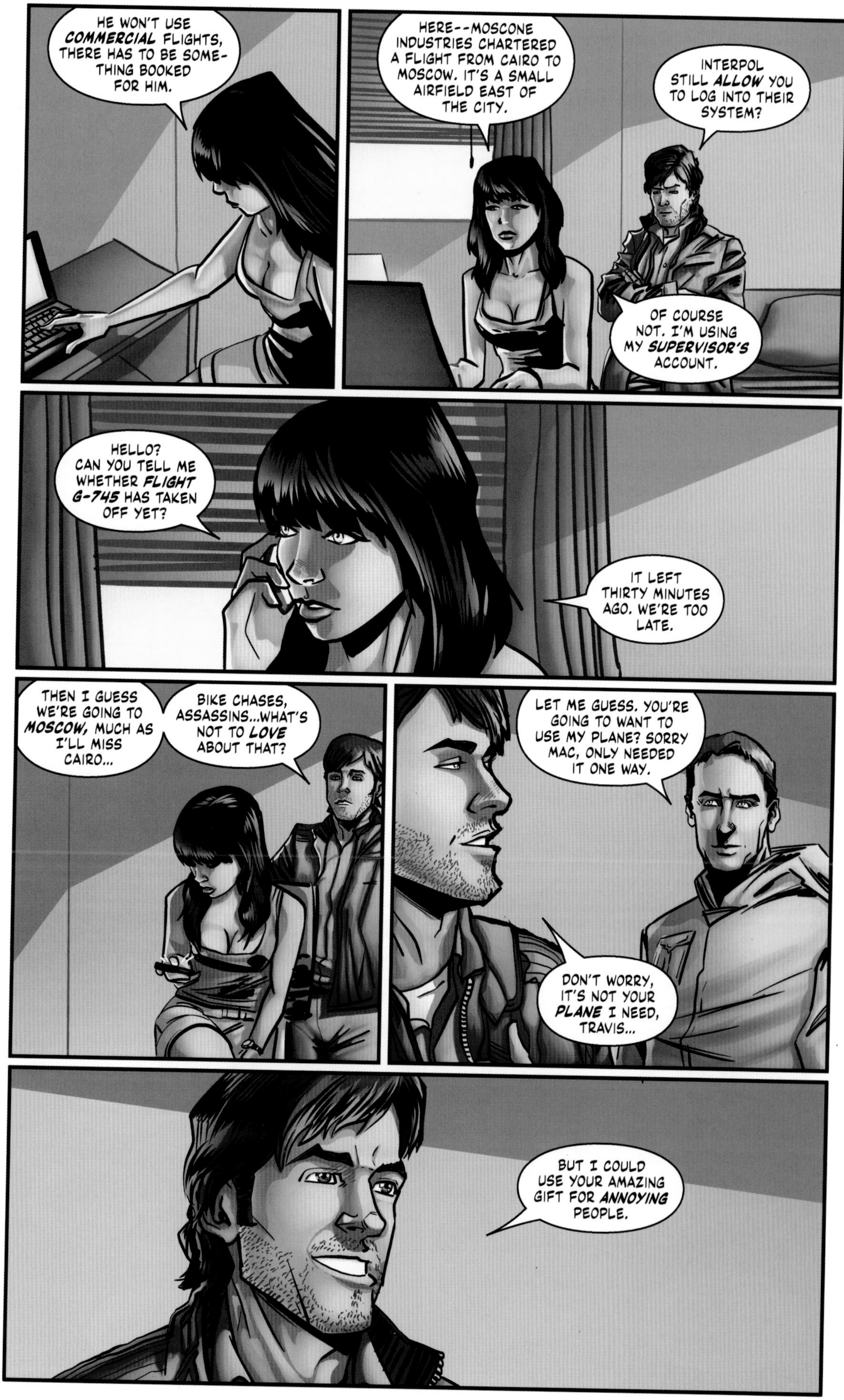
HE WON'T USE COMMERCIAL FLIGHTS, THERE HAS TO BE SOMETHING BOOKED FOR HIM.
HERE--MOSCONE INDUSTRIES CHARTERED A FLIGHT FROM CAIRO TO MOSCOW. IT'S A SMALL AIRFIELD EAST OF THE CITY.
INTERPOL STILL ALLOW YOU TO LOG INTO THEIR SYSTEM?
OF COURSE NOT. I'M USING MY SUPERVISOR'S ACCOUNT.
HELLO? CAN YOU TELL ME WHETHER FLIGHT G-745 HAS TAKEN OFF YET?
IT LEFT THIRTY MINUTES AGO. WE'RE TOO LATE.
THEN I GUESS WE'RE GOING TO MOSCOW, MUCH AS I'LL MISS CAIRO...
BIKE CHASES, ASSASSINS...WHAT'S NOT TO LOVE ABOUT THAT?
LET ME GUESS. YOU'RE GOING TO WANT TO USE MY PLANE? SORRY MAC, ONLY NEEDED IT ONE WAY.
DON'T WORRY, IT'S NOT YOUR PLANE I NEED, TRAVIS...
BUT I COULD USE YOUR AMAZING GIFT FOR ANNOYING PEOPLE.

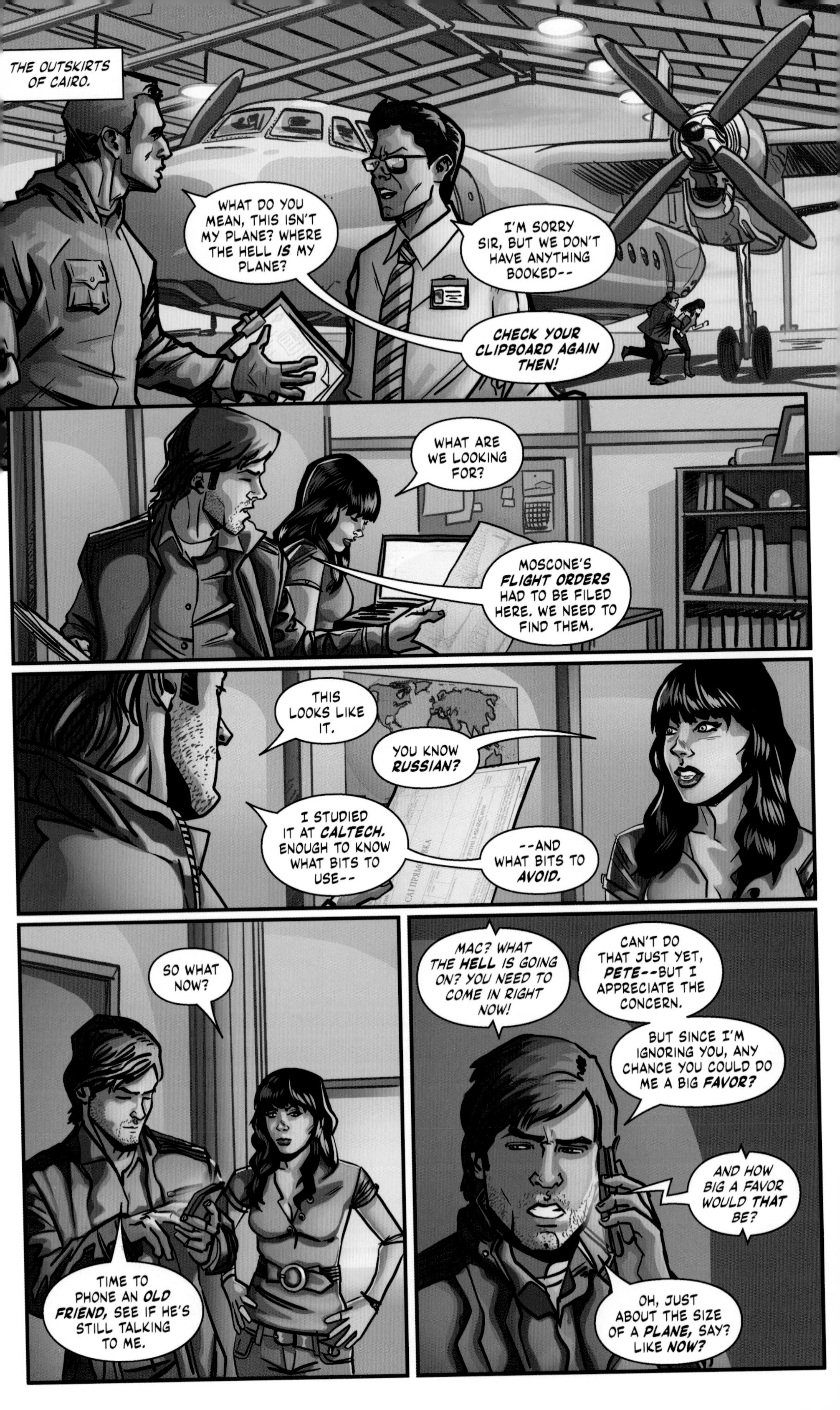
THE OUTSKIRTS OF CAIRO.
WHAT DO YOU MEAN, THIS ISN'T MY PLANE? WHERE THE HELL *IS* MY PLANE?
I'M SORRY SIR, BUT WE DON'T HAVE ANYTHING BOOKED--
CHECK YOUR CLIPBOARD AGAIN THEN!
WHAT ARE WE LOOKING FOR?
MOSCONE'S *FLIGHT ORDERS* HAD TO BE FILED HERE. WE NEED TO FIND THEM.
THIS LOOKS LIKE IT.
YOU KNOW *RUSSIAN?*
I STUDIED IT AT *CALTECH.* ENOUGH TO KNOW WHAT BITS TO USE--
--AND WHAT BITS TO *AVOID.*
SO WHAT NOW?
TIME TO PHONE AN *OLD FRIEND,* SEE IF HE'S STILL TALKING TO ME.
MAC? WHAT THE HELL IS GOING ON? YOU NEED TO COME IN RIGHT NOW!
CAN'T DO THAT JUST YET, *PETE*--BUT I APPRECIATE THE CONCERN.
BUT SINCE I'M IGNORING YOU, ANY CHANCE YOU COULD DO ME A BIG *FAVOR?*
AND HOW BIG A FAVOR WOULD THAT BE?
OH, JUST ABOUT THE SIZE OF A *PLANE,* SAY? LIKE *NOW?*

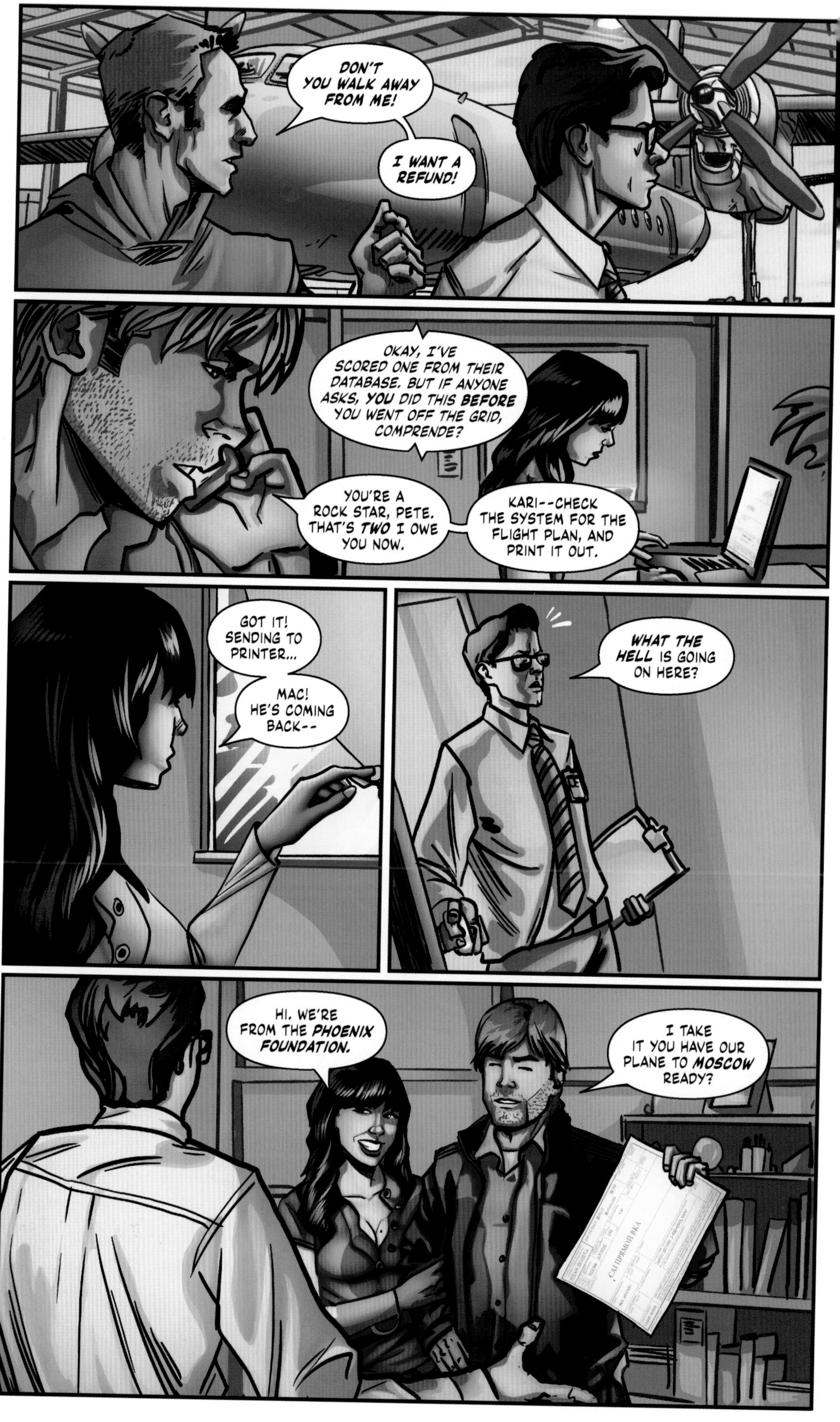
DON'T YOU WALK AWAY FROM ME!
I WANT A REFUND!
OKAY, I'VE SCORED ONE FROM THEIR DATABASE. BUT IF ANYONE ASKS, YOU DID THIS BEFORE YOU WENT OFF THE GRID, COMPRENDE?
YOU'RE A ROCK STAR, PETE. THAT'S TWO I OWE YOU NOW.
KARI--CHECK THE SYSTEM FOR THE FLIGHT PLAN, AND PRINT IT OUT.
GOT IT! SENDING TO PRINTER...
MAC! HE'S COMING BACK--
WHAT THE HELL IS GOING ON HERE?
HI. WE'RE FROM THE PHOENIX FOUNDATION.
I TAKE IT YOU HAVE OUR PLANE TO MOSCOW READY?

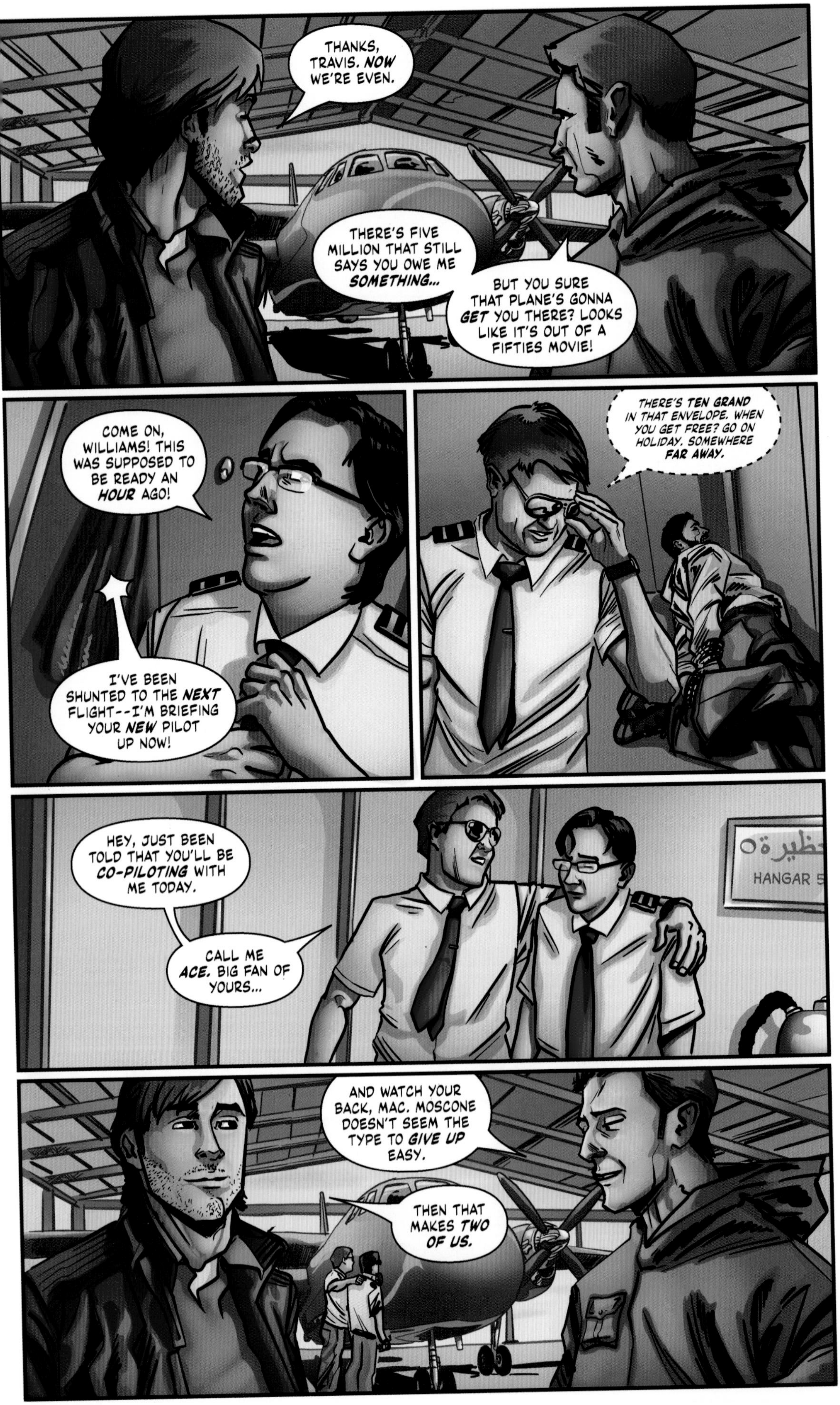
THANKS, TRAVIS. NOW WE'RE EVEN.
THERE'S FIVE MILLION THAT STILL SAYS YOU OWE ME SOMETHING...
BUT YOU SURE THAT PLANE'S GONNA GET YOU THERE? LOOKS LIKE IT'S OUT OF A FIFTIES MOVIE!
COME ON, WILLIAMS! THIS WAS SUPPOSED TO BE READY AN HOUR AGO!
I'VE BEEN SHUNTED TO THE NEXT FLIGHT--I'M BRIEFING YOUR NEW PILOT UP NOW!
THERE'S TEN GRAND IN THAT ENVELOPE. WHEN YOU GET FREE? GO ON HOLIDAY. SOMEWHERE FAR AWAY.
HEY, JUST BEEN TOLD THAT YOU'LL BE CO-PILOTING WITH ME TODAY.
CALL ME ACE. BIG FAN OF YOURS...
HANGAR 5
AND WATCH YOUR BACK, MAC. MOSCONE DOESN'T SEEM THE TYPE TO GIVE UP EASY.
THEN THAT MAKES TWO OF US.

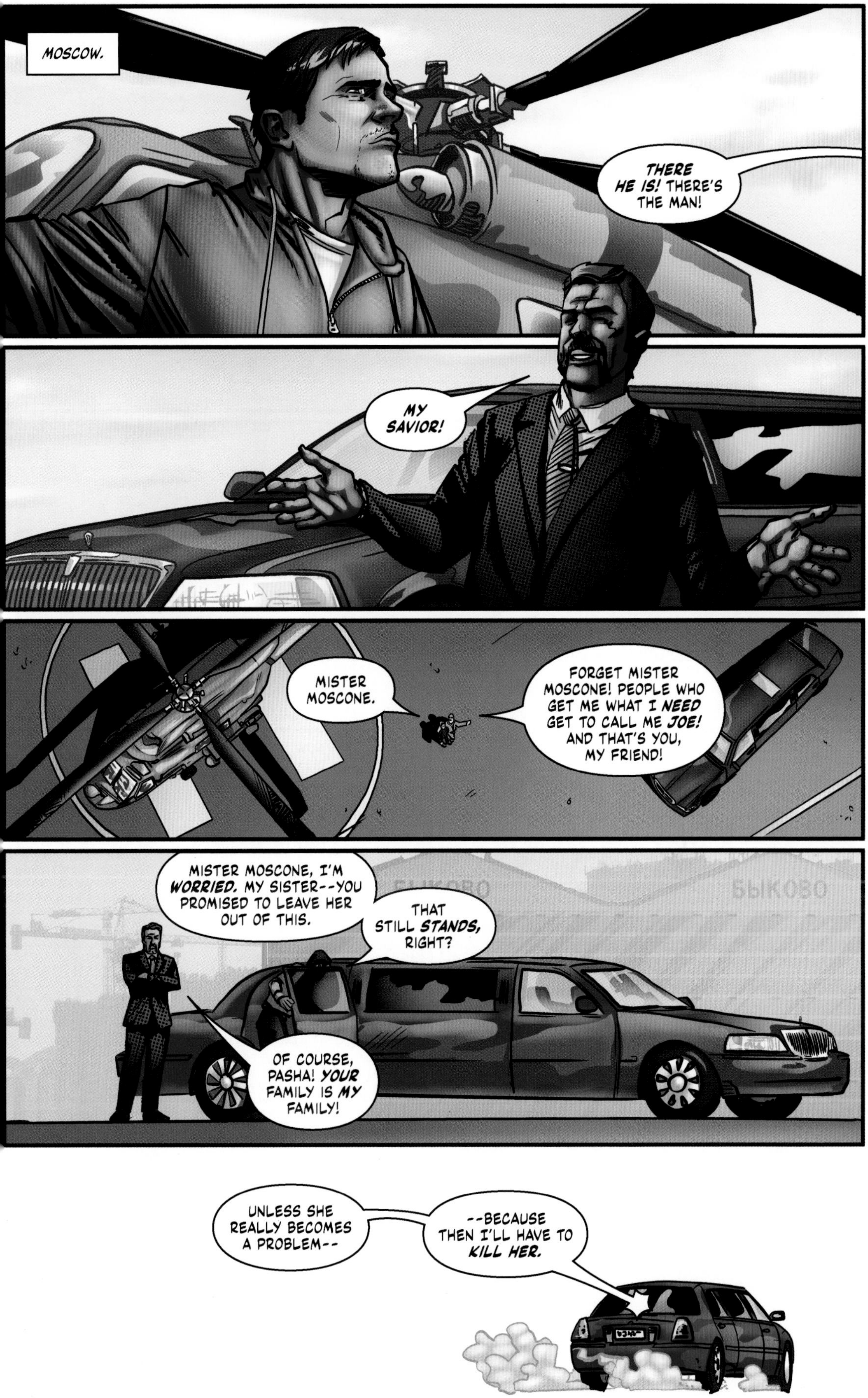
MOSCOW.
THERE HE IS! THERE'S THE MAN!
MY SAVIOR!
MISTER MOSCONE.
FORGET MISTER MOSCONE! PEOPLE WHO GET ME WHAT I NEED GET TO CALL ME JOE! AND THAT'S YOU, MY FRIEND!
БЫКОВО
БЫКОВО
MISTER MOSCONE, I'M WORRIED. MY SISTER--YOU PROMISED TO LEAVE HER OUT OF THIS.
THAT STILL STANDS, RIGHT?
OF COURSE, PASHA! YOUR FAMILY IS MY FAMILY!
UNLESS SHE REALLY BECOMES A PROBLEM--
--BECAUSE THEN I'LL HAVE TO KILL HER.

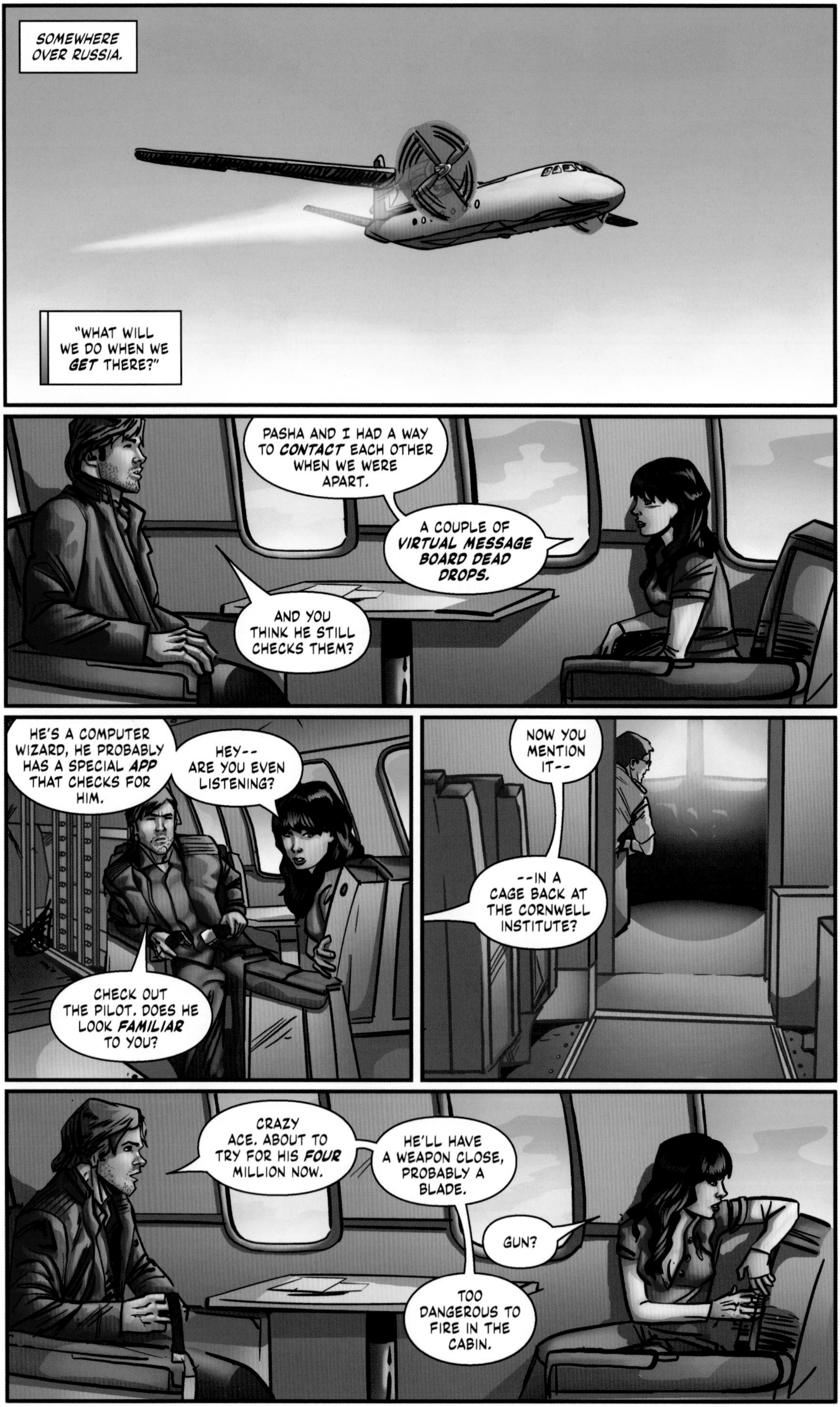
SOMEWHERE OVER RUSSIA.
"WHAT WILL WE DO WHEN WE GET THERE?"
PASHA AND I HAD A WAY TO CONTACT EACH OTHER WHEN WE WERE APART.
A COUPLE OF VIRTUAL MESSAGE BOARD DEAD DROPS.
AND YOU THINK HE STILL CHECKS THEM?
HE'S A COMPUTER WIZARD, HE PROBABLY HAS A SPECIAL APP THAT CHECKS FOR HIM.
HEY-- ARE YOU EVEN LISTENING?
CHECK OUT THE PILOT. DOES HE LOOK FAMILIAR TO YOU?
NOW YOU MENTION IT--
--IN A CAGE BACK AT THE CORNWELL INSTITUTE?
CRAZY ACE. ABOUT TO TRY FOR HIS FOUR MILLION NOW.
HE'LL HAVE A WEAPON CLOSE, PROBABLY A BLADE.
GUN?
TOO DANGEROUS TO FIRE IN THE CABIN.

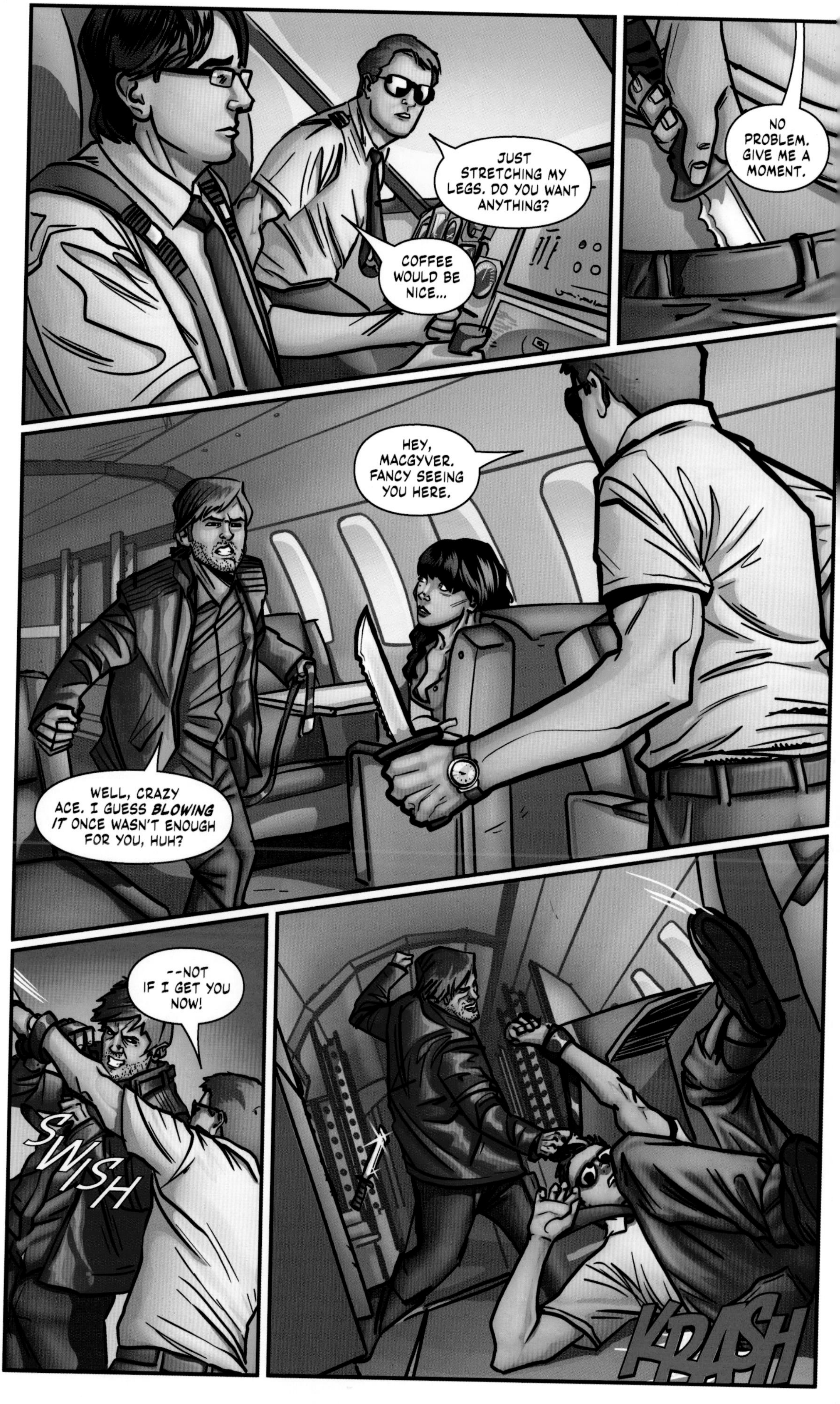
JUST STRETCHING MY LEGS. DO YOU WANT ANYTHING?
COFFEE WOULD BE NICE...
NO PROBLEM. GIVE ME A MOMENT.
HEY, MACGYVER. FANCY SEEING YOU HERE.
WELL, CRAZY ACE. I GUESS *BLOWING IT* ONCE WASN'T ENOUGH FOR YOU, HUH?
--NOT IF I GET YOU NOW!
SWISH
KRASH

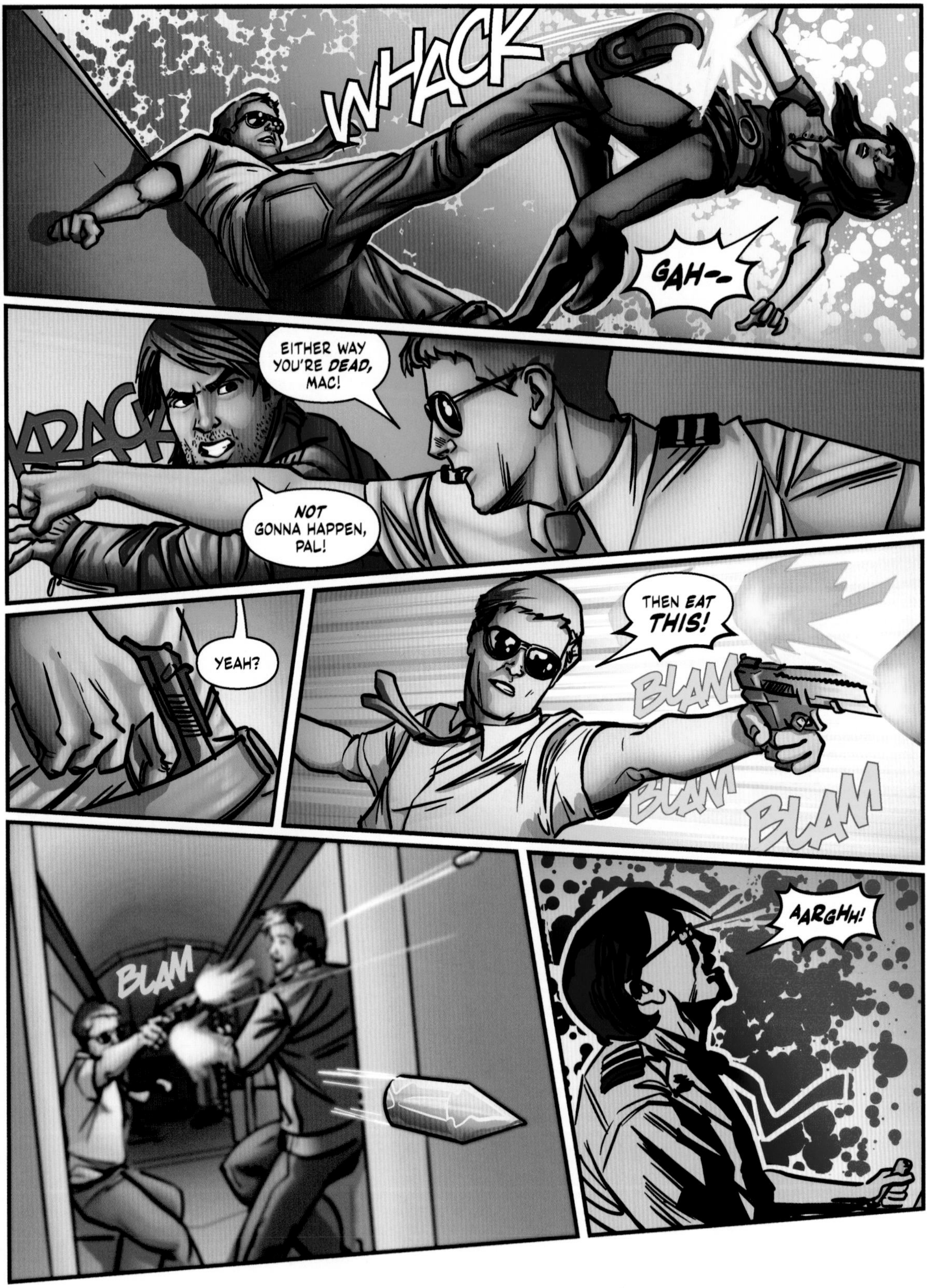
WHACK
GAH--
EITHER WAY YOU'RE *DEAD*, MAC!
KRACK
NOT GONNA HAPPEN, PAL!
YEAH?
THEN *EAT* **THIS!**
BLAM
BLAM
BLAM
BLAM
AARGHH!

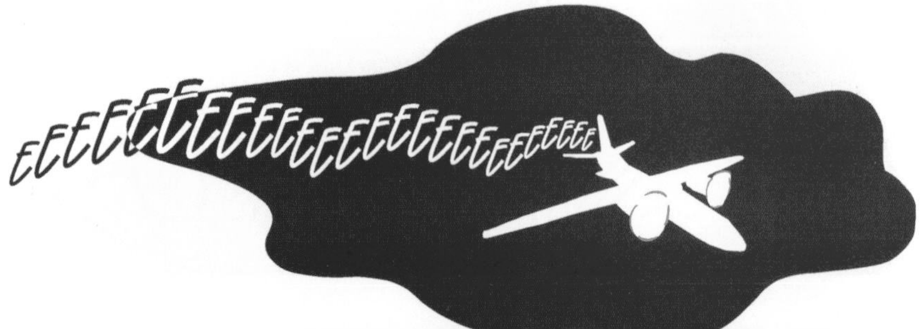
EEEEEEEEEEEEEEEEEEEEEEEEEEE

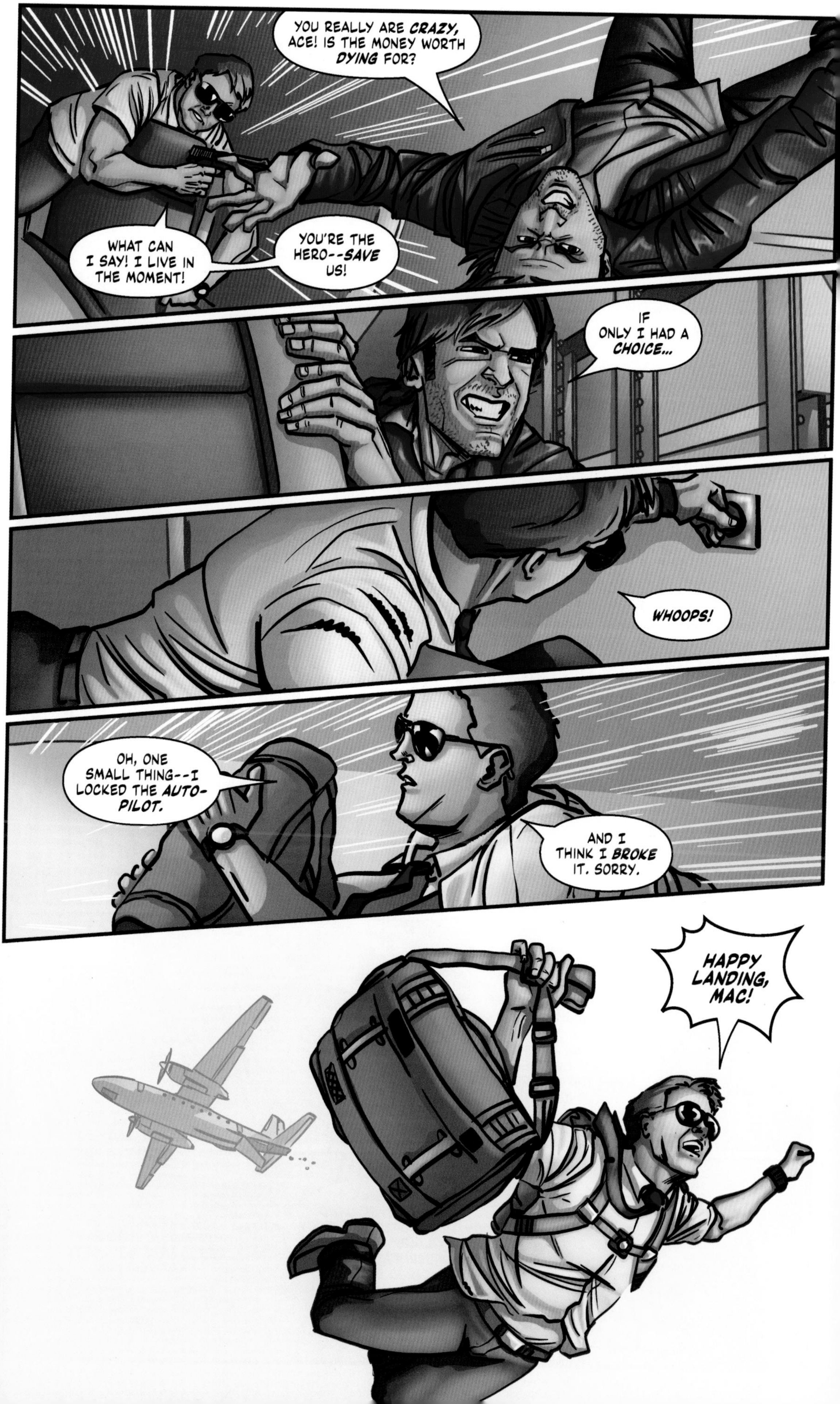
YOU REALLY ARE CRAZY, ACE! IS THE MONEY WORTH DYING FOR?
WHAT CAN I SAY! I LIVE IN THE MOMENT!
YOU'RE THE HERO--SAVE US!
IF ONLY I HAD A CHOICE...
WHOOPS!
OH, ONE SMALL THING--I LOCKED THE AUTO-PILOT.
AND I THINK I BROKE IT. SORRY.
HAPPY LANDING, MAC!

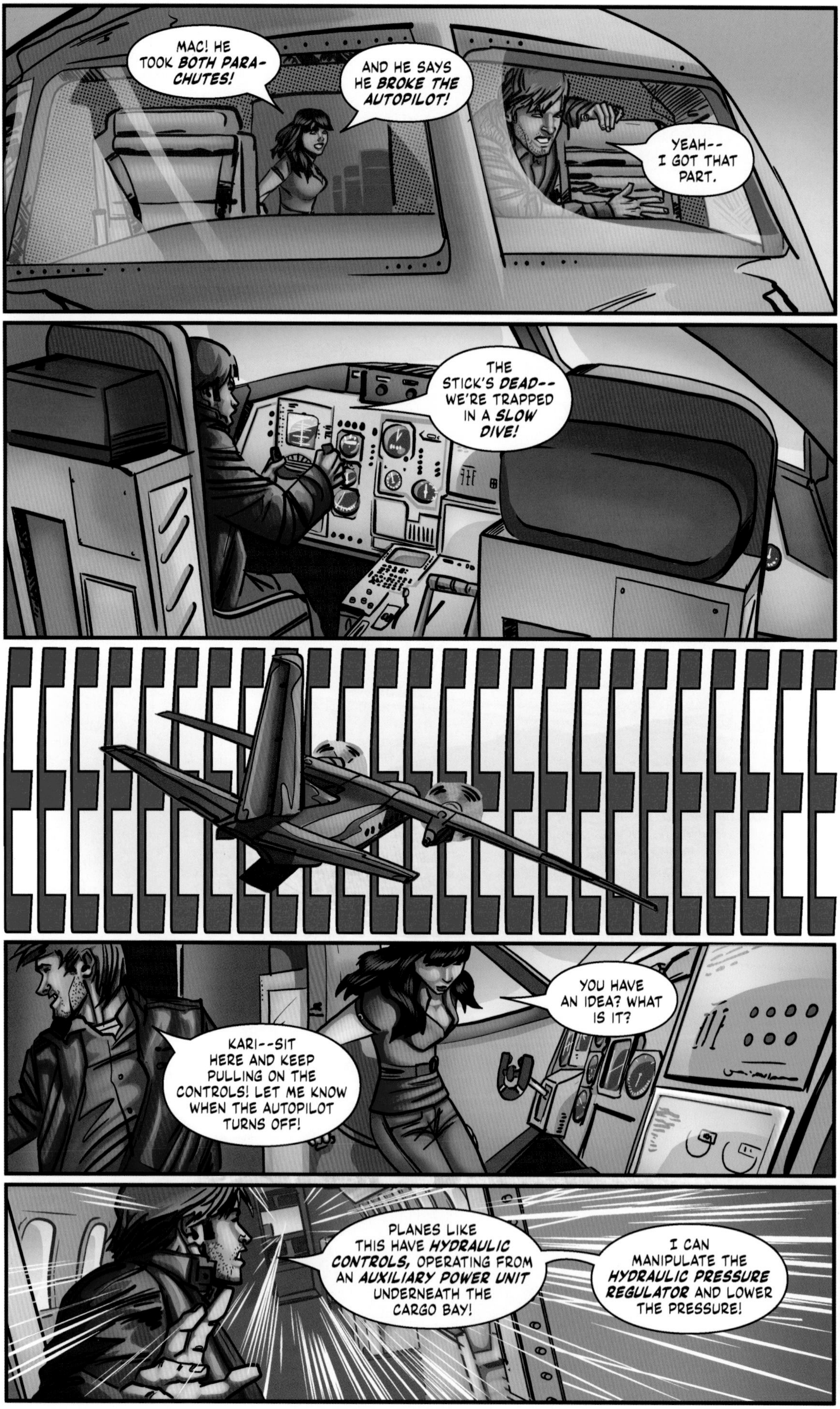
MAC! HE TOOK BOTH PARA-CHUTES!
AND HE SAYS HE BROKE THE AUTOPILOT!
YEAH-- I GOT THAT PART.
THE STICK'S DEAD-- WE'RE TRAPPED IN A SLOW DIVE!
EEEEEEEEEEEEEEEEEEEEEEEEEEEEEEE
YOU HAVE AN IDEA? WHAT IS IT?
KARI--SIT HERE AND KEEP PULLING ON THE CONTROLS! LET ME KNOW WHEN THE AUTOPILOT TURNS OFF!
PLANES LIKE THIS HAVE HYDRAULIC CONTROLS, OPERATING FROM AN AUXILIARY POWER UNIT UNDERNEATH THE CARGO BAY!
I CAN MANIPULATE THE HYDRAULIC PRESSURE REGULATOR AND LOWER THE PRESSURE!

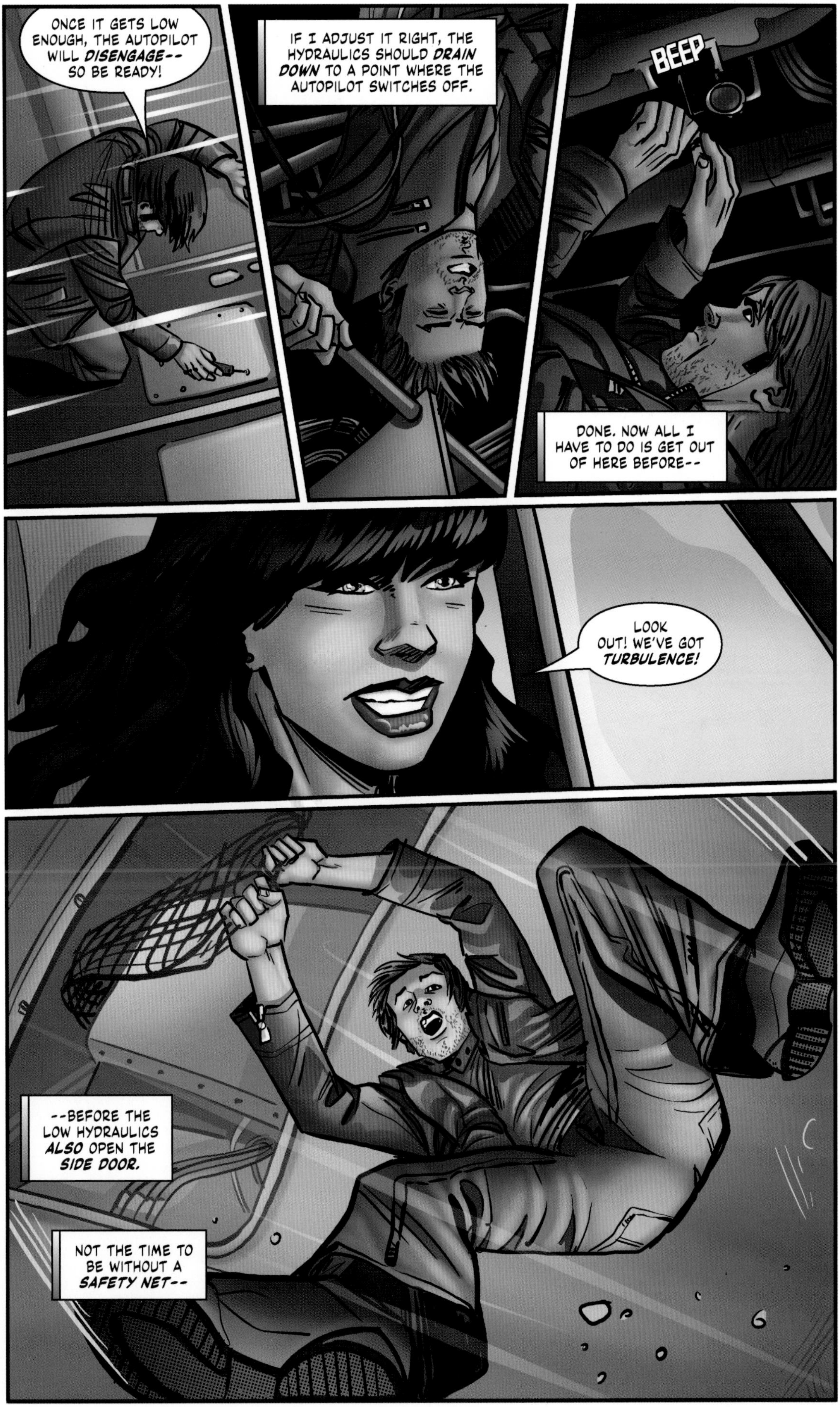
ONCE IT GETS LOW ENOUGH, THE AUTOPILOT WILL *DISENGAGE--* SO BE READY!
IF I ADJUST IT RIGHT, THE HYDRAULICS SHOULD *DRAIN DOWN* TO A POINT WHERE THE AUTOPILOT SWITCHES OFF.
BEEP
DONE. NOW ALL I HAVE TO DO IS GET OUT OF HERE BEFORE--
LOOK OUT! WE'VE GOT *TURBULENCE!*
--BEFORE THE LOW HYDRAULICS *ALSO* OPEN THE *SIDE DOOR.*
NOT THE TIME TO BE WITHOUT A *SAFETY NET--*

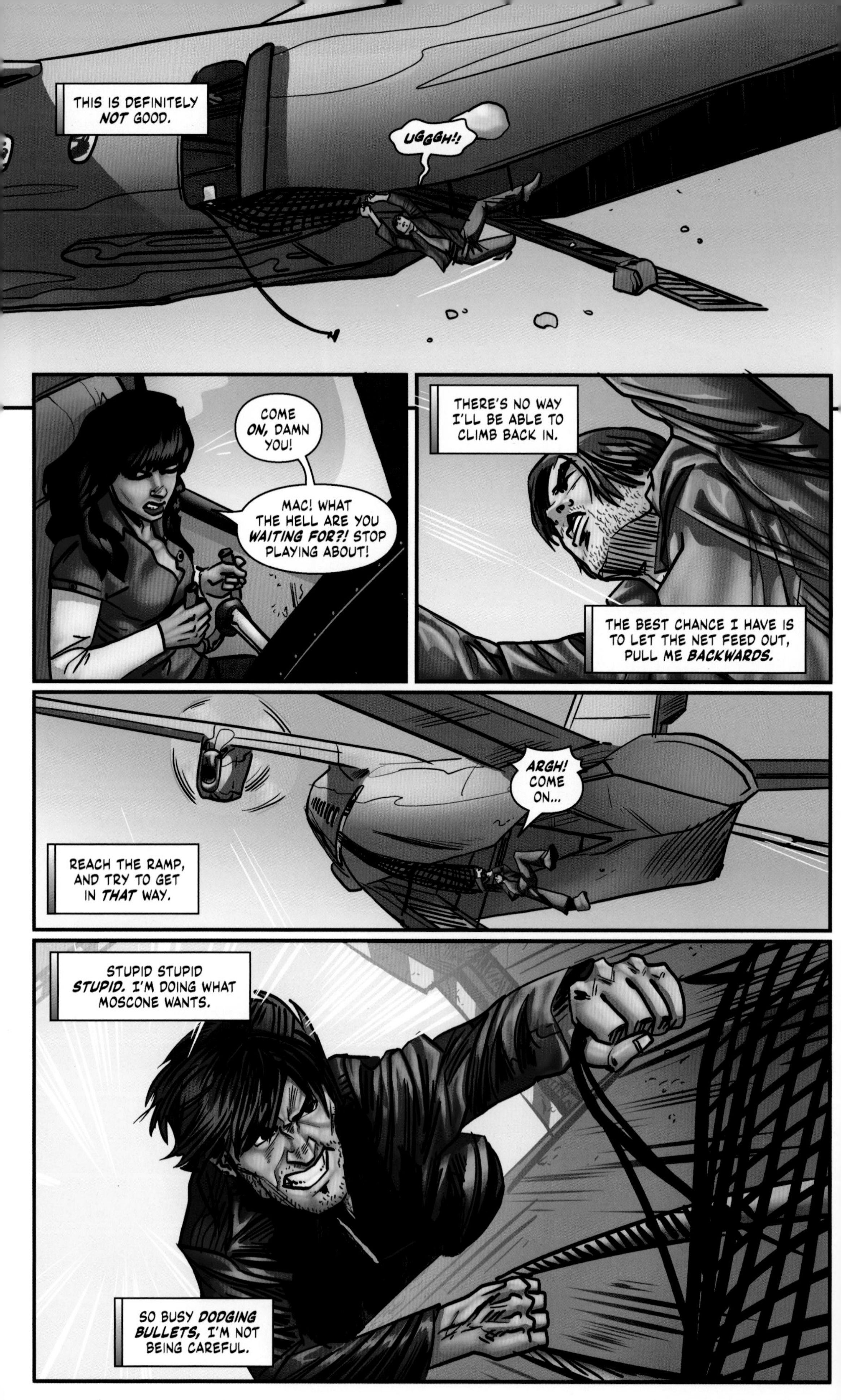
THIS IS DEFINITELY *NOT* GOOD.
UGGGH!!
COME *ON,* DAMN YOU!
MAC! WHAT THE HELL ARE YOU *WAITING FOR?!* STOP PLAYING ABOUT!
THERE'S NO WAY I'LL BE ABLE TO CLIMB BACK IN.
THE BEST CHANCE I HAVE IS TO LET THE NET FEED OUT, PULL ME *BACKWARDS.*
REACH THE RAMP, AND TRY TO GET IN *THAT* WAY.
ARGH! COME ON...
STUPID STUPID *STUPID.* I'M DOING WHAT MOSCONE WANTS.
SO BUSY *DODGING BULLETS,* I'M NOT BEING CAREFUL.

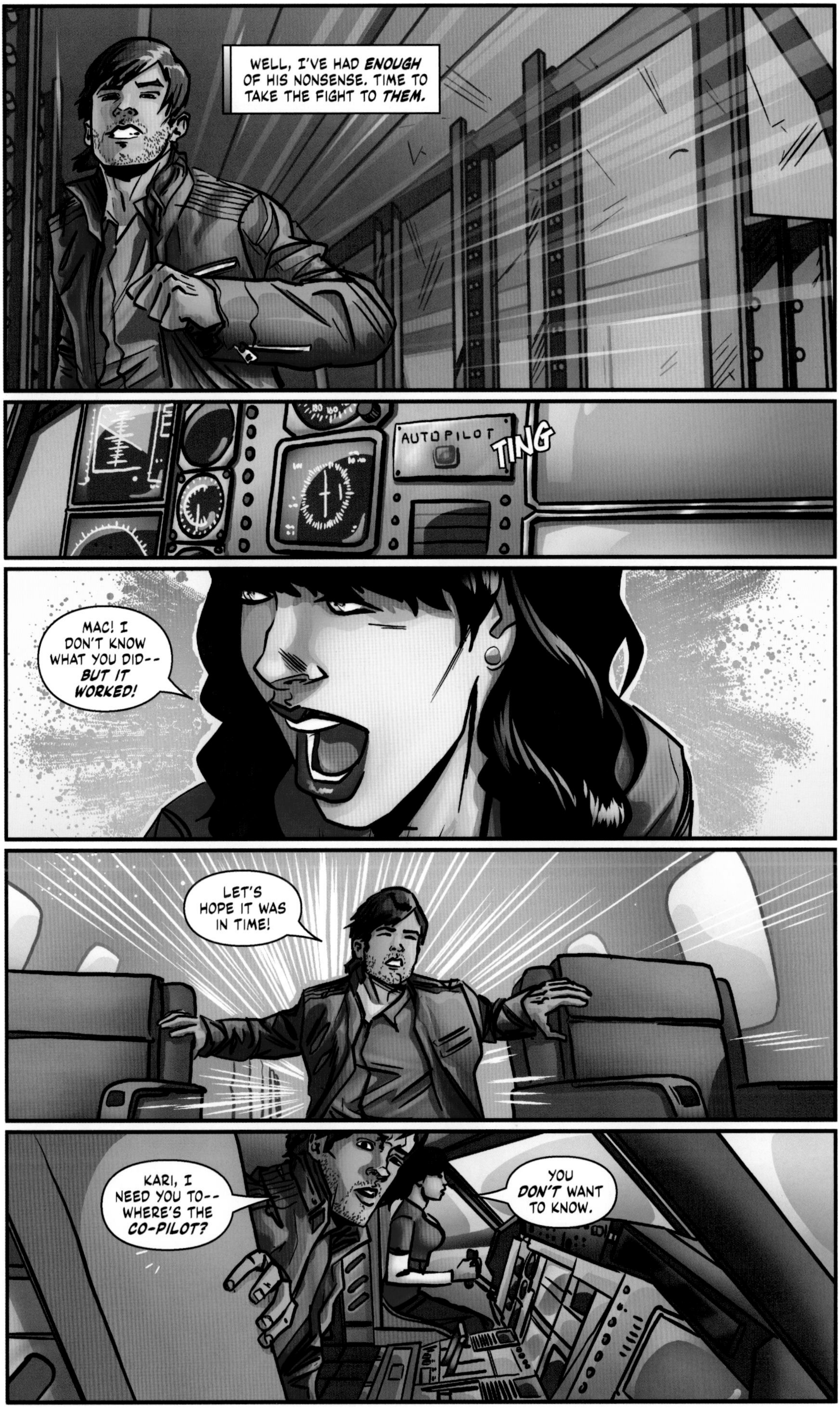
WELL, I'VE HAD *ENOUGH* OF HIS NONSENSE. TIME TO TAKE THE FIGHT TO *THEM.*
AUTOPILOT
TING
MAC! I DON'T KNOW WHAT YOU DID-- *BUT IT WORKED!*
LET'S HOPE IT WAS IN TIME!
KARI, I NEED YOU TO-- WHERE'S THE *CO-PILOT?*
YOU *DON'T* WANT TO KNOW.

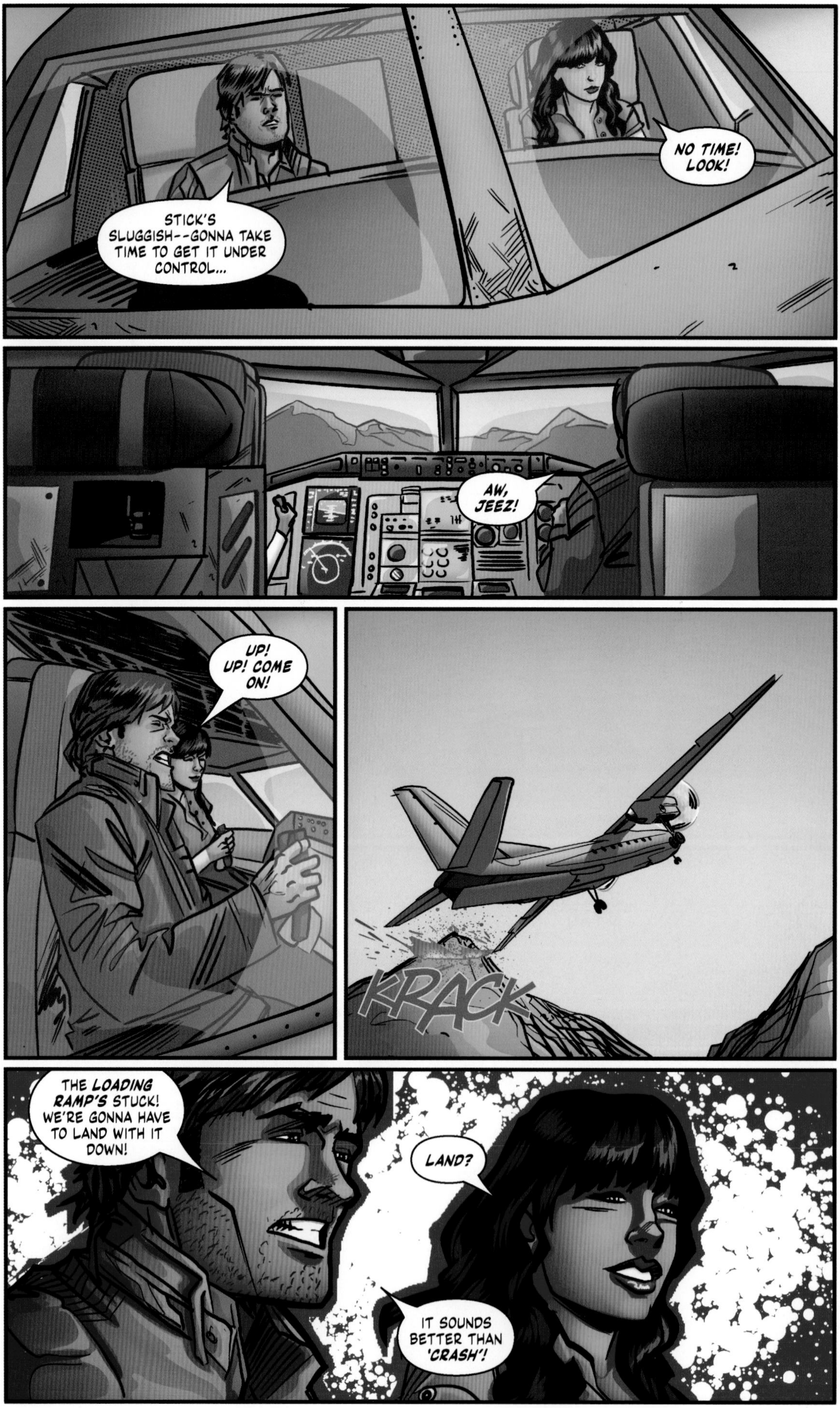
STICK'S SLUGGISH--GONNA TAKE TIME TO GET IT UNDER CONTROL...
NO TIME! LOOK!
AW, JEEZ!
UP! UP! COME ON!
KRACK
THE LOADING RAMP'S STUCK! WE'RE GONNA HAVE TO LAND WITH IT DOWN!
LAND?
IT SOUNDS BETTER THAN 'CRASH'!

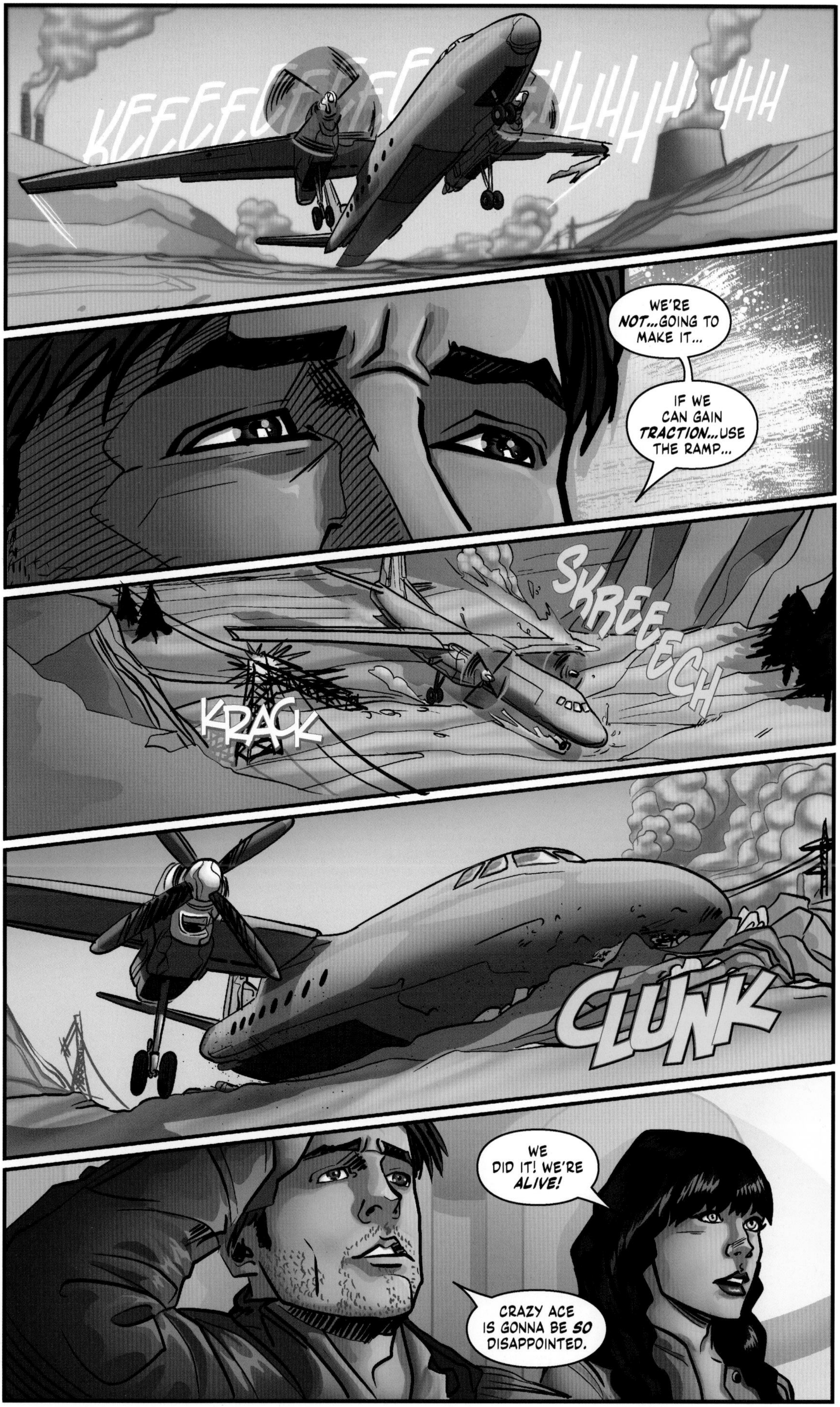
KEEEEEEEEEEEEHHHHHHHHHHH
WE'RE NOT...GOING TO MAKE IT...
IF WE CAN GAIN TRACTION...USE THE RAMP...
SKREEEECH
KRACK
CLUNK
WE DID IT! WE'RE ALIVE!
CRAZY ACE IS GONNA BE SO DISAPPOINTED.

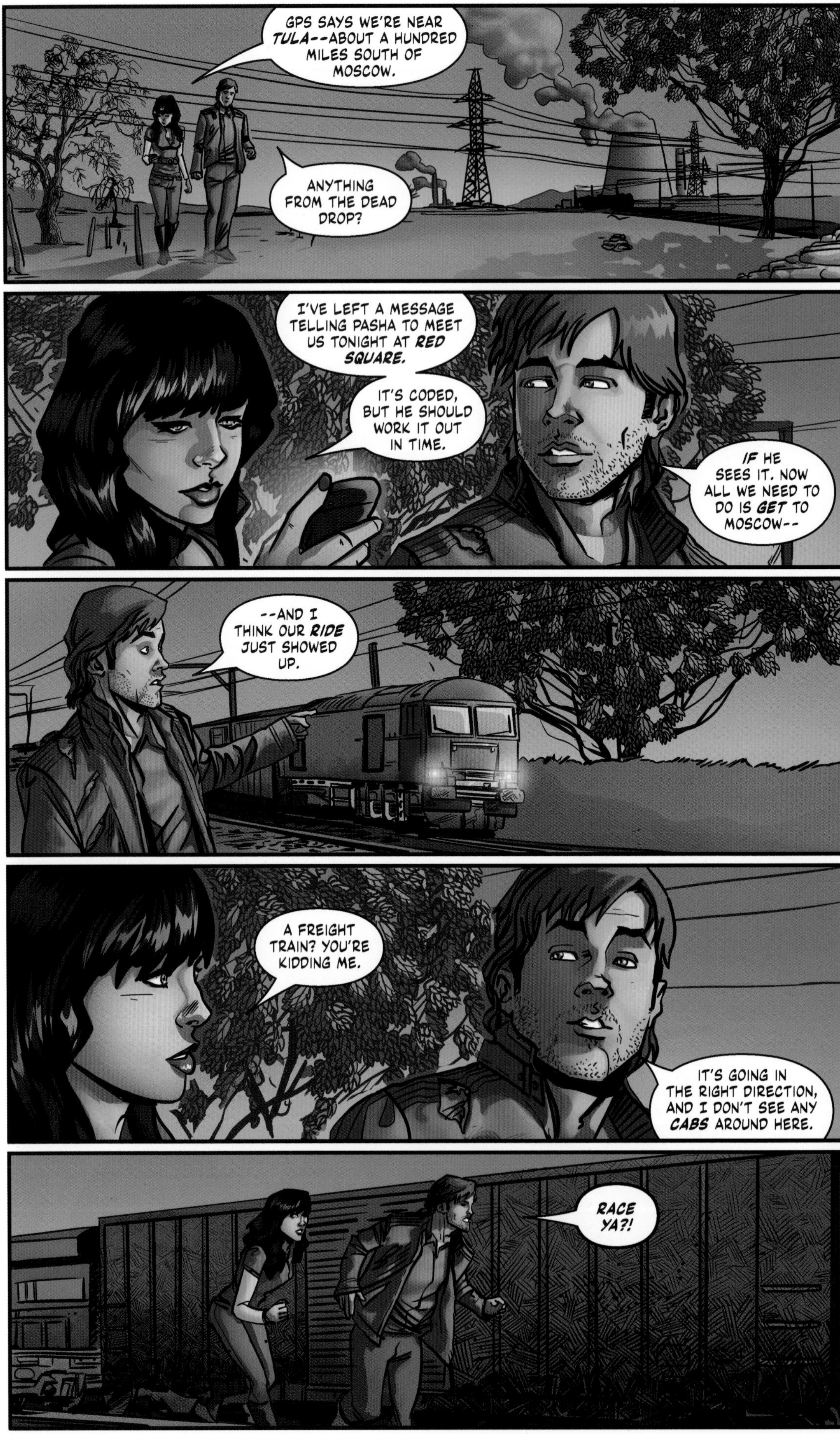
GPS SAYS WE'RE NEAR TULA--ABOUT A HUNDRED MILES SOUTH OF MOSCOW.
ANYTHING FROM THE DEAD DROP?
I'VE LEFT A MESSAGE TELLING PASHA TO MEET US TONIGHT AT RED SQUARE.
IT'S CODED, BUT HE SHOULD WORK IT OUT IN TIME.
IF HE SEES IT. NOW ALL WE NEED TO DO IS GET TO MOSCOW--
--AND I THINK OUR RIDE JUST SHOWED UP.
A FREIGHT TRAIN? YOU'RE KIDDING ME.
IT'S GOING IN THE RIGHT DIRECTION, AND I DON'T SEE ANY CABS AROUND HERE.
RACE YA?!

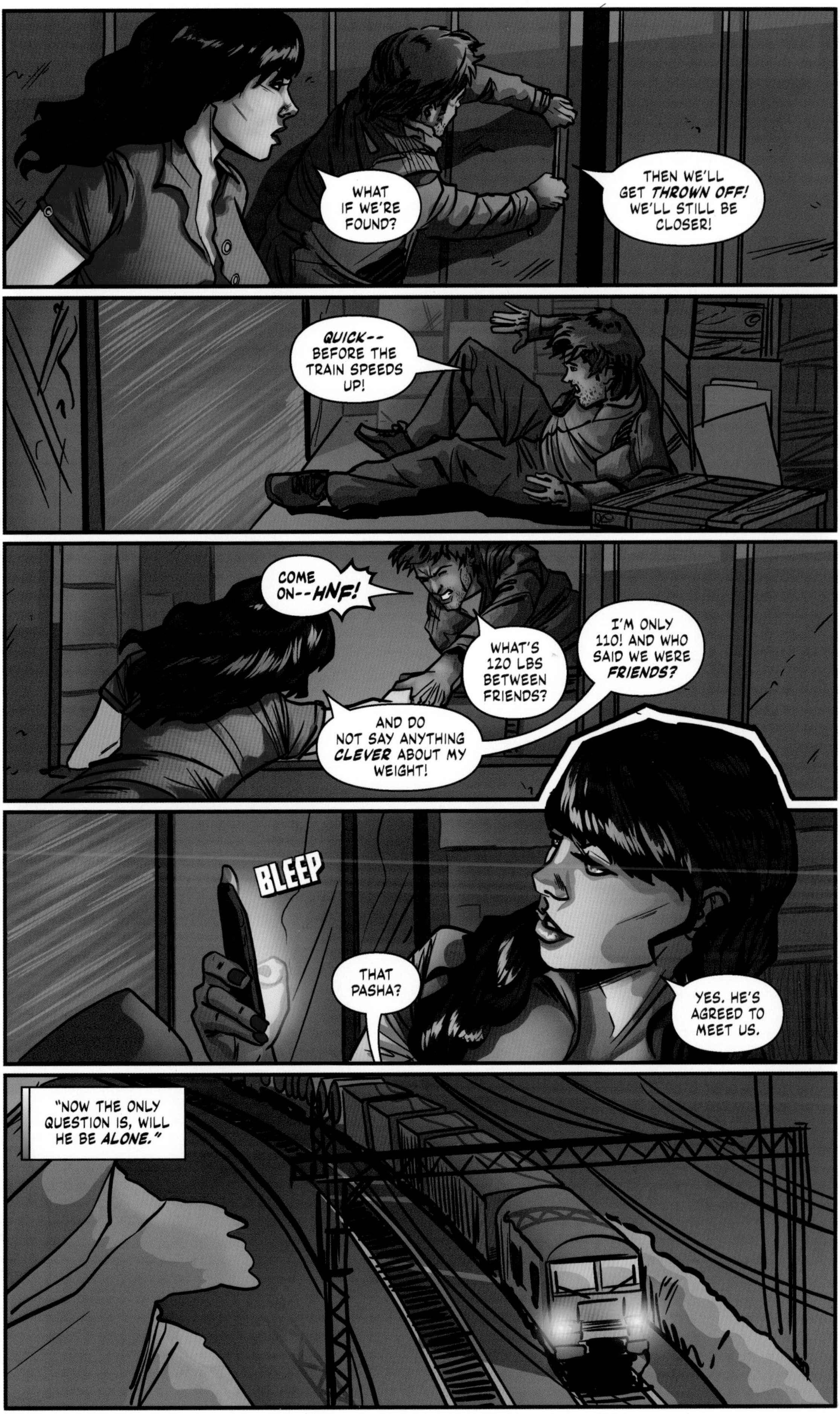
WHAT IF WE'RE FOUND?
THEN WE'LL GET *THROWN OFF!* WE'LL STILL BE CLOSER!
QUICK-- BEFORE THE TRAIN SPEEDS UP!
COME ON--*HNF!*
WHAT'S 120 LBS BETWEEN FRIENDS?
I'M ONLY 110! AND WHO SAID WE WERE *FRIENDS?*
AND DO NOT SAY ANYTHING *CLEVER* ABOUT MY WEIGHT!
BLEEP
THAT PASHA?
YES. HE'S AGREED TO MEET US.
"NOW THE ONLY QUESTION IS, WILL HE BE *ALONE.*"

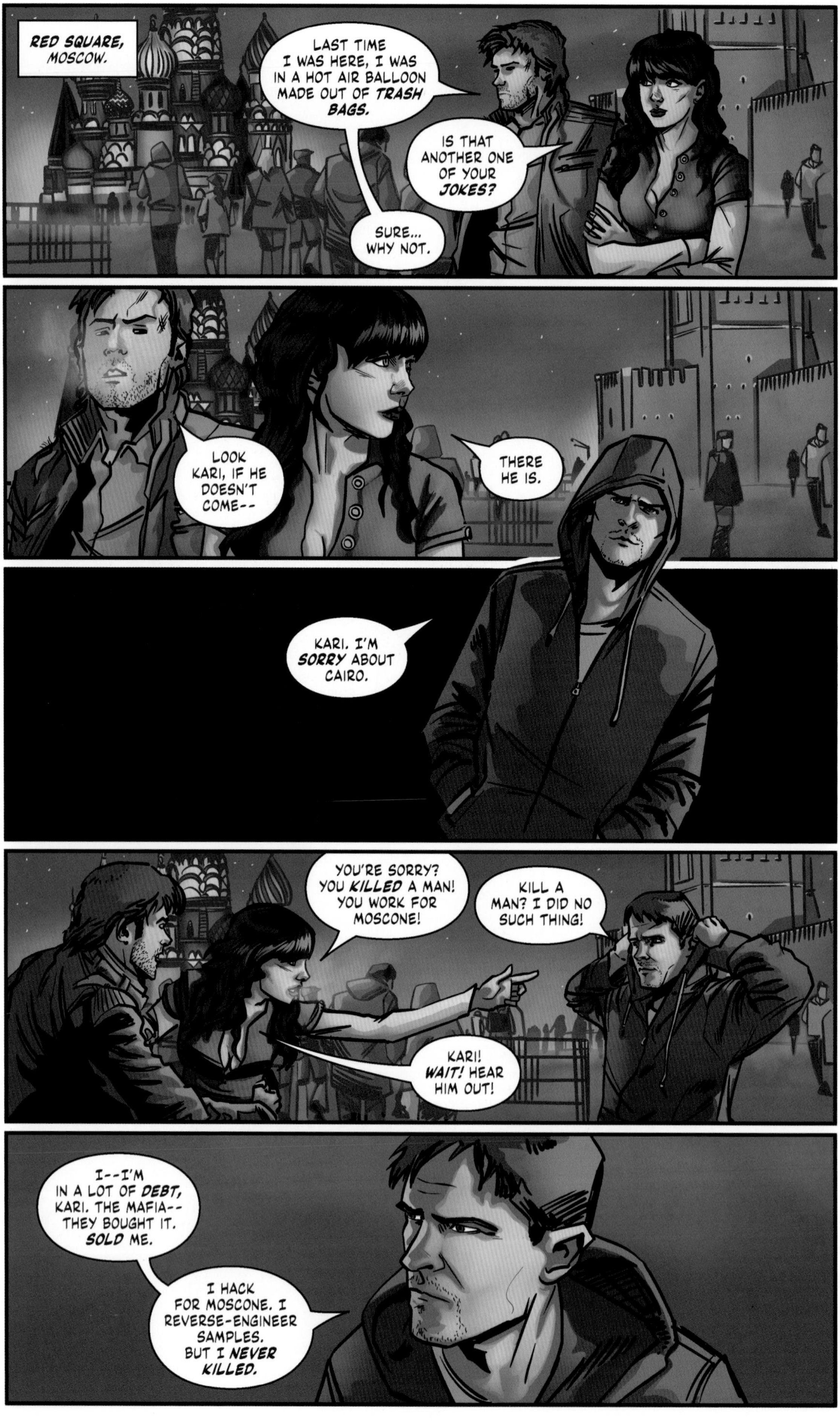
RED SQUARE, MOSCOW.
LAST TIME I WAS HERE, I WAS IN A HOT AIR BALLOON MADE OUT OF TRASH BAGS.
IS THAT ANOTHER ONE OF YOUR JOKES?
SURE... WHY NOT.
LOOK KARI, IF HE DOESN'T COME--
THERE HE IS.
KARI. I'M SORRY ABOUT CAIRO.
YOU'RE SORRY? YOU KILLED A MAN! YOU WORK FOR MOSCONE!
KILL A MAN? I DID NO SUCH THING!
KARI! WAIT! HEAR HIM OUT!
I--I'M IN A LOT OF DEBT, KARI. THE MAFIA--THEY BOUGHT IT. SOLD ME.
I HACK FOR MOSCONE. I REVERSE-ENGINEER SAMPLES. BUT I NEVER KILLED.

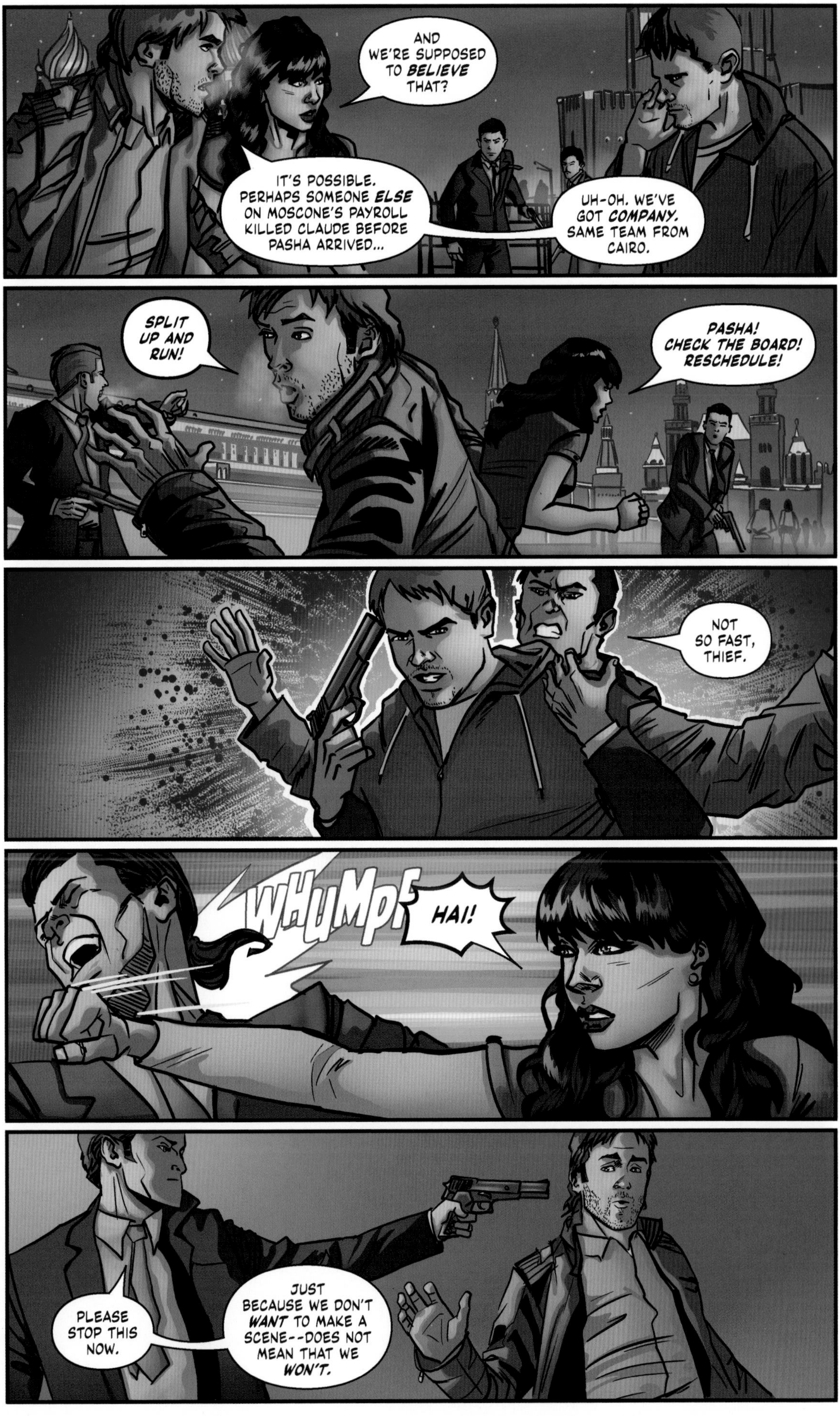
AND WE'RE SUPPOSED TO BELIEVE THAT?
IT'S POSSIBLE. PERHAPS SOMEONE ELSE ON MOSCONE'S PAYROLL KILLED CLAUDE BEFORE PASHA ARRIVED...
UH-OH. WE'VE GOT COMPANY. SAME TEAM FROM CAIRO.
SPLIT UP AND RUN!
PASHA! CHECK THE BOARD! RESCHEDULE!
NOT SO FAST, THIEF.
WHUMPF
HAI!
JUST BECAUSE WE DON'T WANT TO MAKE A SCENE--DOES NOT MEAN THAT WE WON'T.
PLEASE STOP THIS NOW.

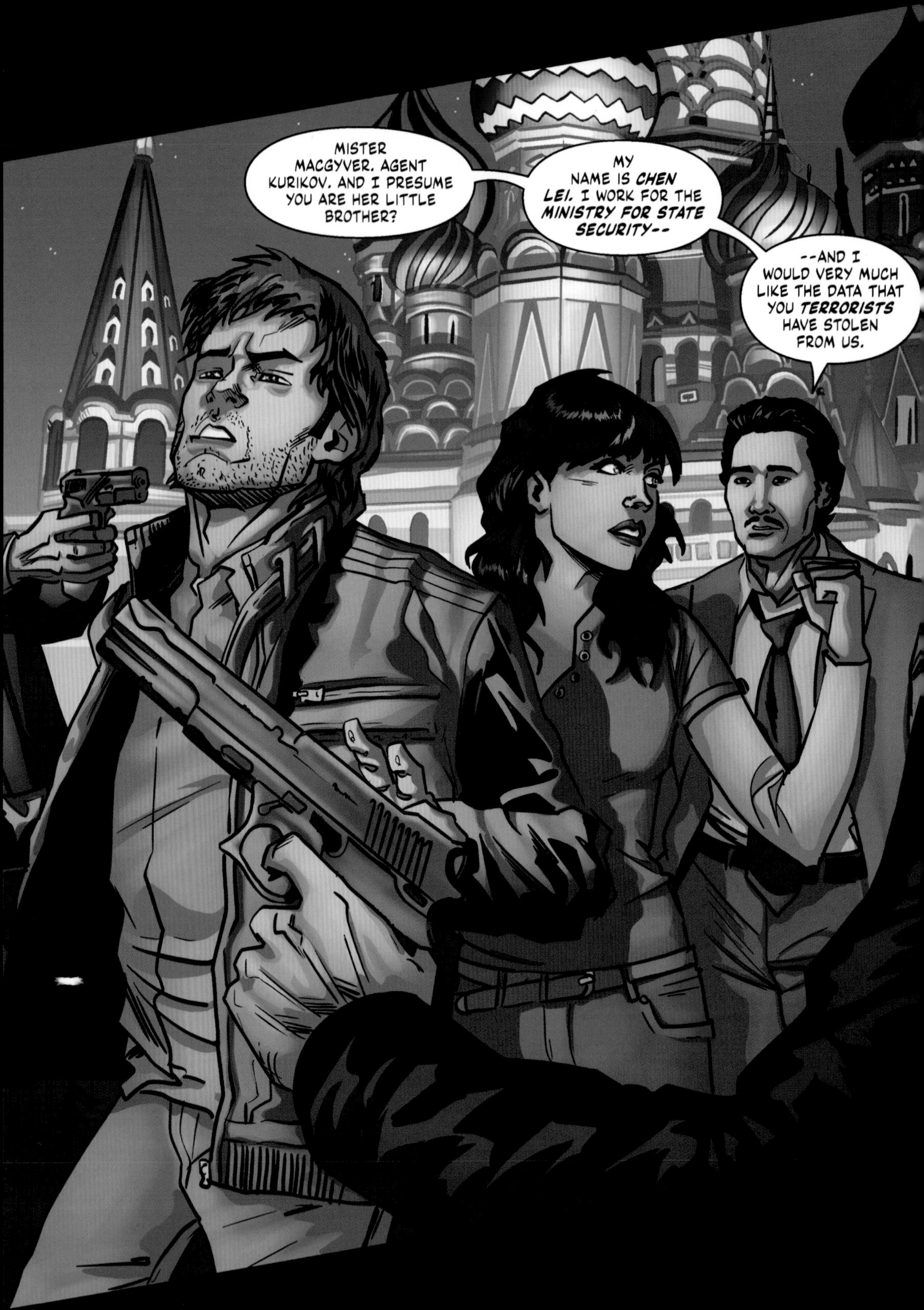
MISTER MACGYVER. AGENT KURIKOV. AND I PRESUME YOU ARE HER LITTLE BROTHER?
MY NAME IS *CHEN LEI.* I WORK FOR THE *MINISTRY FOR STATE SECURITY--*
--AND I WOULD VERY MUCH LIKE THE DATA THAT YOU *TERRORISTS* HAVE STOLEN FROM US.

END OF PART THREE.

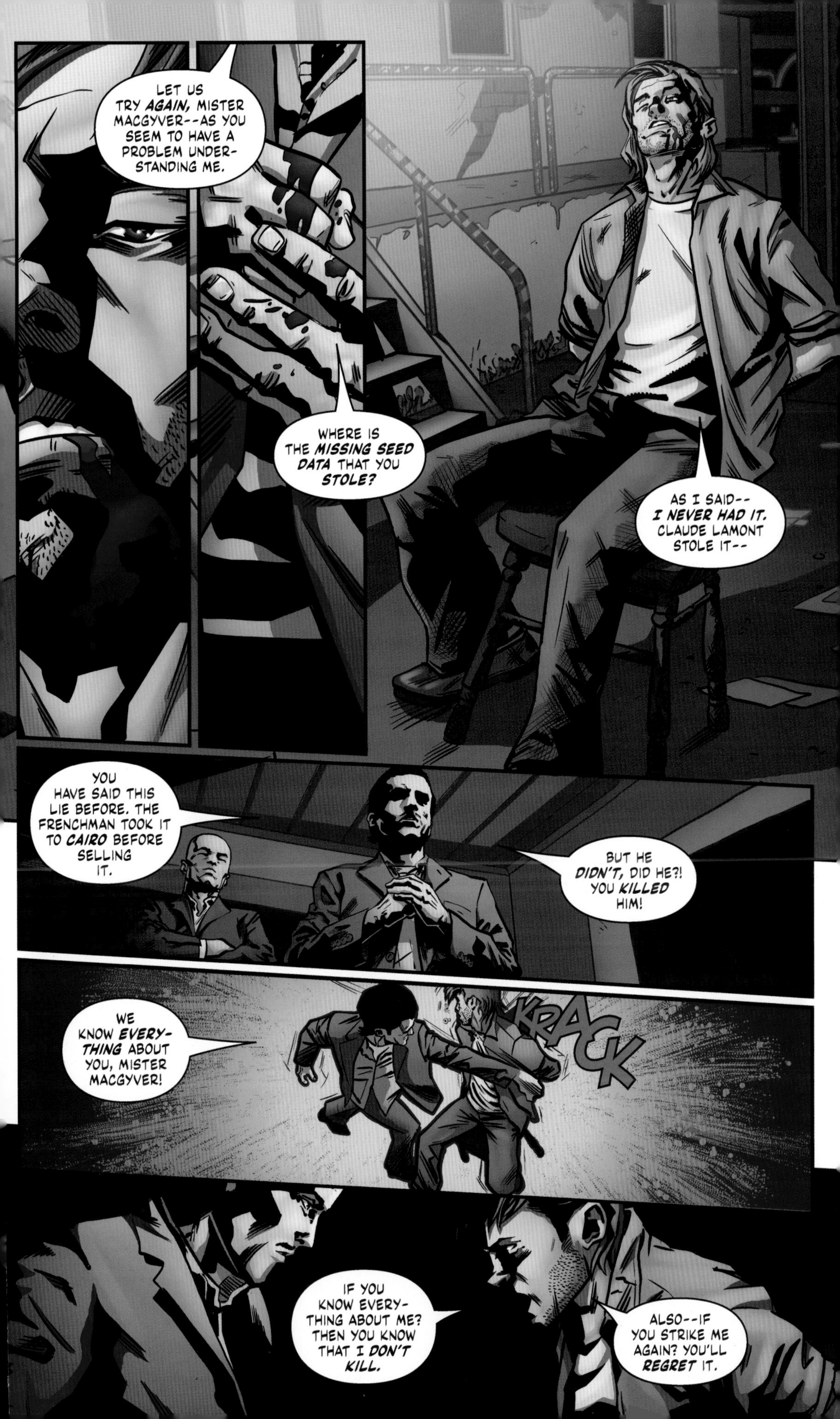

LET US TRY AGAIN, MISTER MACGYVER--AS YOU SEEM TO HAVE A PROBLEM UNDER-STANDING ME.
WHERE IS THE MISSING SEED DATA THAT YOU STOLE?
AS I SAID-- I NEVER HAD IT. CLAUDE LAMONT STOLE IT--
YOU HAVE SAID THIS LIE BEFORE. THE FRENCHMAN TOOK IT TO CAIRO BEFORE SELLING IT.
BUT HE DIDN'T, DID HE?! YOU KILLED HIM!
WE KNOW EVERY-THING ABOUT YOU, MISTER MACGYVER!
KRACK
IF YOU KNOW EVERY-THING ABOUT ME? THEN YOU KNOW THAT I DON'T KILL.
ALSO--IF YOU STRIKE ME AGAIN? YOU'LL REGRET IT.

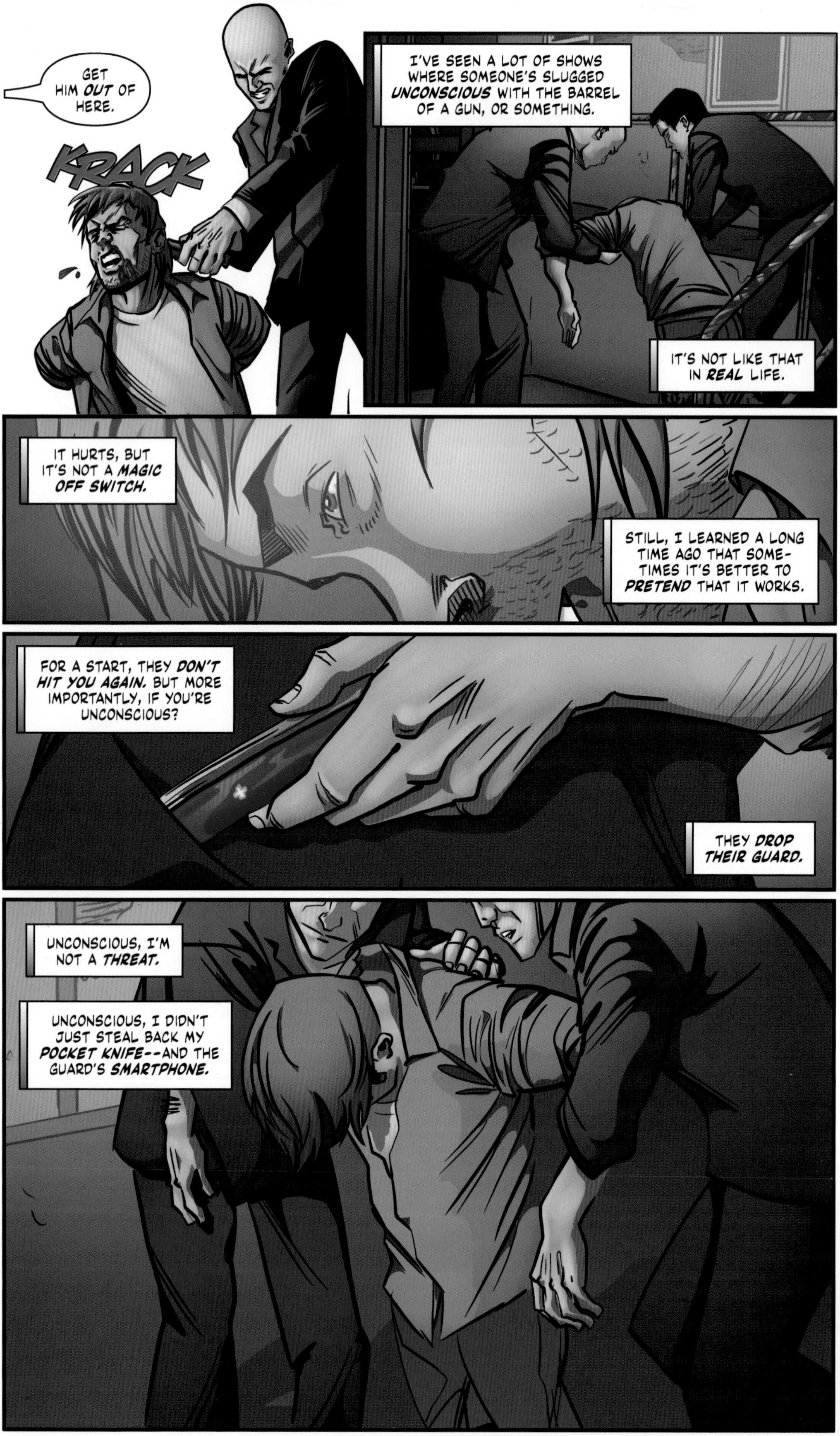
GET HIM OUT OF HERE.
KRACK
I'VE SEEN A LOT OF SHOWS WHERE SOMEONE'S SLUGGED UNCONSCIOUS WITH THE BARREL OF A GUN, OR SOMETHING.
IT'S NOT LIKE THAT IN REAL LIFE.
IT HURTS, BUT IT'S NOT A MAGIC OFF SWITCH.
STILL, I LEARNED A LONG TIME AGO THAT SOME-TIMES IT'S BETTER TO PRETEND THAT IT WORKS.
FOR A START, THEY DON'T HIT YOU AGAIN. BUT MORE IMPORTANTLY, IF YOU'RE UNCONSCIOUS?
THEY DROP THEIR GUARD.
UNCONSCIOUS, I'M NOT A THREAT.
UNCONSCIOUS, I DIDN'T JUST STEAL BACK MY POCKET KNIFE--AND THE GUARD'S SMARTPHONE.

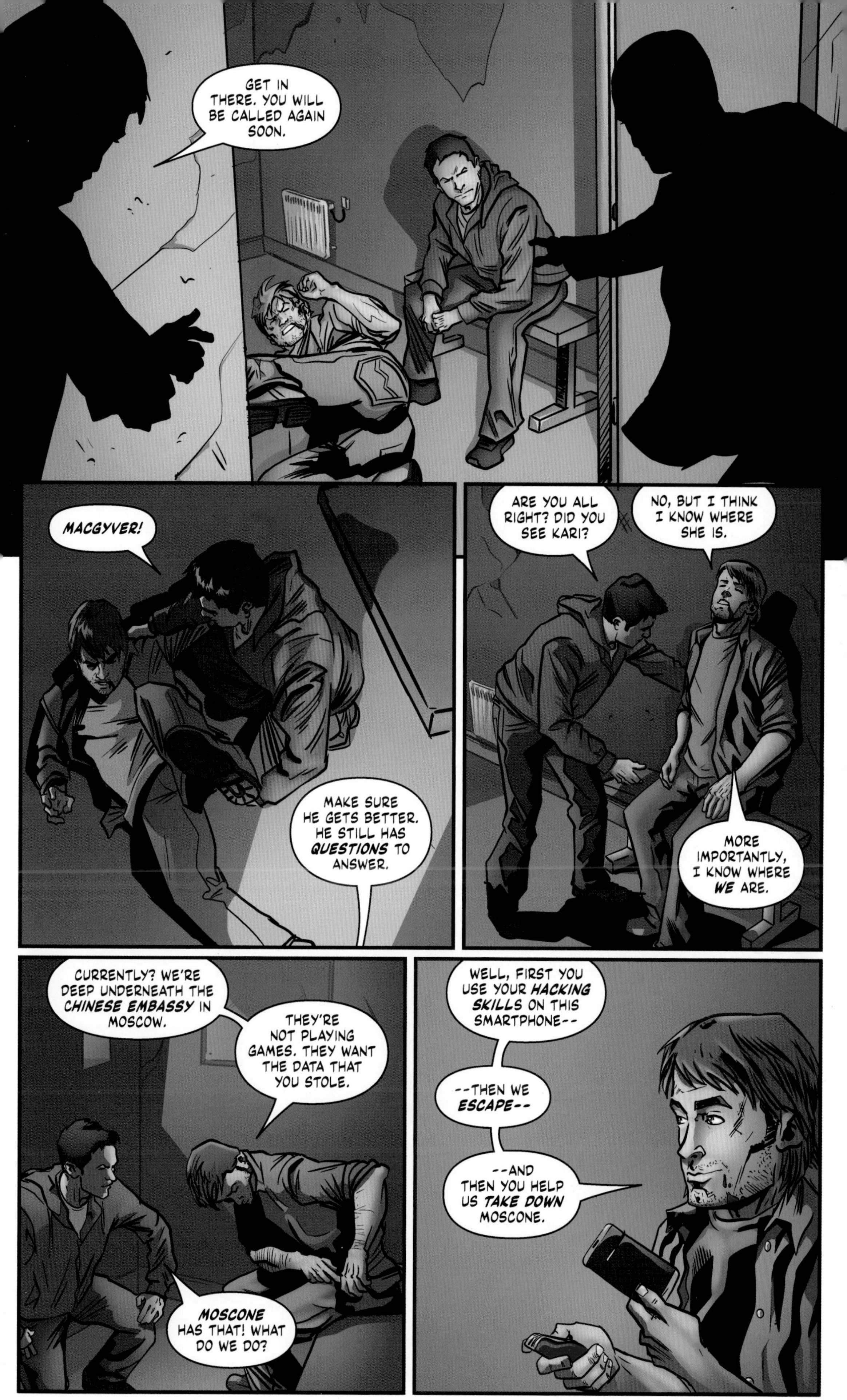
GET IN THERE. YOU WILL BE CALLED AGAIN SOON.
MACGYVER!
MAKE SURE HE GETS BETTER. HE STILL HAS QUESTIONS TO ANSWER.
ARE YOU ALL RIGHT? DID YOU SEE KARI?
NO, BUT I THINK I KNOW WHERE SHE IS.
MORE IMPORTANTLY, I KNOW WHERE WE ARE.
CURRENTLY? WE'RE DEEP UNDERNEATH THE CHINESE EMBASSY IN MOSCOW.
THEY'RE NOT PLAYING GAMES. THEY WANT THE DATA THAT YOU STOLE.
MOSCONE HAS THAT! WHAT DO WE DO?
WELL, FIRST YOU USE YOUR HACKING SKILLS ON THIS SMARTPHONE--
--THEN WE ESCAPE--
--AND THEN YOU HELP US TAKE DOWN MOSCONE.

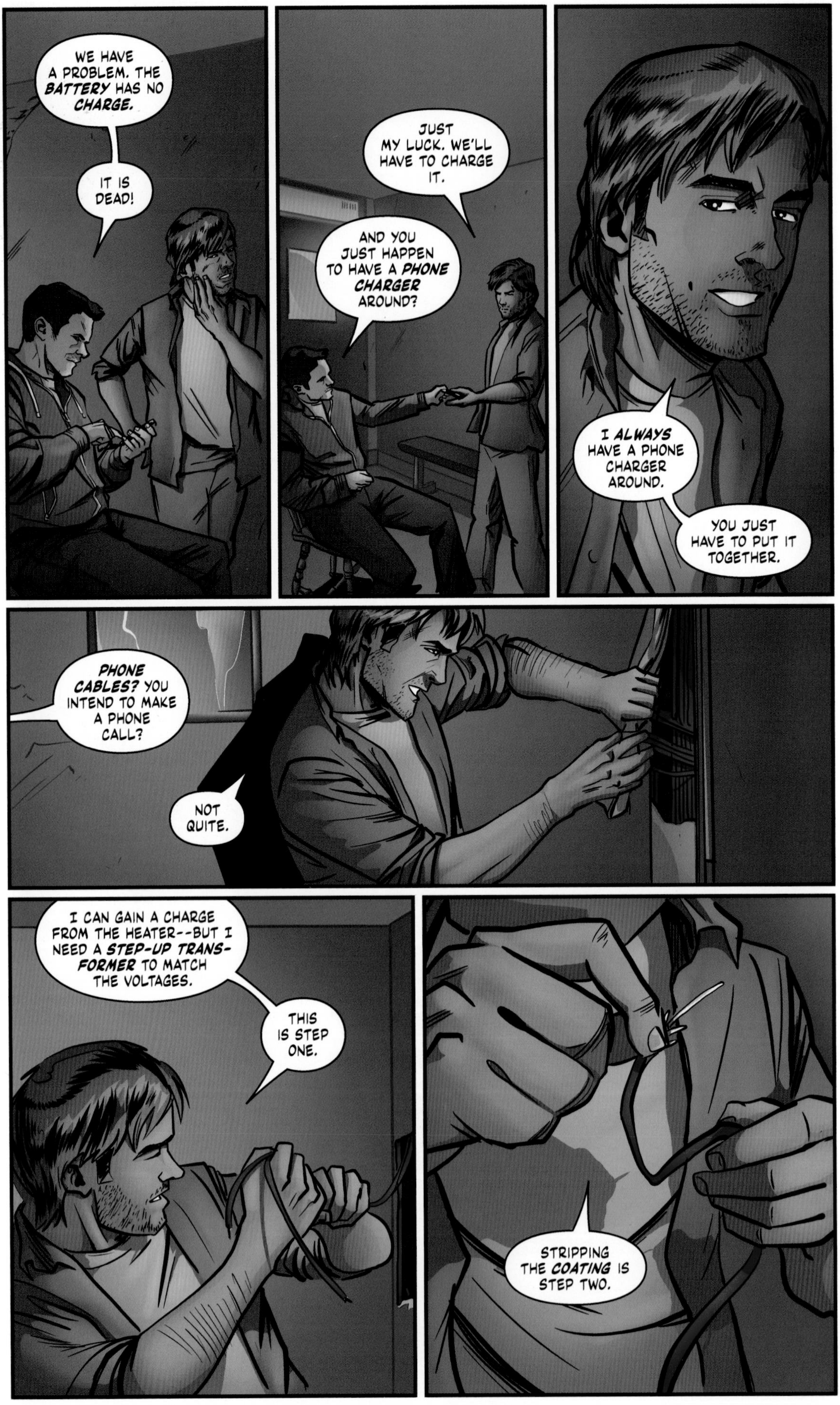
WE HAVE A PROBLEM. THE BATTERY HAS NO CHARGE.
IT IS DEAD!
JUST MY LUCK. WE'LL HAVE TO CHARGE IT.
AND YOU JUST HAPPEN TO HAVE A PHONE CHARGER AROUND?
I ALWAYS HAVE A PHONE CHARGER AROUND.
YOU JUST HAVE TO PUT IT TOGETHER.
PHONE CABLES? YOU INTEND TO MAKE A PHONE CALL?
NOT QUITE.
I CAN GAIN A CHARGE FROM THE HEATER--BUT I NEED A STEP-UP TRANS-FORMER TO MATCH THE VOLTAGES.
THIS IS STEP ONE.
STRIPPING THE COATING IS STEP TWO.

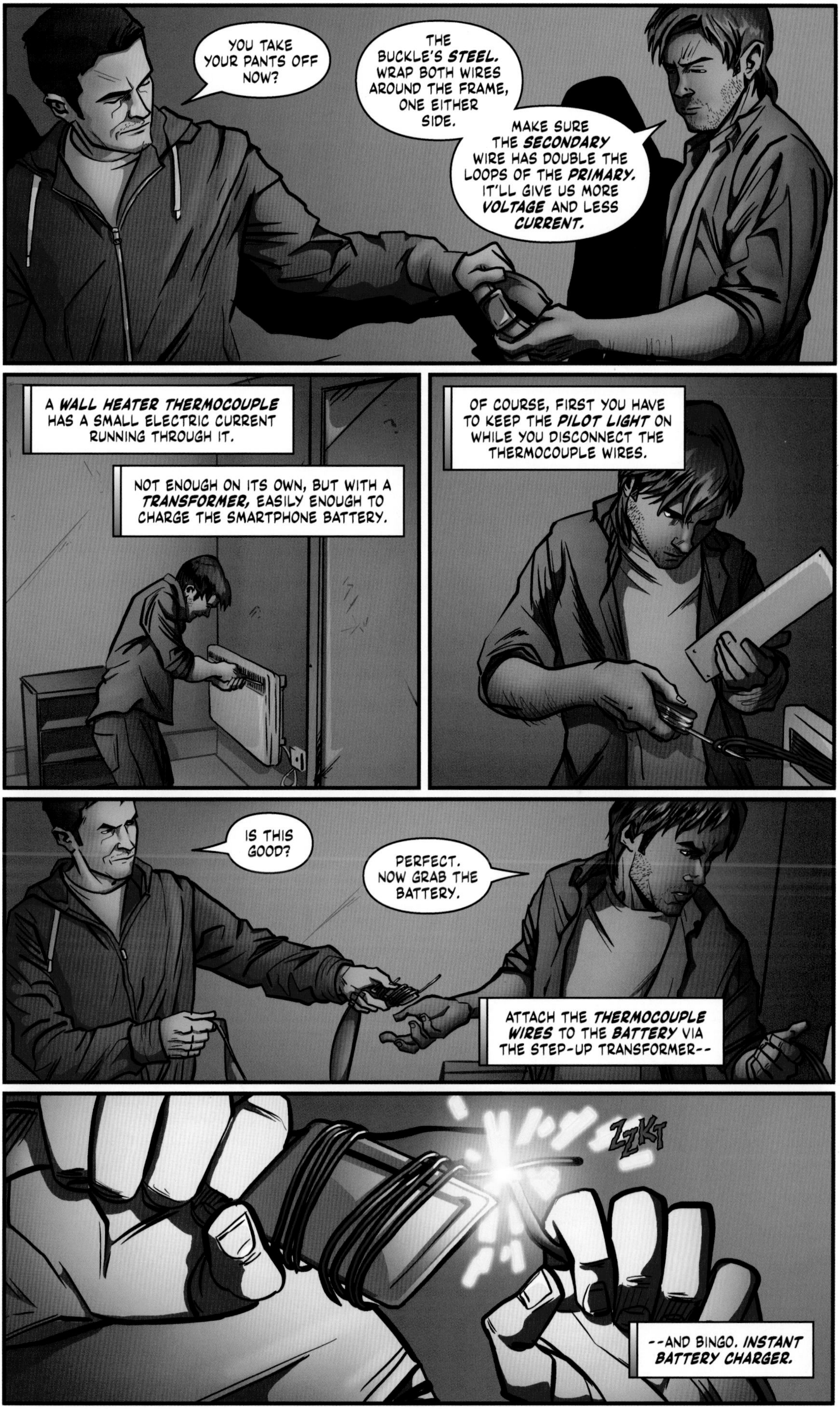
YOU TAKE YOUR PANTS OFF NOW?
THE BUCKLE'S STEEL. WRAP BOTH WIRES AROUND THE FRAME, ONE EITHER SIDE.
MAKE SURE THE SECONDARY WIRE HAS DOUBLE THE LOOPS OF THE PRIMARY. IT'LL GIVE US MORE VOLTAGE AND LESS CURRENT.
A WALL HEATER THERMOCOUPLE HAS A SMALL ELECTRIC CURRENT RUNNING THROUGH IT.
NOT ENOUGH ON ITS OWN, BUT WITH A TRANSFORMER, EASILY ENOUGH TO CHARGE THE SMARTPHONE BATTERY.
OF COURSE, FIRST YOU HAVE TO KEEP THE PILOT LIGHT ON WHILE YOU DISCONNECT THE THERMOCOUPLE WIRES.
IS THIS GOOD?
PERFECT. NOW GRAB THE BATTERY.
ATTACH THE THERMOCOUPLE WIRES TO THE BATTERY VIA THE STEP-UP TRANSFORMER--
ZZKT
--AND BINGO. INSTANT BATTERY CHARGER.

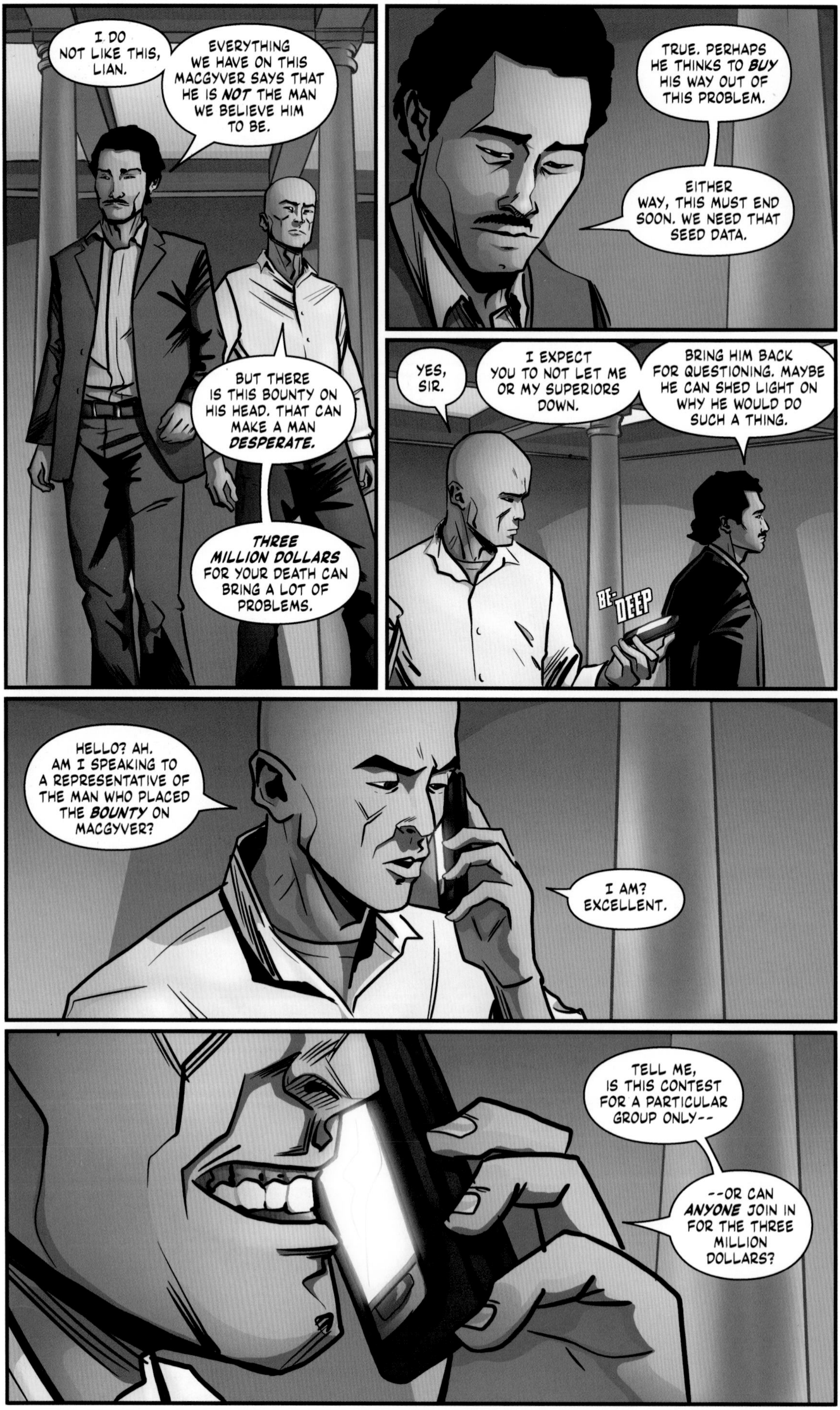
I DO NOT LIKE THIS, LIAN.
EVERYTHING WE HAVE ON THIS MACGYVER SAYS THAT HE IS *NOT* THE MAN WE BELIEVE HIM TO BE.
BUT THERE IS THIS BOUNTY ON HIS HEAD. THAT CAN MAKE A MAN *DESPERATE.*
THREE MILLION DOLLARS FOR YOUR DEATH CAN BRING A LOT OF PROBLEMS.
TRUE. PERHAPS HE THINKS TO *BUY* HIS WAY OUT OF THIS PROBLEM.
EITHER WAY, THIS MUST END SOON. WE NEED THAT SEED DATA.
BRING HIM BACK FOR QUESTIONING. MAYBE HE CAN SHED LIGHT ON WHY HE WOULD DO SUCH A THING.
I EXPECT YOU TO NOT LET ME OR MY SUPERIORS DOWN.
YES, SIR.
BE-DEEP
HELLO? AH. AM I SPEAKING TO A REPRESENTATIVE OF THE MAN WHO PLACED THE *BOUNTY* ON MACGYVER?
I AM? EXCELLENT.
TELL ME, IS THIS CONTEST FOR A PARTICULAR GROUP ONLY--
--OR CAN *ANYONE* JOIN IN FOR THE THREE MILLION DOLLARS?

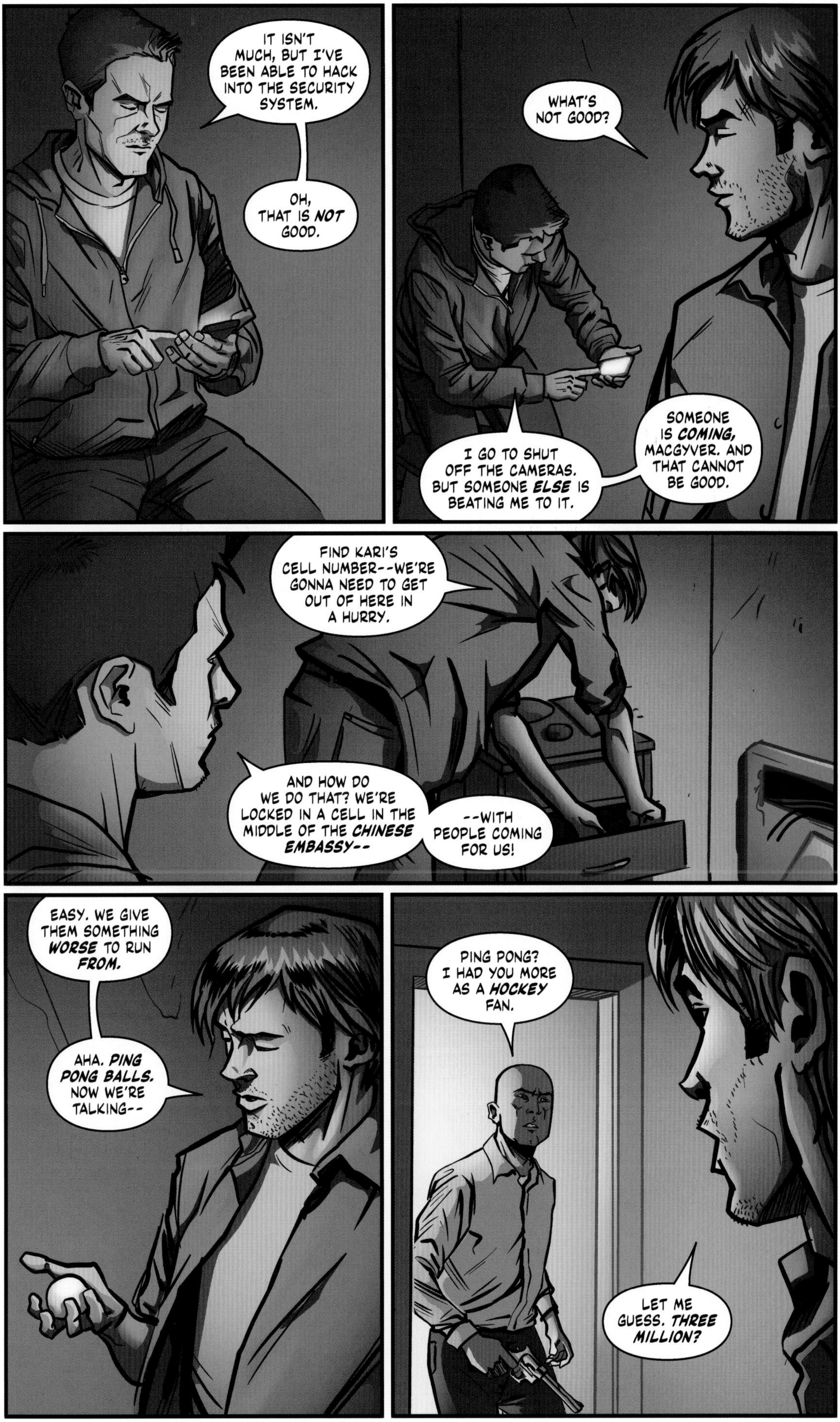
IT ISN'T MUCH, BUT I'VE BEEN ABLE TO HACK INTO THE SECURITY SYSTEM.
OH, THAT IS *NOT* GOOD.
WHAT'S NOT GOOD?
I GO TO SHUT OFF THE CAMERAS. BUT SOMEONE *ELSE* IS BEATING ME TO IT.
SOMEONE IS *COMING,* MACGYVER. AND THAT CANNOT BE GOOD.
FIND KARI'S CELL NUMBER--WE'RE GONNA NEED TO GET OUT OF HERE IN A HURRY.
AND HOW DO WE DO THAT? WE'RE LOCKED IN A CELL IN THE MIDDLE OF THE *CHINESE EMBASSY--*
--WITH PEOPLE COMING FOR US!
EASY. WE GIVE THEM SOMETHING *WORSE* TO RUN *FROM.*
AHA. *PING PONG BALLS.* NOW WE'RE TALKING--
PING PONG? I HAD YOU MORE AS A *HOCKEY* FAN.
LET ME GUESS. *THREE MILLION?*

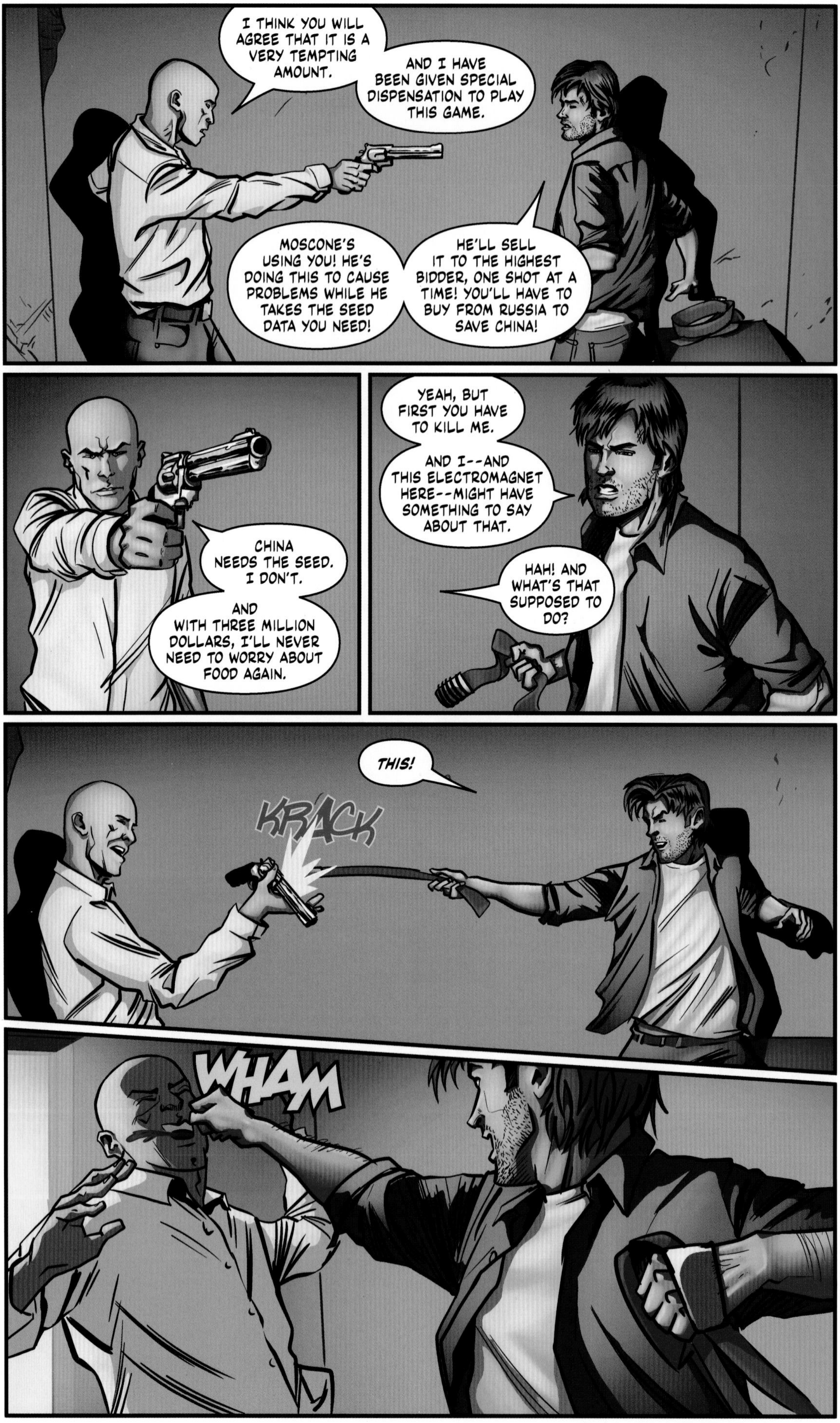
I THINK YOU WILL AGREE THAT IT IS A VERY TEMPTING AMOUNT.
AND I HAVE BEEN GIVEN SPECIAL DISPENSATION TO PLAY THIS GAME.
MOSCONE'S USING YOU! HE'S DOING THIS TO CAUSE PROBLEMS WHILE HE TAKES THE SEED DATA YOU NEED!
HE'LL SELL IT TO THE HIGHEST BIDDER, ONE SHOT AT A TIME! YOU'LL HAVE TO BUY FROM RUSSIA TO SAVE CHINA!
CHINA NEEDS THE SEED. I DON'T.
AND WITH THREE MILLION DOLLARS, I'LL NEVER NEED TO WORRY ABOUT FOOD AGAIN.
YEAH, BUT FIRST YOU HAVE TO KILL ME.
AND I--AND THIS ELECTROMAGNET HERE--MIGHT HAVE SOMETHING TO SAY ABOUT THAT.
HAH! AND WHAT'S THAT SUPPOSED TO DO?
THIS!
KRACK
WHAM

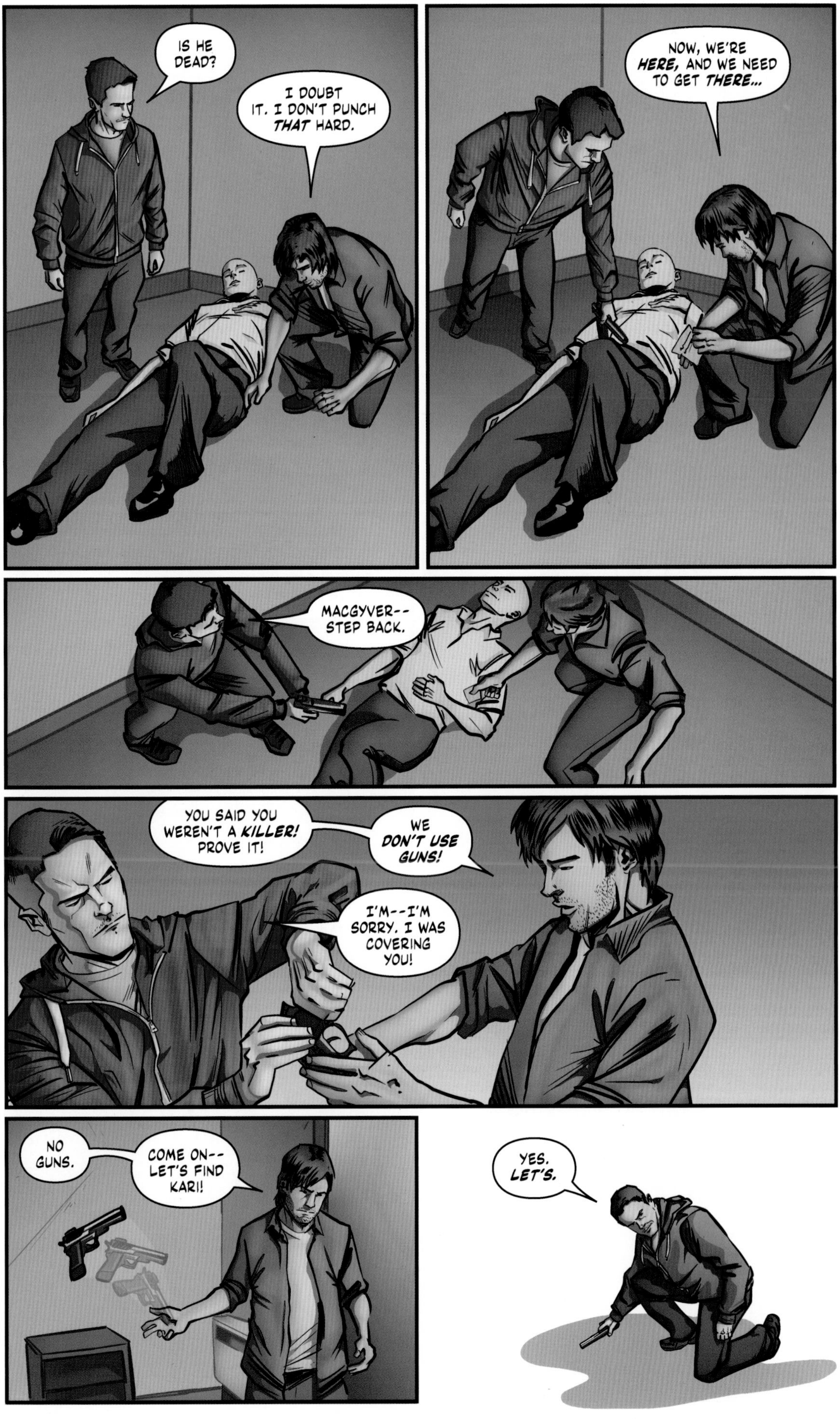
IS HE DEAD?
I DOUBT IT. I DON'T PUNCH *THAT* HARD.
NOW, WE'RE *HERE,* AND WE NEED TO GET *THERE...*
MACGYVER-- STEP BACK.
YOU SAID YOU WEREN'T A *KILLER!* PROVE IT!
WE *DON'T USE GUNS!*
I'M--I'M SORRY. I WAS COVERING YOU!
NO GUNS.
COME ON-- LET'S FIND KARI!
YES. *LET'S.*

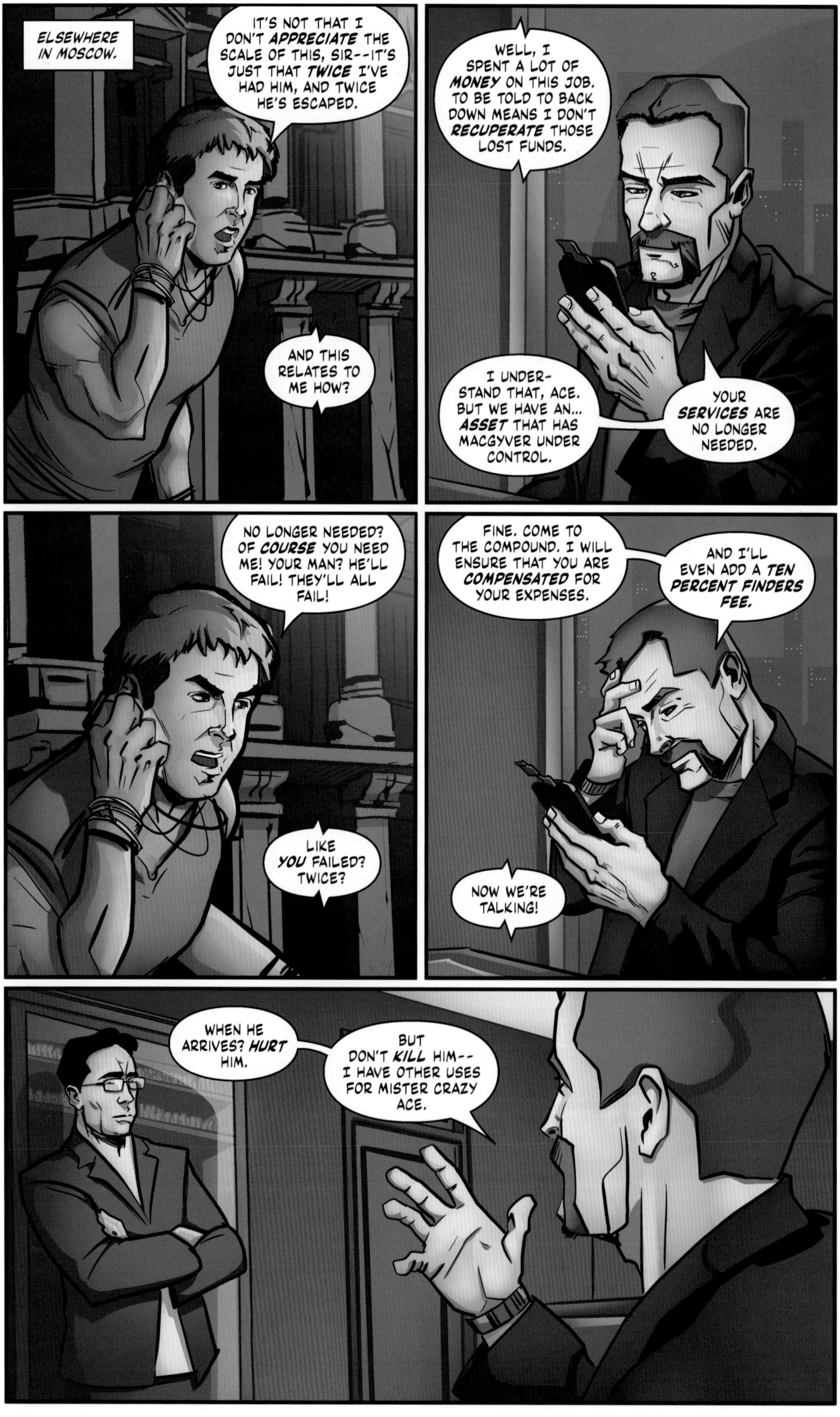
ELSEWHERE IN MOSCOW.
IT'S NOT THAT I DON'T **APPRECIATE** THE SCALE OF THIS, SIR--IT'S JUST THAT **TWICE** I'VE HAD HIM, AND TWICE HE'S ESCAPED.
AND THIS RELATES TO ME HOW?
WELL, I SPENT A LOT OF **MONEY** ON THIS JOB. TO BE TOLD TO BACK DOWN MEANS I DON'T **RECUPERATE** THOSE LOST FUNDS.
I UNDERSTAND THAT, ACE. BUT WE HAVE AN... **ASSET** THAT HAS MACGYVER UNDER CONTROL.
YOUR **SERVICES** ARE NO LONGER NEEDED.
NO LONGER NEEDED? OF **COURSE** YOU NEED ME! YOUR MAN? HE'LL FAIL! THEY'LL ALL FAIL!
LIKE **YOU** FAILED? TWICE?
FINE. COME TO THE COMPOUND. I WILL ENSURE THAT YOU ARE **COMPENSATED** FOR YOUR EXPENSES.
AND I'LL EVEN ADD A **TEN PERCENT FINDERS FEE.**
NOW WE'RE TALKING!
WHEN HE ARRIVES? **HURT** HIM.
BUT DON'T **KILL** HIM--I HAVE OTHER USES FOR MISTER CRAZY ACE.

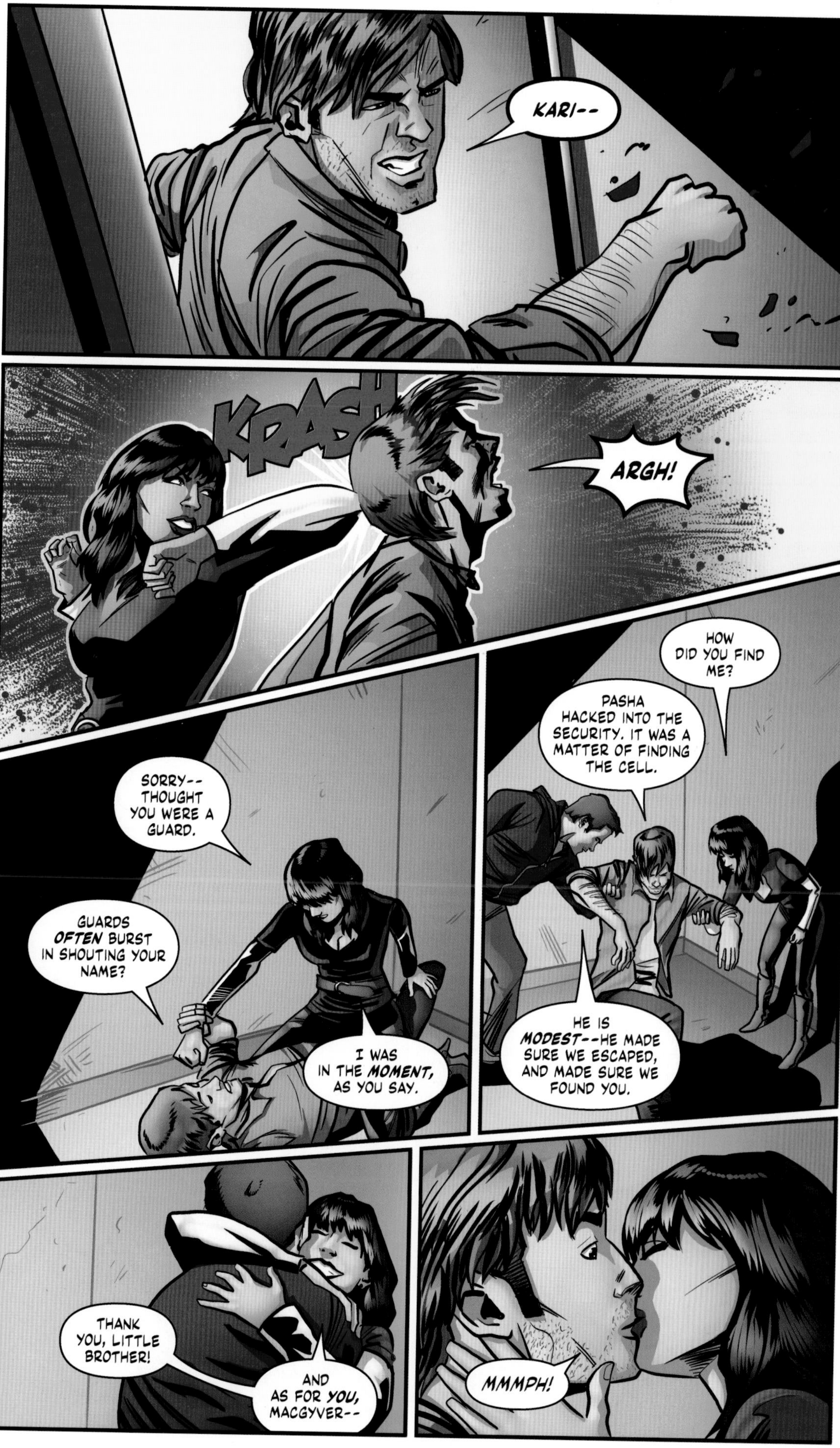
KARI--
KRASH
ARGH!
SORRY--THOUGHT YOU WERE A GUARD.
GUARDS *OFTEN* BURST IN SHOUTING YOUR NAME?
I WAS IN THE *MOMENT,* AS YOU SAY.
HOW DID YOU FIND ME?
PASHA HACKED INTO THE SECURITY. IT WAS A MATTER OF FINDING THE CELL.
HE IS *MODEST*--HE MADE SURE WE ESCAPED, AND MADE SURE WE FOUND YOU.
THANK YOU, LITTLE BROTHER!
AND AS FOR *YOU,* MACGYVER--
MMMPH!

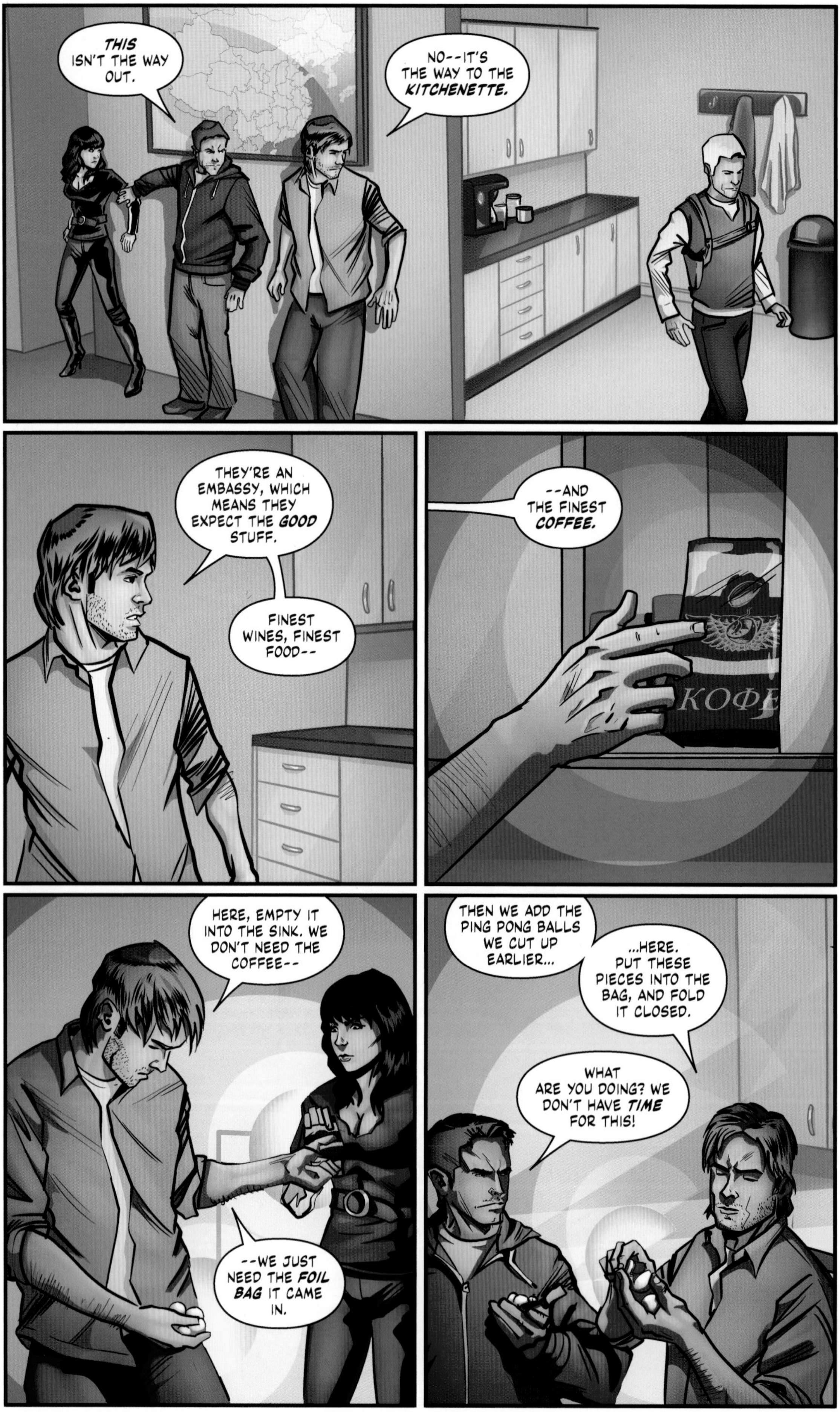
THIS ISN'T THE WAY OUT.
NO--IT'S THE WAY TO THE KITCHENETTE.
THEY'RE AN EMBASSY, WHICH MEANS THEY EXPECT THE GOOD STUFF.
FINEST WINES, FINEST FOOD--
--AND THE FINEST COFFEE.
КОФЕ
HERE, EMPTY IT INTO THE SINK. WE DON'T NEED THE COFFEE--
--WE JUST NEED THE FOIL BAG IT CAME IN.
THEN WE ADD THE PING PONG BALLS WE CUT UP EARLIER...
...HERE. PUT THESE PIECES INTO THE BAG, AND FOLD IT CLOSED.
WHAT ARE YOU DOING? WE DON'T HAVE TIME FOR THIS!

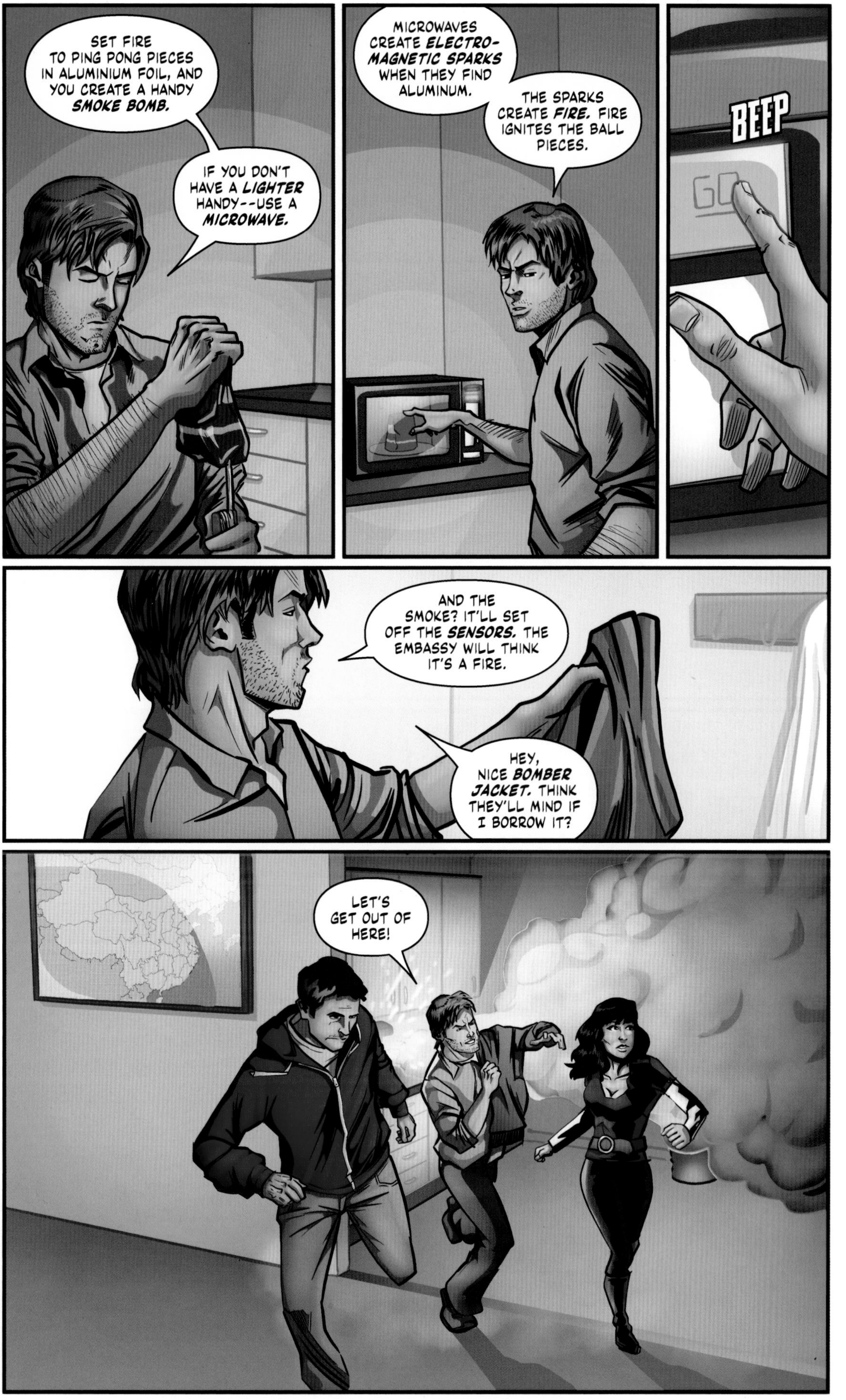
SET FIRE TO PING PONG PIECES IN ALUMINIUM FOIL, AND YOU CREATE A HANDY SMOKE BOMB.
IF YOU DON'T HAVE A LIGHTER HANDY--USE A MICROWAVE.
MICROWAVES CREATE ELECTRO-MAGNETIC SPARKS WHEN THEY FIND ALUMINUM.
THE SPARKS CREATE FIRE. FIRE IGNITES THE BALL PIECES.
BEEP
GO
AND THE SMOKE? IT'LL SET OFF THE SENSORS. THE EMBASSY WILL THINK IT'S A FIRE.
HEY, NICE BOMBER JACKET. THINK THEY'LL MIND IF I BORROW IT?
LET'S GET OUT OF HERE!

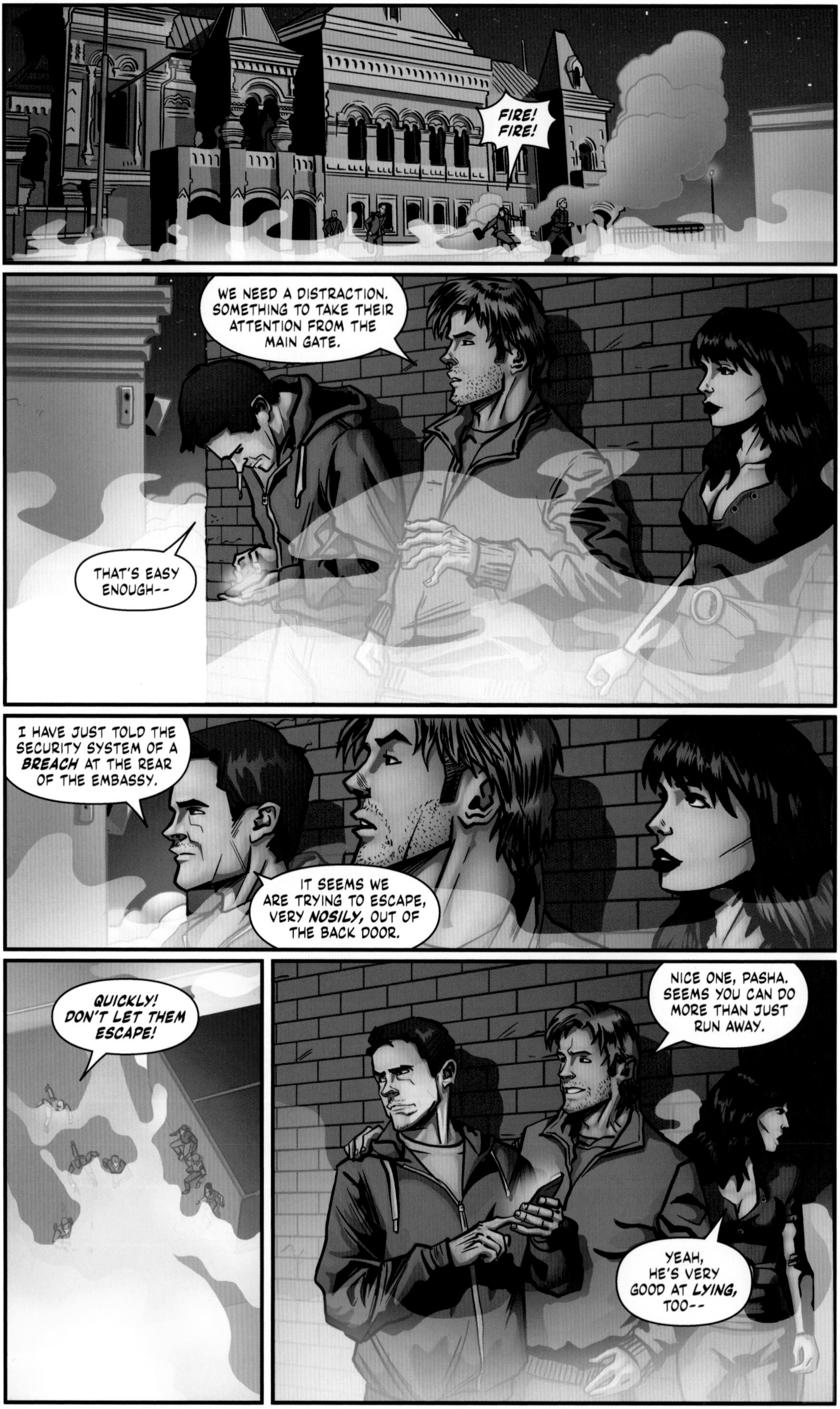
FIRE! FIRE!
WE NEED A DISTRACTION. SOMETHING TO TAKE THEIR ATTENTION FROM THE MAIN GATE.
THAT'S EASY ENOUGH--
I HAVE JUST TOLD THE SECURITY SYSTEM OF A *BREACH* AT THE REAR OF THE EMBASSY.
IT SEEMS WE ARE TRYING TO ESCAPE, VERY *NOSILY*, OUT OF THE BACK DOOR.
QUICKLY! DON'T LET THEM ESCAPE!
NICE ONE, PASHA. SEEMS YOU CAN DO MORE THAN JUST RUN AWAY.
YEAH, HE'S VERY GOOD AT *LYING,* TOO--

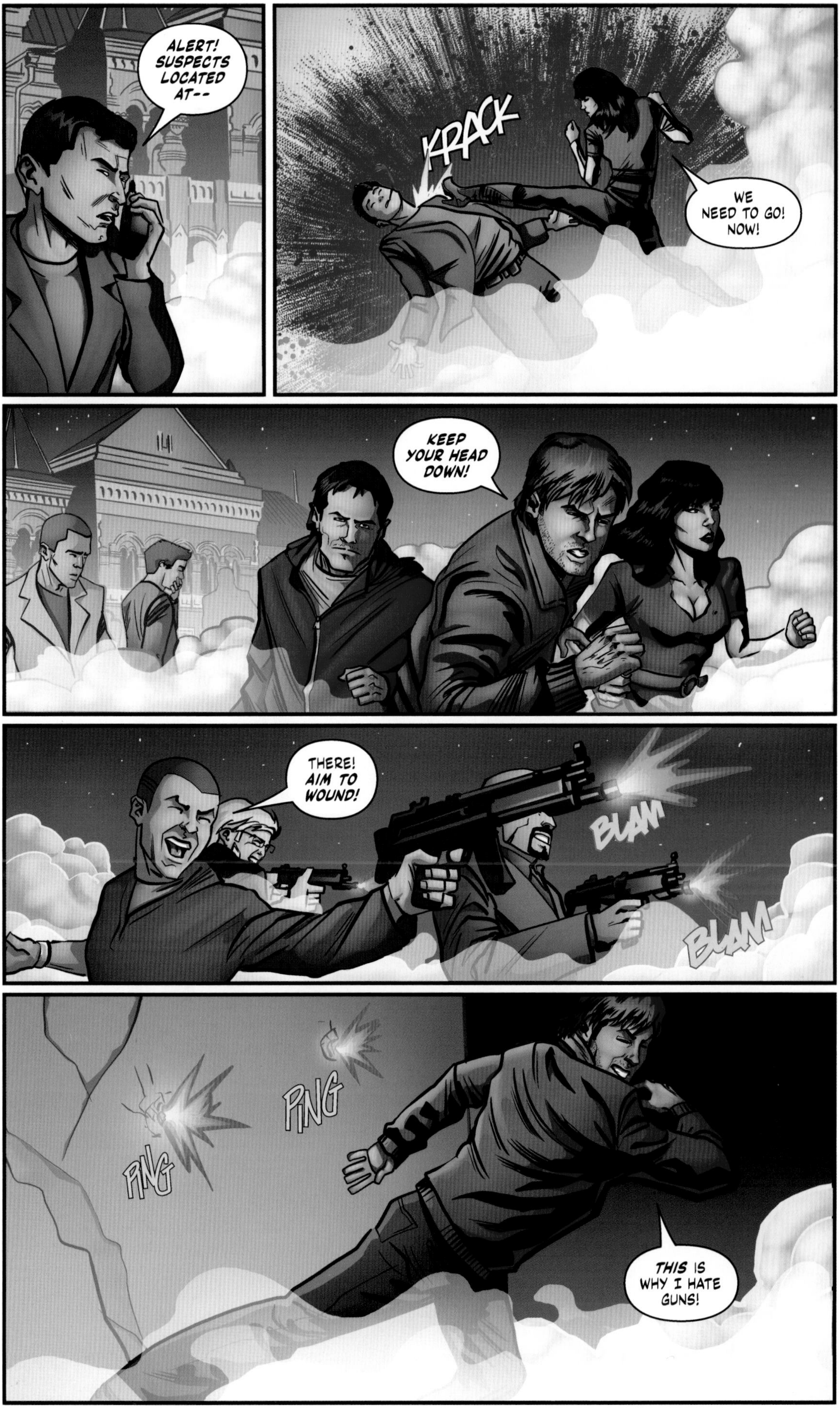
ALERT! SUSPECTS LOCATED AT--
KRACK
WE NEED TO GO! NOW!
KEEP YOUR HEAD DOWN!
THERE! AIM TO WOUND!
BLAM
BLAM
PING
PING
THIS IS WHY I HATE GUNS!

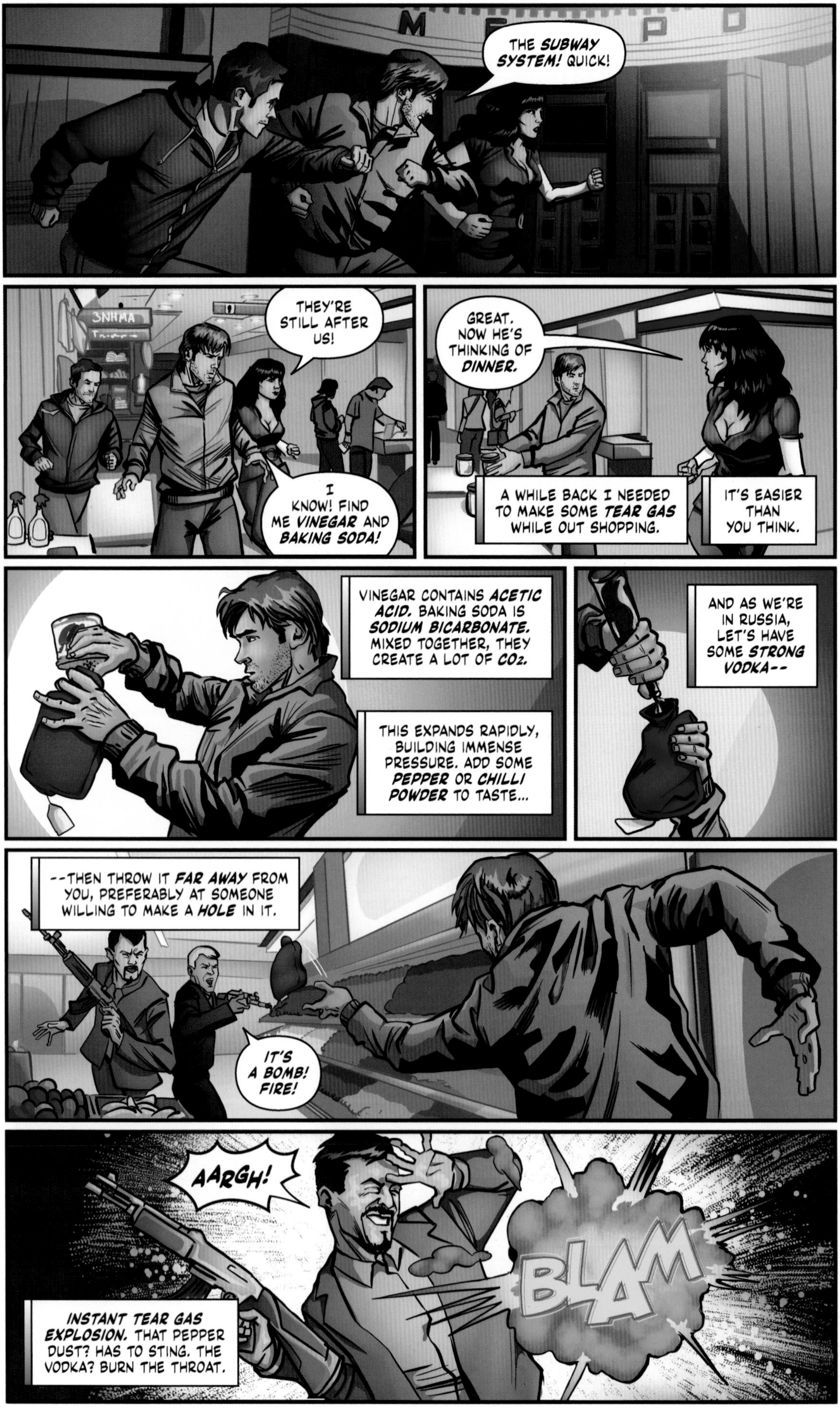
M P
THE SUBWAY SYSTEM! QUICK!
THEY'RE STILL AFTER US!
I KNOW! FIND ME VINEGAR AND BAKING SODA!
GREAT. NOW HE'S THINKING OF DINNER.
A WHILE BACK I NEEDED TO MAKE SOME TEAR GAS WHILE OUT SHOPPING.
IT'S EASIER THAN YOU THINK.
VINEGAR CONTAINS ACETIC ACID. BAKING SODA IS SODIUM BICARBONATE. MIXED TOGETHER, THEY CREATE A LOT OF CO2.
THIS EXPANDS RAPIDLY, BUILDING IMMENSE PRESSURE. ADD SOME PEPPER OR CHILLI POWDER TO TASTE...
AND AS WE'RE IN RUSSIA, LET'S HAVE SOME STRONG VODKA--
--THEN THROW IT FAR AWAY FROM YOU, PREFERABLY AT SOMEONE WILLING TO MAKE A HOLE IN IT.
IT'S A BOMB! FIRE!
AARGH!
BLAM
INSTANT TEAR GAS EXPLOSION. THAT PEPPER DUST? HAS TO STING. THE VODKA? BURN THE THROAT.

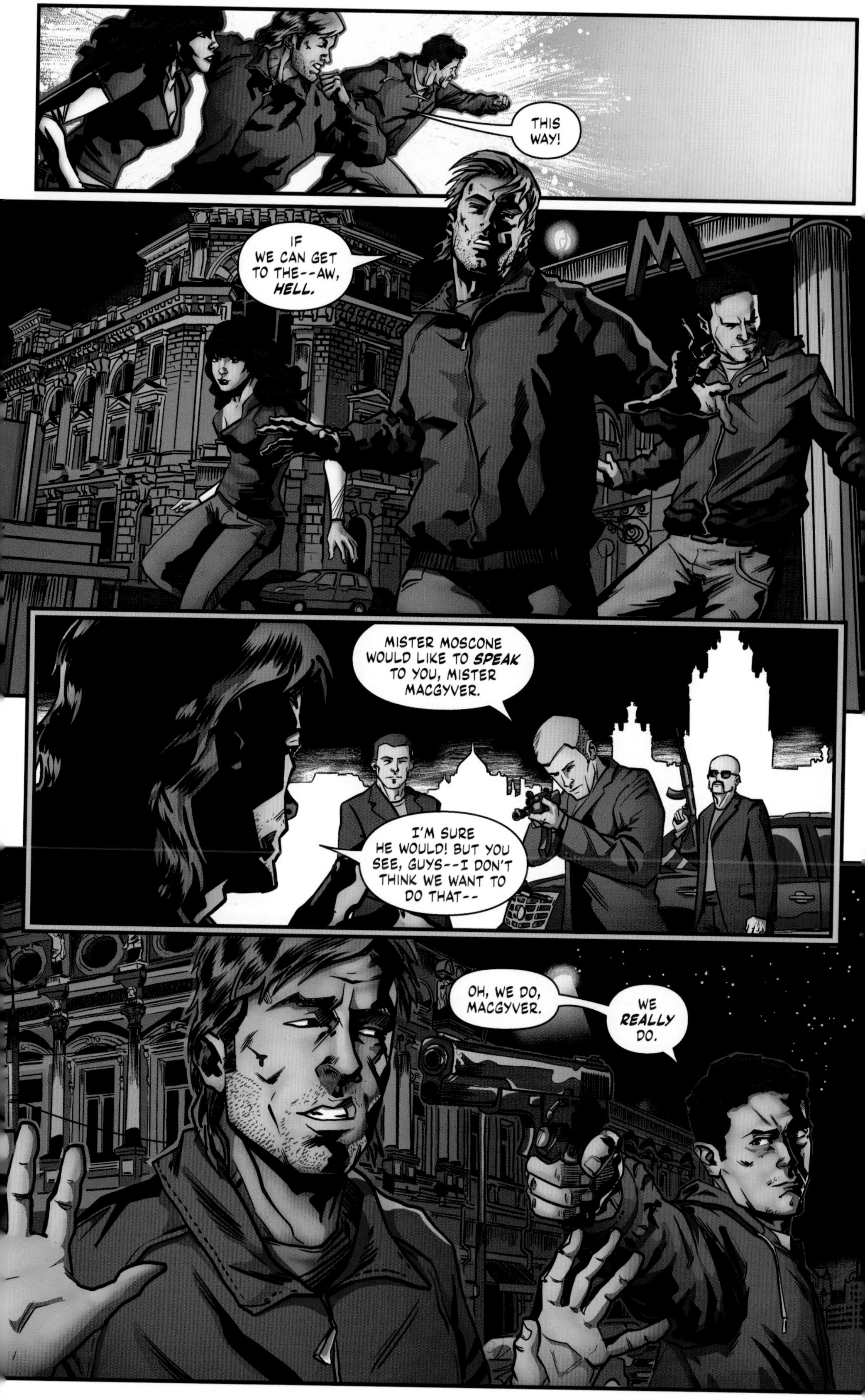
THIS WAY!
IF WE CAN GET TO THE--AW, HELL.
MISTER MOSCONE WOULD LIKE TO SPEAK TO YOU, MISTER MACGYVER.
I'M SURE HE WOULD! BUT YOU SEE, GUYS--I DON'T THINK WE WANT TO DO THAT--
OH, WE DO, MACGYVER.
WE REALLY DO.

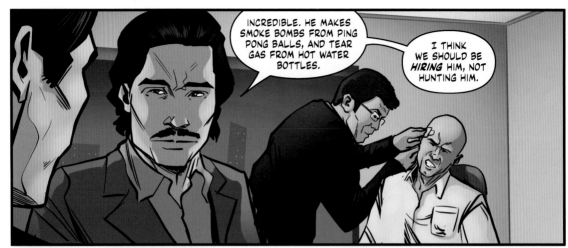

INCREDIBLE. HE MAKES SMOKE BOMBS FROM PING PONG BALLS, AND TEAR GAS FROM HOT WATER BOTTLES.

I THINK WE SHOULD BE *HIRING* HIM, NOT HUNTING HIM.

AH, LIAN--WE'LL DISCUSS YOUR FAILED ATTEMPT TO GAIN *BLOOD MONEY* LATER.

NOW, I NEED TO KNOW WHETHER MACGYVER OR HIS FRIEND GAVE ANY *CLUES* AS TO WHERE THEY WERE HEADING.

HE DID BETTER THAN THAT, SIR--

--HE GAVE ME *THIS* TO PASS TO YOU.

IMPOSSIBLE! THIS HAS TO BE A *TRICK!* HOW DO YOU KNOW WE CAN TRUST HIM?

BECAUSE THAT WASN'T THE *ONLY* THING HE GAVE ME, SIR--

--HE ALSO GAVE ME *THESE.*

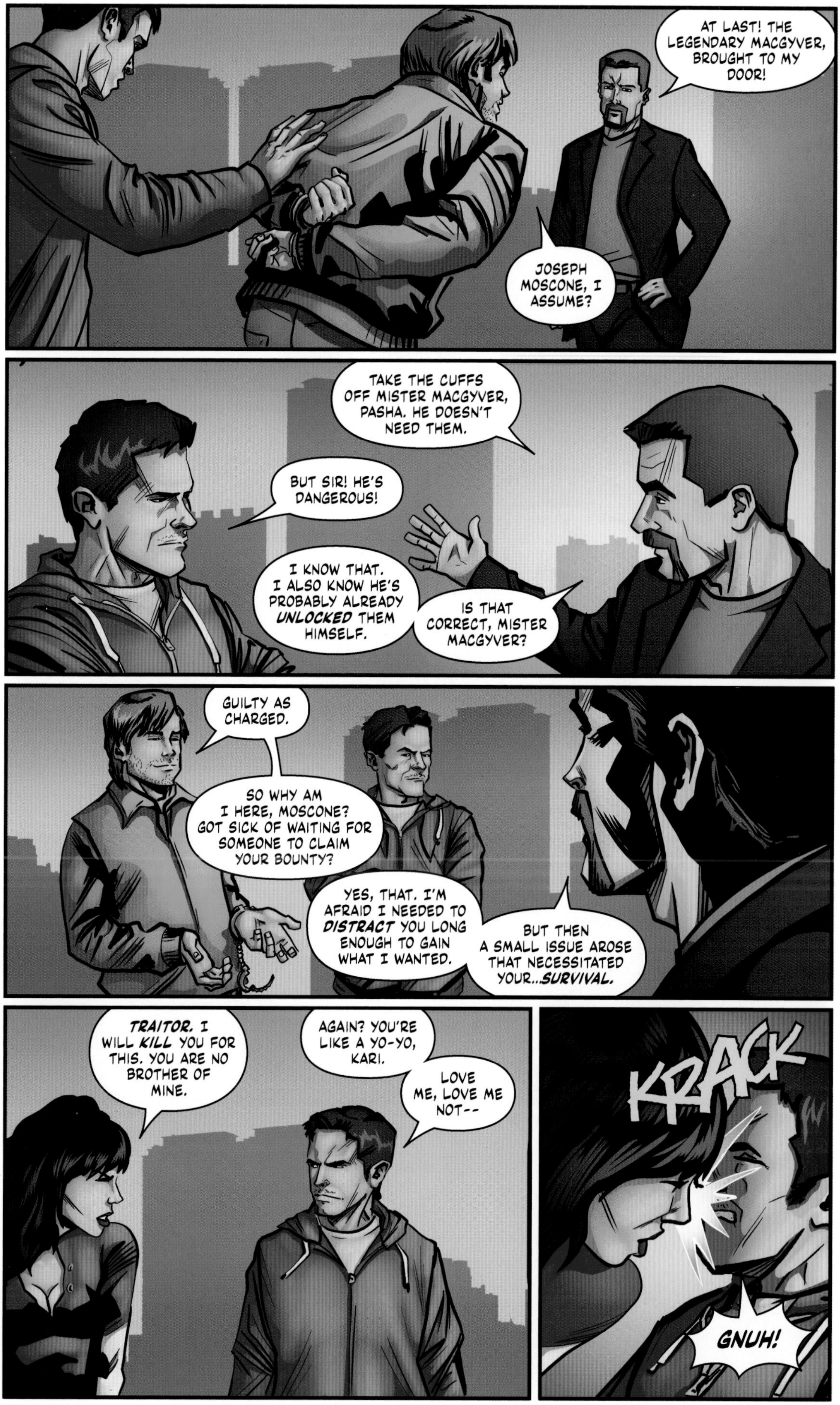
AT LAST! THE LEGENDARY MACGYVER, BROUGHT TO MY DOOR!
JOSEPH MOSCONE, I ASSUME?
TAKE THE CUFFS OFF MISTER MACGYVER, PASHA. HE DOESN'T NEED THEM.
BUT SIR! HE'S DANGEROUS!
I KNOW THAT. I ALSO KNOW HE'S PROBABLY ALREADY *UNLOCKED* THEM HIMSELF.
IS THAT CORRECT, MISTER MACGYVER?
GUILTY AS CHARGED.
SO WHY AM I HERE, MOSCONE? GOT SICK OF WAITING FOR SOMEONE TO CLAIM YOUR BOUNTY?
YES, THAT. I'M AFRAID I NEEDED TO *DISTRACT* YOU LONG ENOUGH TO GAIN WHAT I WANTED.
BUT THEN A SMALL ISSUE AROSE THAT NECESSITATED YOUR...*SURVIVAL.*
TRAITOR. I WILL *KILL* YOU FOR THIS. YOU ARE NO BROTHER OF MINE.
AGAIN? YOU'RE LIKE A YO-YO, KARI.
LOVE ME, LOVE ME NOT--
KRACK
GNUH!

IF SHE DOES THAT AGAIN, SHOOT HER IN THE BACK OF THE KNEE. *EITHER,* I DON'T CARE WHICH.

SO--YOU WERE SAYING? I TAKE IT *YOU* SENT THE CHINESE GUARD IN TO KILL ME, HOPING WE'D ESCAPE?

I KNEW THAT IF *YOU* FAILED, THEN *PASHA* COULD STOP HIM FROM SUCCEEDING. HE'S PROVED *VERY ADEPT* IN THE WAYS OF KILLING.

COME, FOLLOW ME.

IT WAS SUPPOSED TO BE *SO EASY,* YOU SEE.

CORNWELL INVITES YOU OVER, I SEND SOME HITMEN, THEY *KILL* YOU--

--AND IN THE CONFUSION, THE DATA *AND* DOCTOR CORNWELL ARE TAKEN 'TO SAFETY' BY CLAUDE.

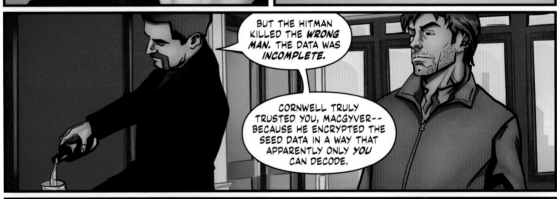

BUT THE HITMAN KILLED THE *WRONG MAN.* THE DATA WAS *INCOMPLETE.*

CORNWELL TRULY TRUSTED YOU, MACGYVER-- BECAUSE HE ENCRYPTED THE SEED DATA IN A WAY THAT APPARENTLY ONLY *YOU* CAN DECODE.

SO ALL THIS TIME YOU'VE BEEN TRYING TO *KILL* ME WHEN ACTUALLY YOU NEEDED TO *SAVE* ME?

I APPRECIATE THE *IRONY* OF THE SITUATION. AND I HAVE A *PROPOSITION* FOR YOU.

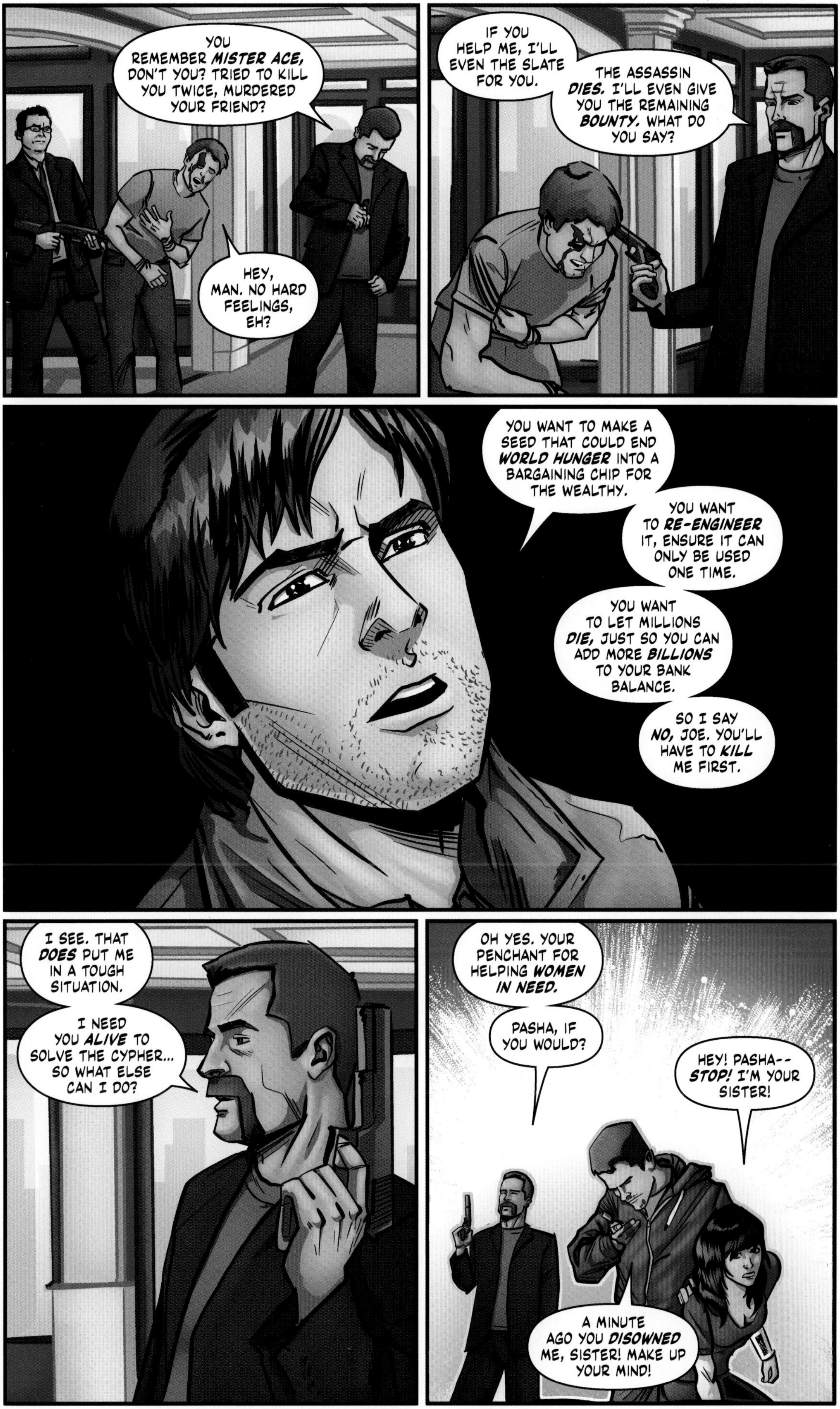
YOU REMEMBER MISTER ACE, DON'T YOU? TRIED TO KILL YOU TWICE, MURDERED YOUR FRIEND?
HEY, MAN. NO HARD FEELINGS, EH?
IF YOU HELP ME, I'LL EVEN THE SLATE FOR YOU.
THE ASSASSIN DIES. I'LL EVEN GIVE YOU THE REMAINING BOUNTY. WHAT DO YOU SAY?
YOU WANT TO MAKE A SEED THAT COULD END WORLD HUNGER INTO A BARGAINING CHIP FOR THE WEALTHY.
YOU WANT TO RE-ENGINEER IT, ENSURE IT CAN ONLY BE USED ONE TIME.
YOU WANT TO LET MILLIONS DIE, JUST SO YOU CAN ADD MORE BILLIONS TO YOUR BANK BALANCE.
SO I SAY NO, JOE. YOU'LL HAVE TO KILL ME FIRST.
I SEE. THAT DOES PUT ME IN A TOUGH SITUATION.
I NEED YOU ALIVE TO SOLVE THE CYPHER... SO WHAT ELSE CAN I DO?
OH YES. YOUR PENCHANT FOR HELPING WOMEN IN NEED.
PASHA, IF YOU WOULD?
HEY! PASHA-- STOP! I'M YOUR SISTER!
A MINUTE AGO YOU DISOWNED ME, SISTER! MAKE UP YOUR MIND!

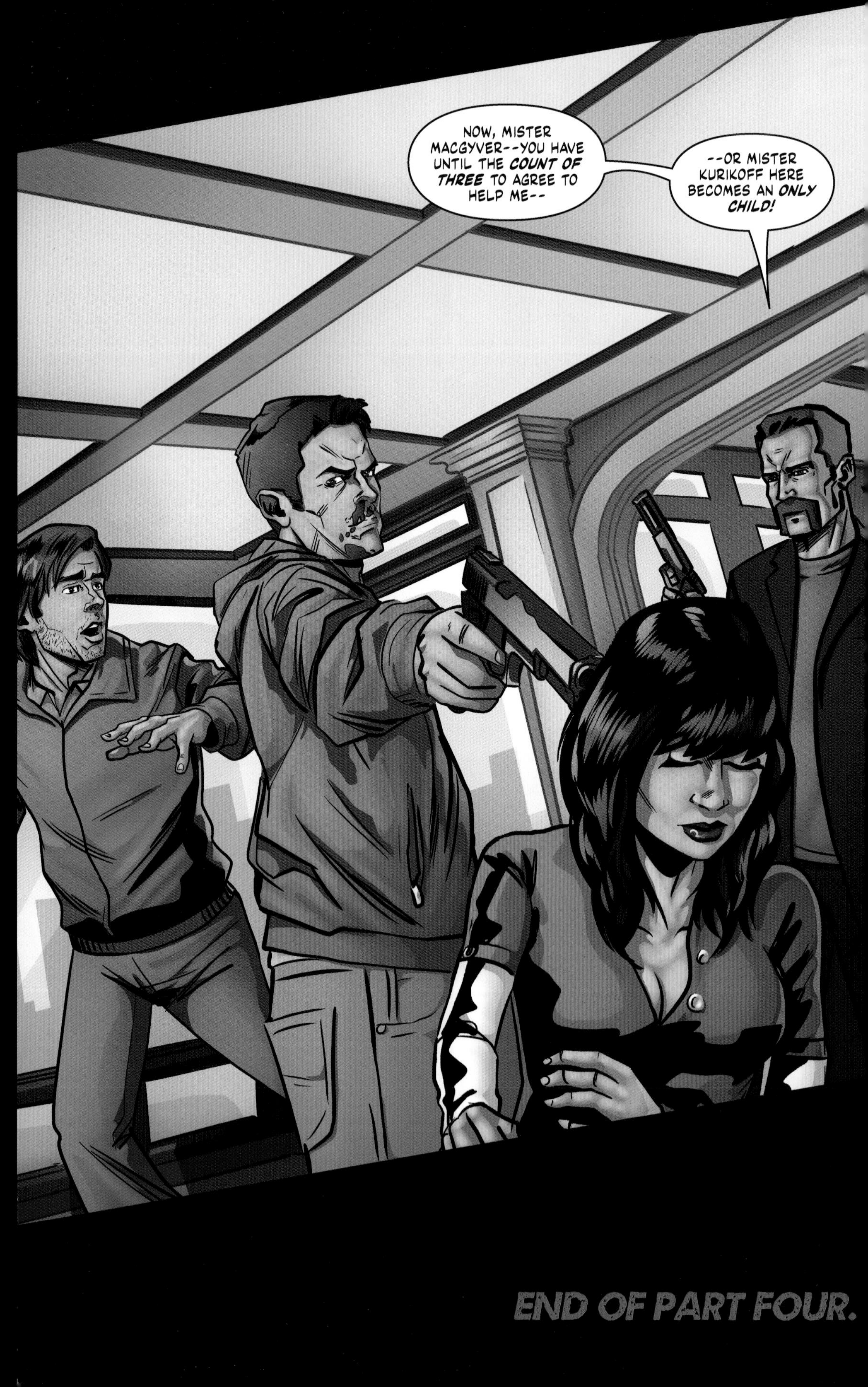
NOW, MISTER MACGYVER--YOU HAVE UNTIL THE COUNT OF THREE TO AGREE TO HELP ME--
--OR MISTER KURIKOFF HERE BECOMES AN ONLY CHILD!

END OF PART FOUR.

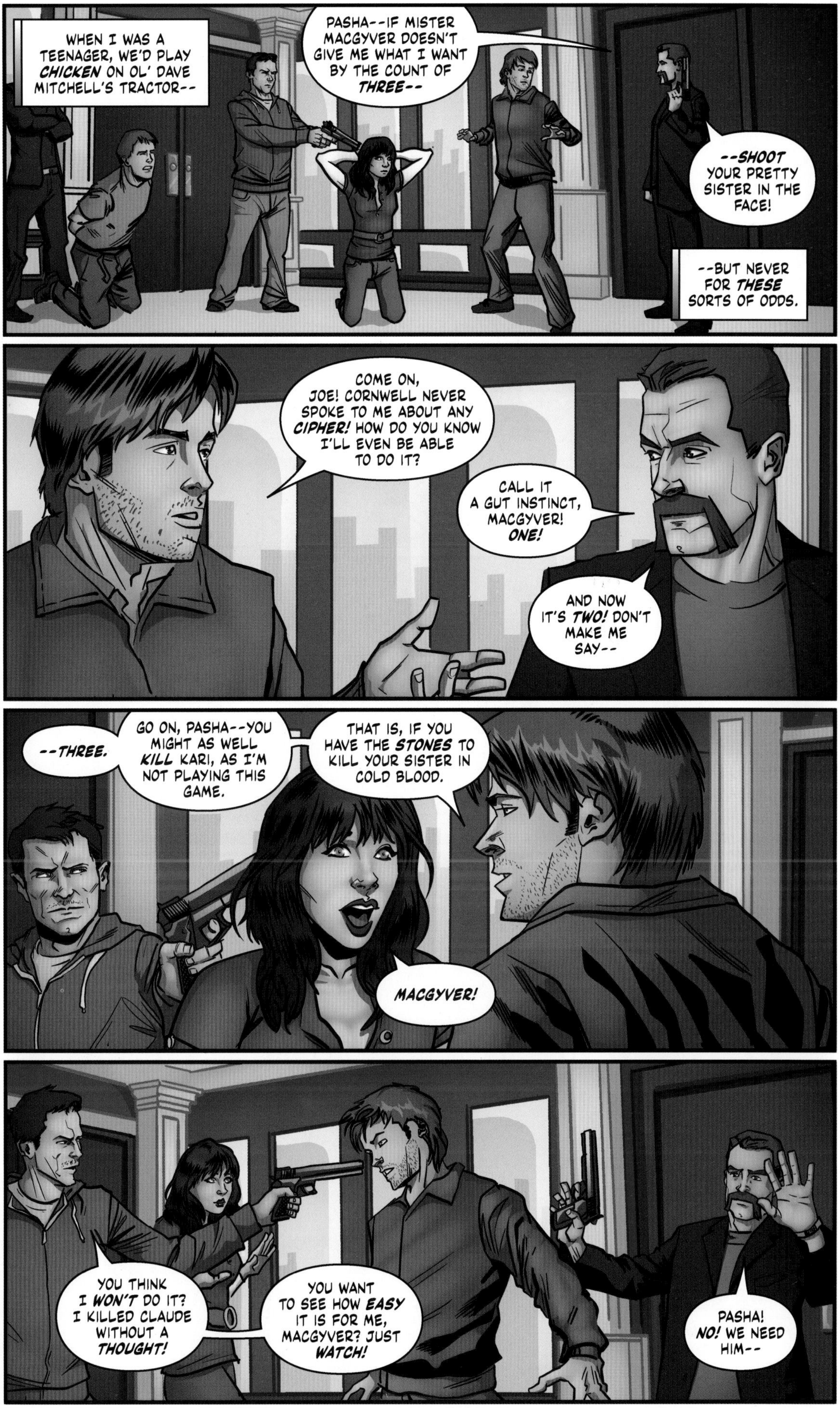

WHEN I WAS A TEENAGER, WE'D PLAY CHICKEN ON OL' DAVE MITCHELL'S TRACTOR--
PASHA--IF MISTER MACGYVER DOESN'T GIVE ME WHAT I WANT BY THE COUNT OF THREE--
--SHOOT YOUR PRETTY SISTER IN THE FACE!
--BUT NEVER FOR THESE SORTS OF ODDS.
COME ON, JOE! CORNWELL NEVER SPOKE TO ME ABOUT ANY CIPHER! HOW DO YOU KNOW I'LL EVEN BE ABLE TO DO IT?
CALL IT A GUT INSTINCT, MACGYVER! ONE!
AND NOW IT'S TWO! DON'T MAKE ME SAY--
--THREE.
GO ON, PASHA--YOU MIGHT AS WELL KILL KARI, AS I'M NOT PLAYING THIS GAME.
THAT IS, IF YOU HAVE THE STONES TO KILL YOUR SISTER IN COLD BLOOD.
MACGYVER!
YOU THINK I WON'T DO IT? I KILLED CLAUDE WITHOUT A THOUGHT!
YOU WANT TO SEE HOW EASY IT IS FOR ME, MACGYVER? JUST WATCH!
PASHA! NO! WE NEED HIM--

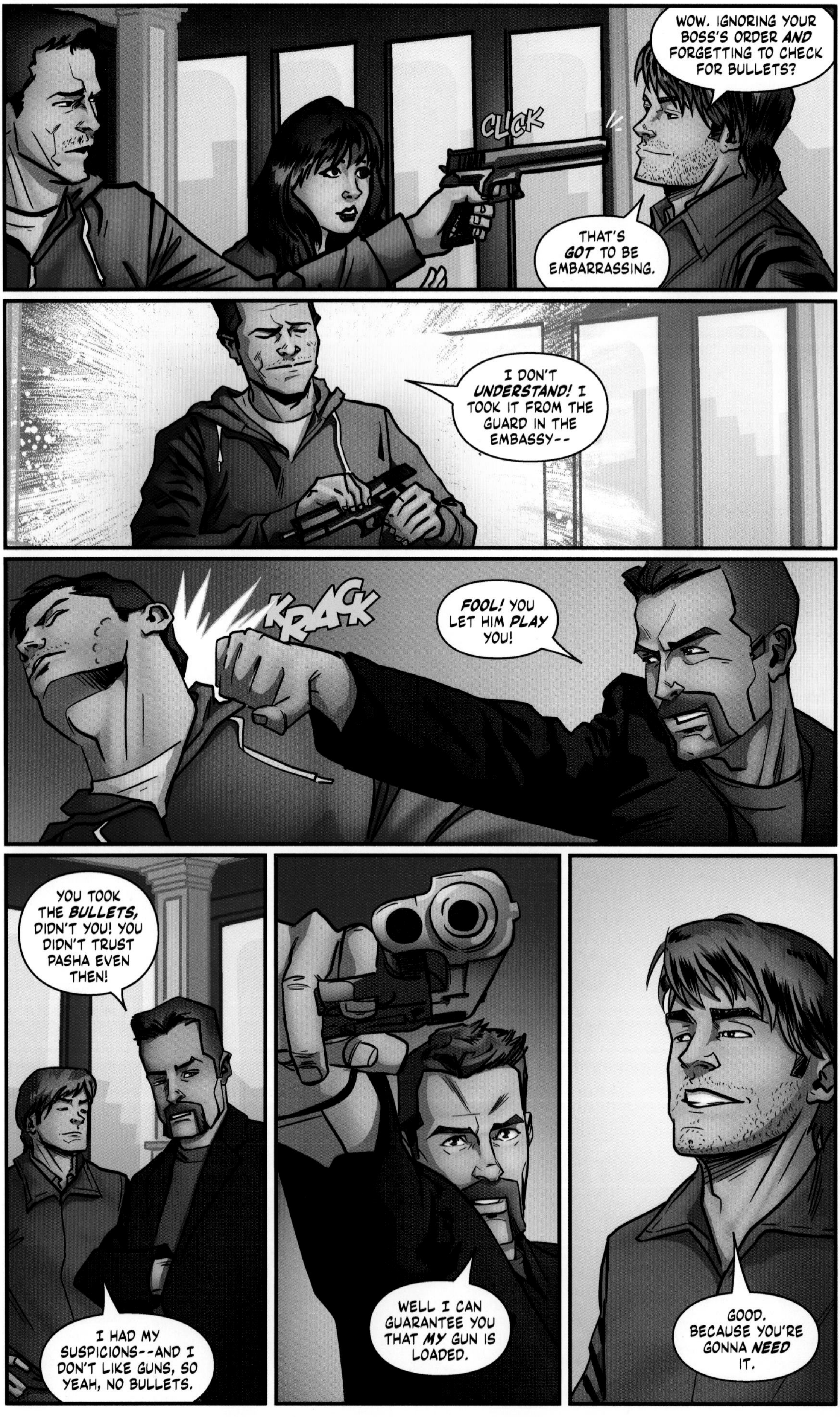
WOW. IGNORING YOUR BOSS'S ORDER AND FORGETTING TO CHECK FOR BULLETS?
CLICK
THAT'S GOT TO BE EMBARRASSING.
I DON'T UNDERSTAND! I TOOK IT FROM THE GUARD IN THE EMBASSY--
KRACK
FOOL! YOU LET HIM PLAY YOU!
YOU TOOK THE BULLETS, DIDN'T YOU! YOU DIDN'T TRUST PASHA EVEN THEN!
I HAD MY SUSPICIONS--AND I DON'T LIKE GUNS, SO YEAH, NO BULLETS.
WELL I CAN GUARANTEE YOU THAT MY GUN IS LOADED.
GOOD. BECAUSE YOU'RE GONNA NEED IT.

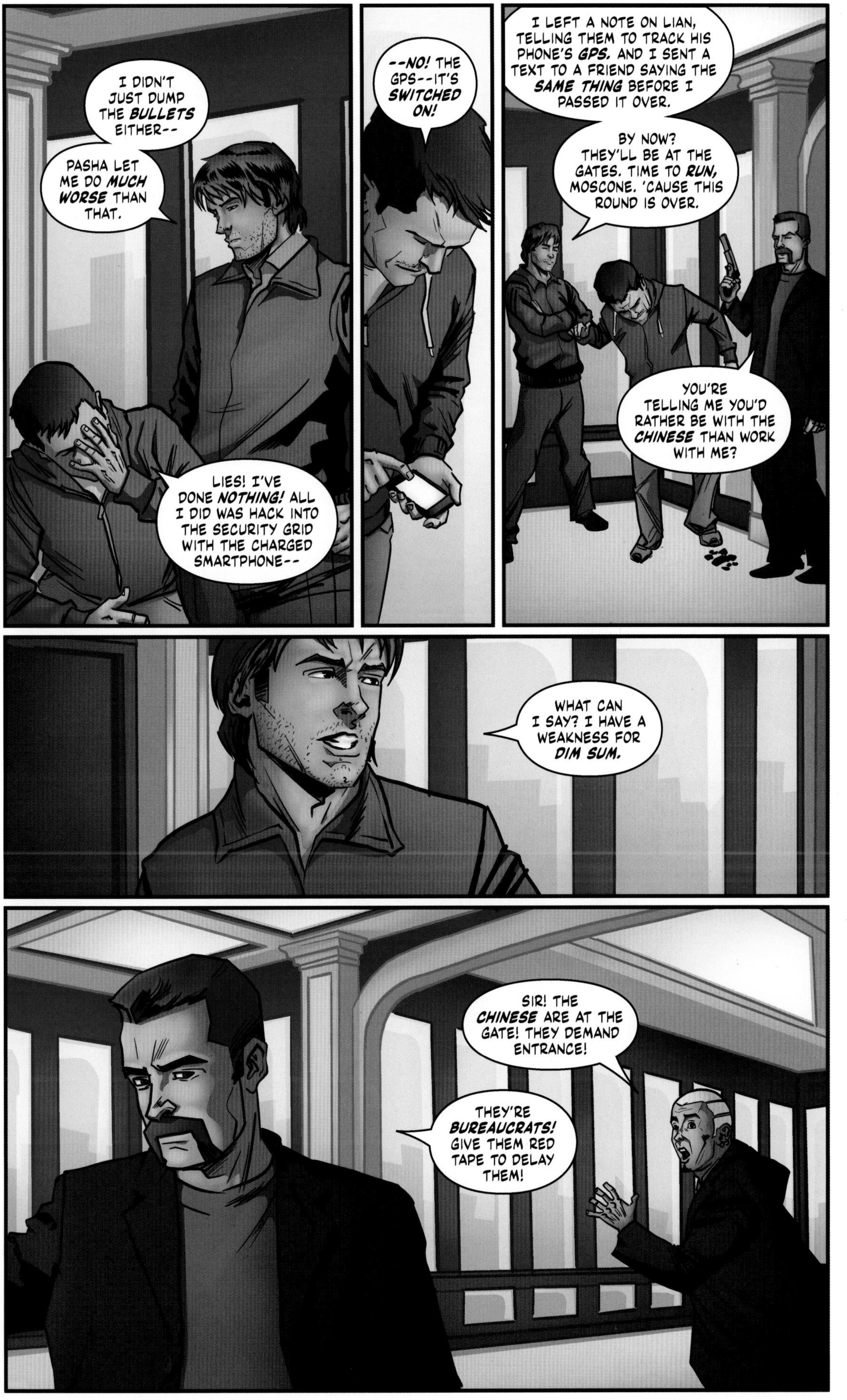
I DIDN'T JUST DUMP THE BULLETS EITHER--
PASHA LET ME DO MUCH WORSE THAN THAT.
LIES! I'VE DONE NOTHING! ALL I DID WAS HACK INTO THE SECURITY GRID WITH THE CHARGED SMARTPHONE--
--NO! THE GPS--IT'S SWITCHED ON!
I LEFT A NOTE ON LIAN, TELLING THEM TO TRACK HIS PHONE'S GPS. AND I SENT A TEXT TO A FRIEND SAYING THE SAME THING BEFORE I PASSED IT OVER.
BY NOW? THEY'LL BE AT THE GATES. TIME TO RUN, MOSCONE. 'CAUSE THIS ROUND IS OVER.
YOU'RE TELLING ME YOU'D RATHER BE WITH THE CHINESE THAN WORK WITH ME?
WHAT CAN I SAY? I HAVE A WEAKNESS FOR DIM SUM.
SIR! THE CHINESE ARE AT THE GATE! THEY DEMAND ENTRANCE!
THEY'RE BUREAUCRATS! GIVE THEM RED TAPE TO DELAY THEM!

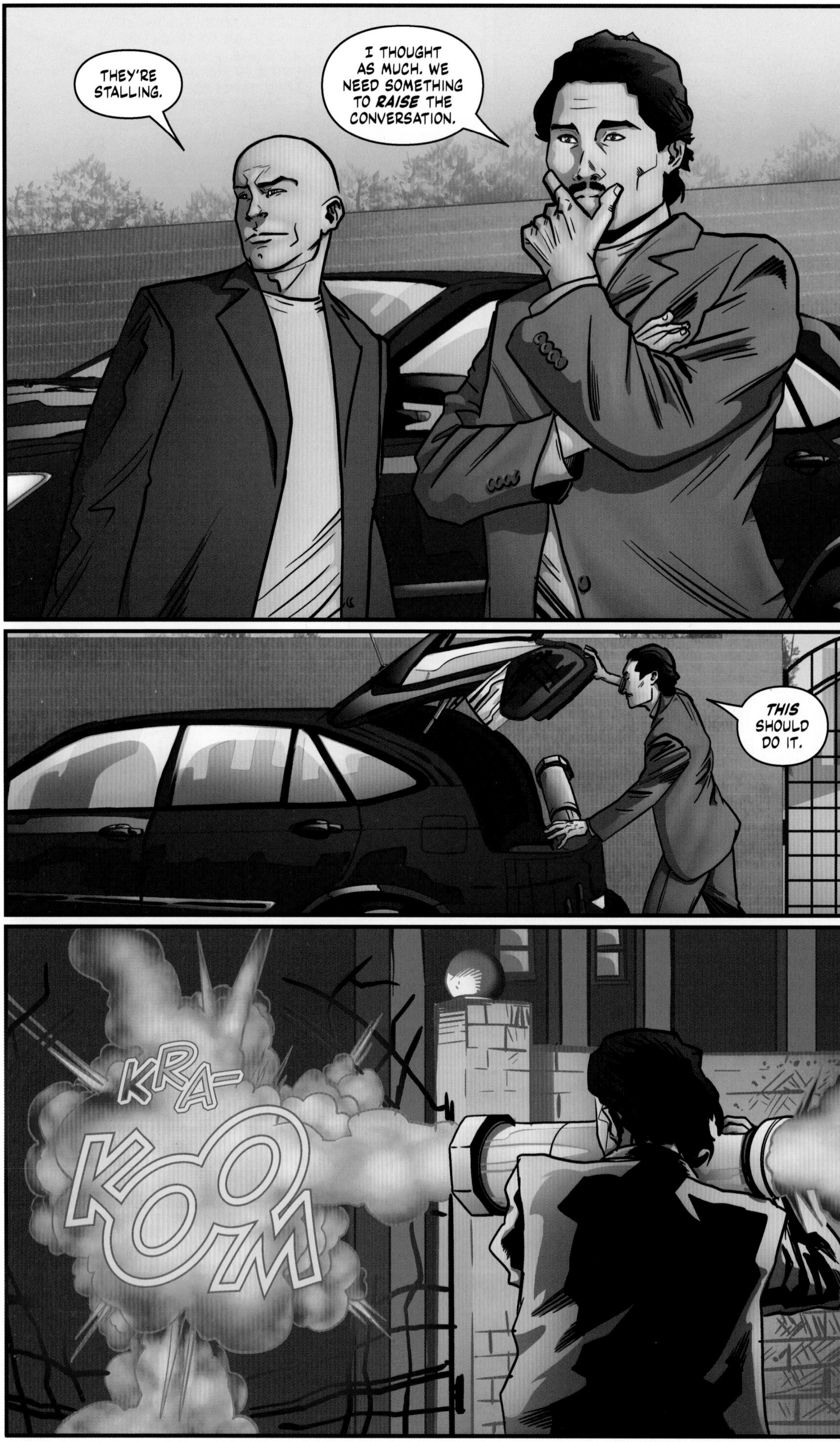
THEY'RE STALLING.
I THOUGHT AS MUCH. WE NEED SOMETHING TO *RAISE* THE CONVERSATION.
THIS SHOULD DO IT.
KRA-KOOM

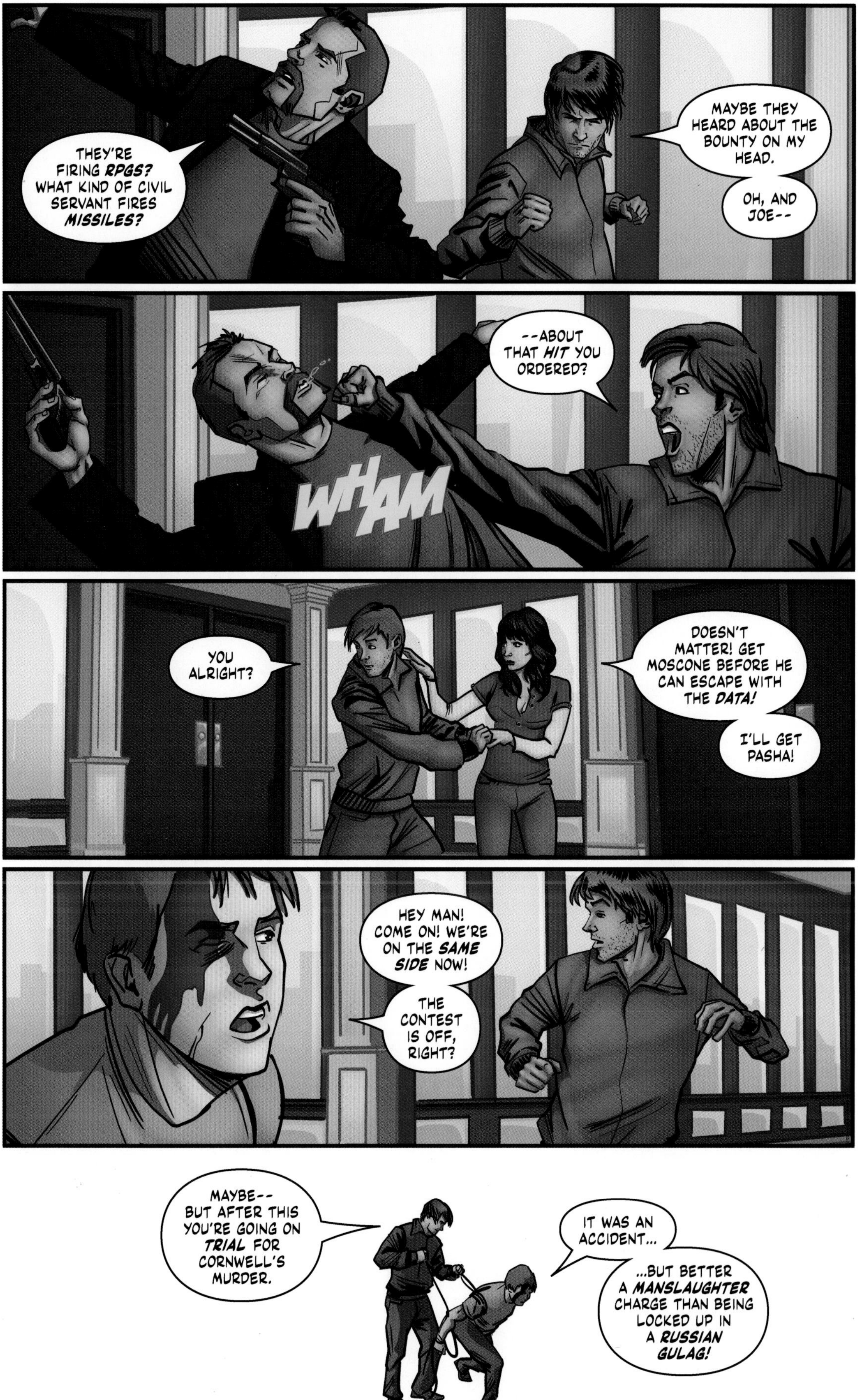
THEY'RE FIRING RPGS? WHAT KIND OF CIVIL SERVANT FIRES MISSILES?
MAYBE THEY HEARD ABOUT THE BOUNTY ON MY HEAD.
OH, AND JOE--
--ABOUT THAT HIT YOU ORDERED?
WHAM
YOU ALRIGHT?
DOESN'T MATTER! GET MOSCONE BEFORE HE CAN ESCAPE WITH THE DATA!
I'LL GET PASHA!
HEY MAN! COME ON! WE'RE ON THE SAME SIDE NOW!
THE CONTEST IS OFF, RIGHT?
MAYBE-- BUT AFTER THIS YOU'RE GOING ON TRIAL FOR CORNWELL'S MURDER.
IT WAS AN ACCIDENT...
...BUT BETTER A MANSLAUGHTER CHARGE THAN BEING LOCKED UP IN A RUSSIAN GULAG!

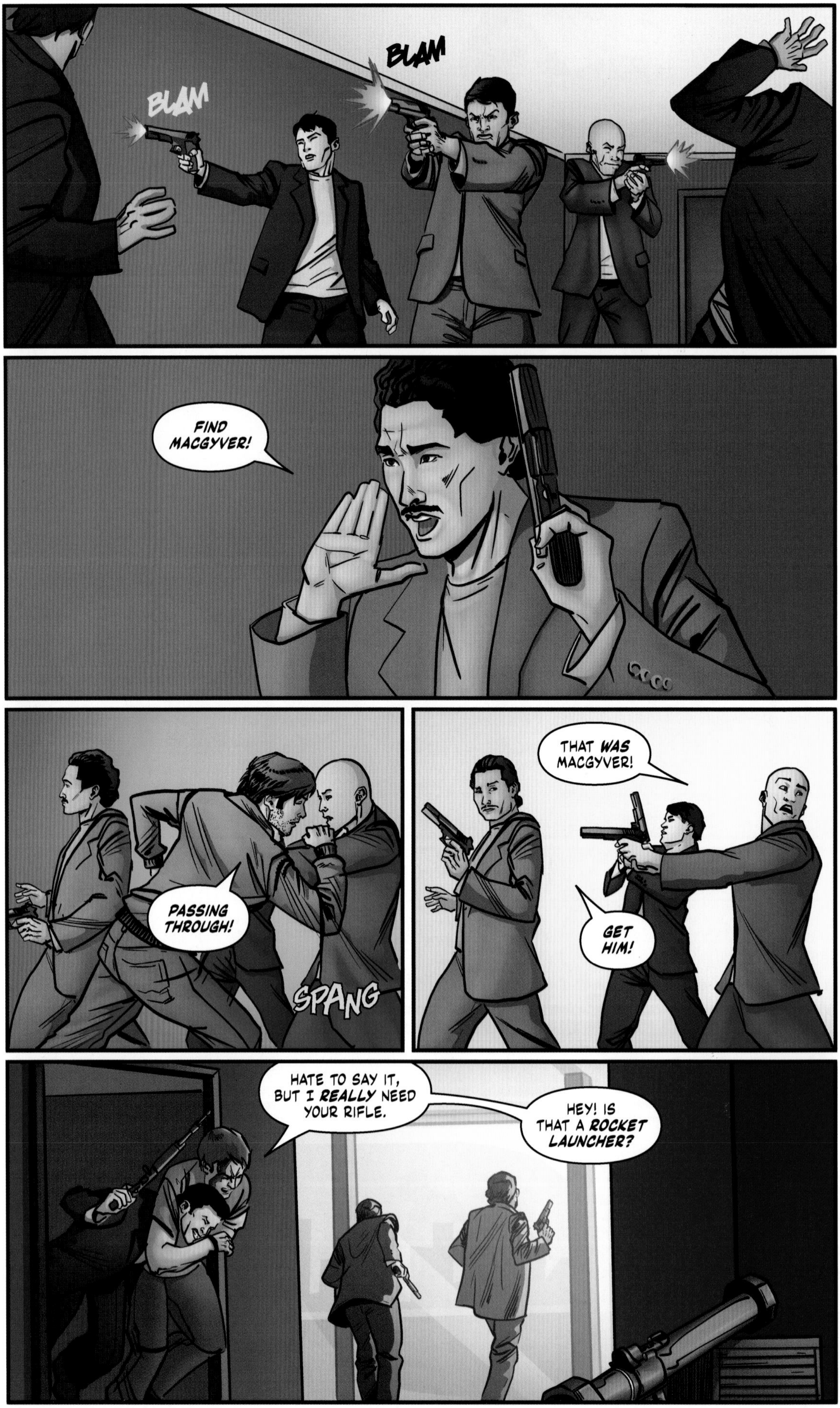
BLAM
BLAM
FIND MACGYVER!
PASSING THROUGH!
SPANG
THAT WAS MACGYVER!
GET HIM!
HATE TO SAY IT, BUT I REALLY NEED YOUR RIFLE.
HEY! IS THAT A ROCKET LAUNCHER?

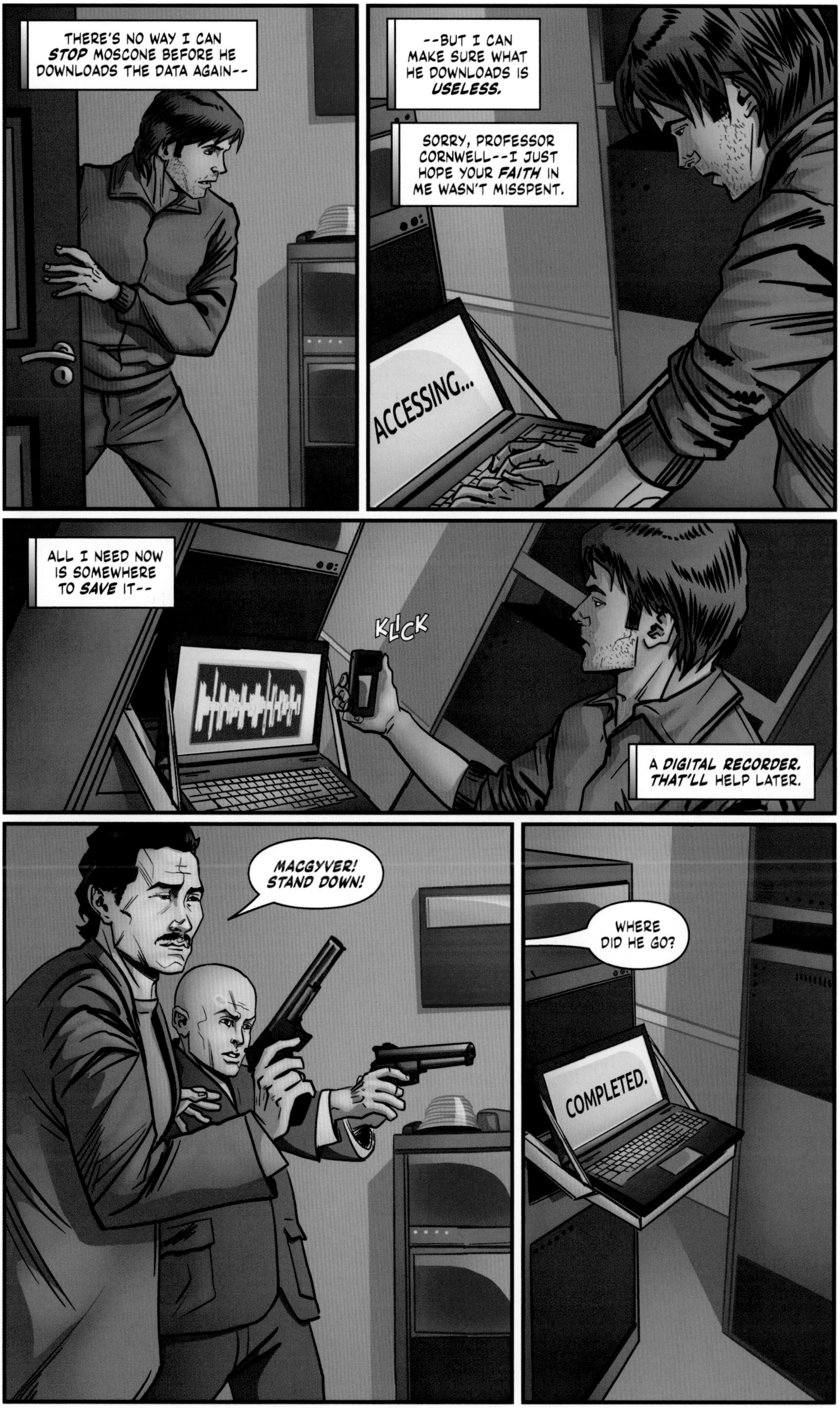
THERE'S NO WAY I CAN STOP MOSCONE BEFORE HE DOWNLOADS THE DATA AGAIN--
--BUT I CAN MAKE SURE WHAT HE DOWNLOADS IS USELESS.
SORRY, PROFESSOR CORNWELL--I JUST HOPE YOUR FAITH IN ME WASN'T MISSPENT.
ACCESSING...
ALL I NEED NOW IS SOMEWHERE TO SAVE IT--
KLICK
A DIGITAL RECORDER. THAT'LL HELP LATER.
MACGYVER! STAND DOWN!
WHERE DID HE GO?
COMPLETED.

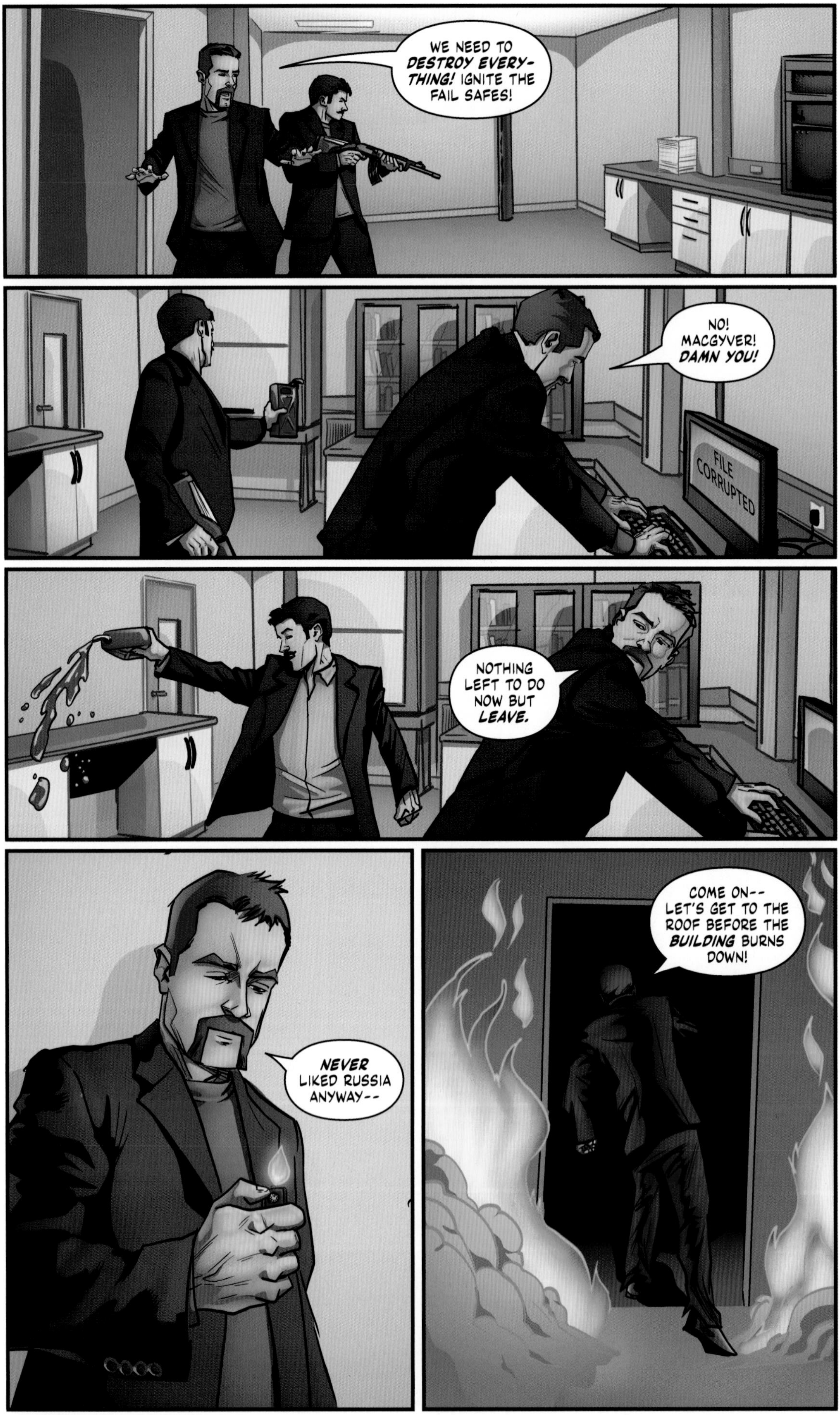
WE NEED TO DESTROY EVERYTHING! IGNITE THE FAIL SAFES!
NO! MACGYVER! DAMN YOU!
FILE CORRUPTED
NOTHING LEFT TO DO NOW BUT LEAVE.
NEVER LIKED RUSSIA ANYWAY--
COME ON-- LET'S GET TO THE ROOF BEFORE THE BUILDING BURNS DOWN!

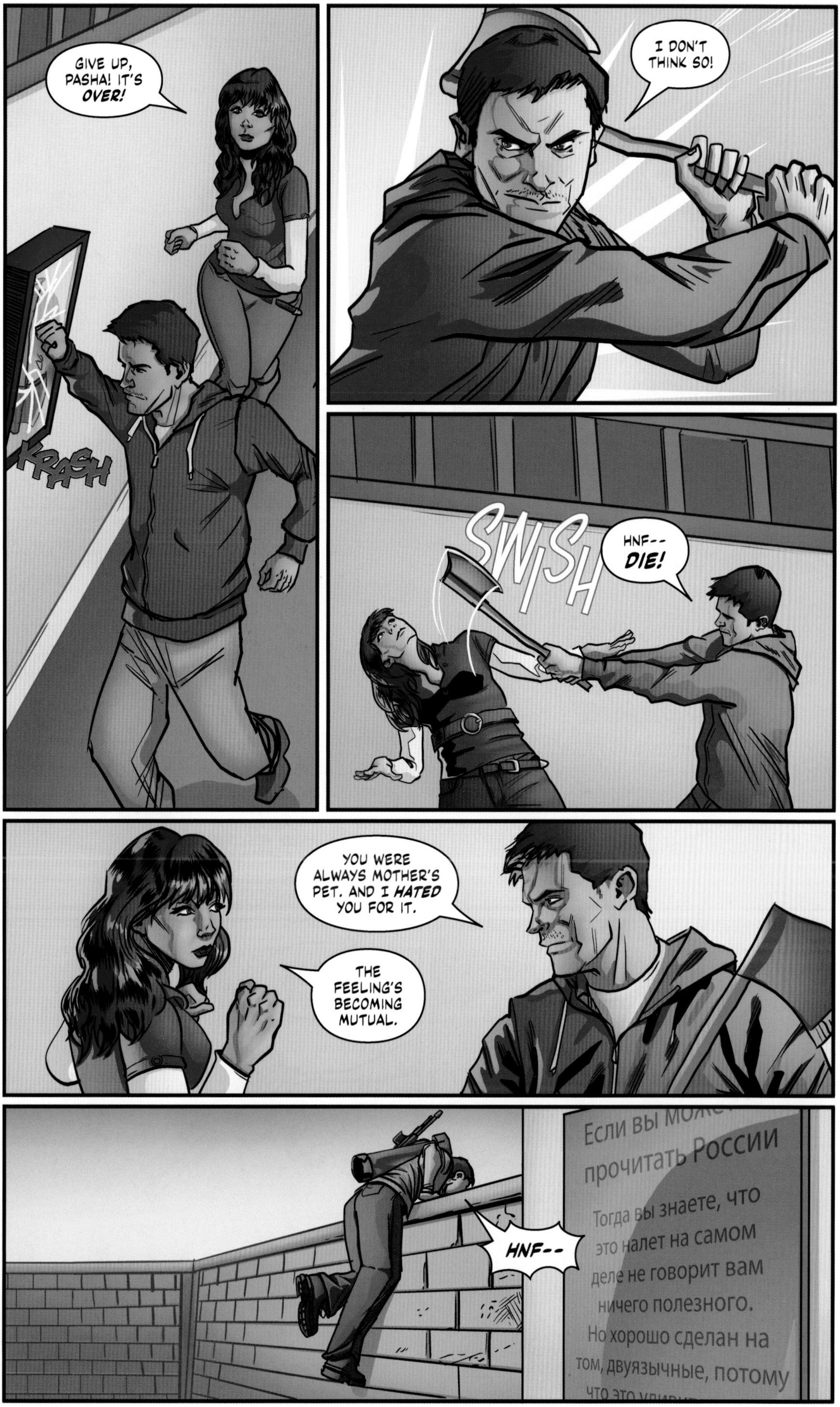

GIVE UP, PASHA! IT'S *OVER!*
KRASH
I DON'T THINK SO!
SWISH
HNF-- *DIE!*
YOU WERE ALWAYS MOTHER'S PET. AND I *HATED* YOU FOR IT.
THE FEELING'S BECOMING MUTUAL.
Если вы мож
прочитать России
Тогда вы знаете, что
это налет на самом
деле не говорит вам
ничего полезного.
Но хорошо сделан на
том, двуязычные, потому
HNF--

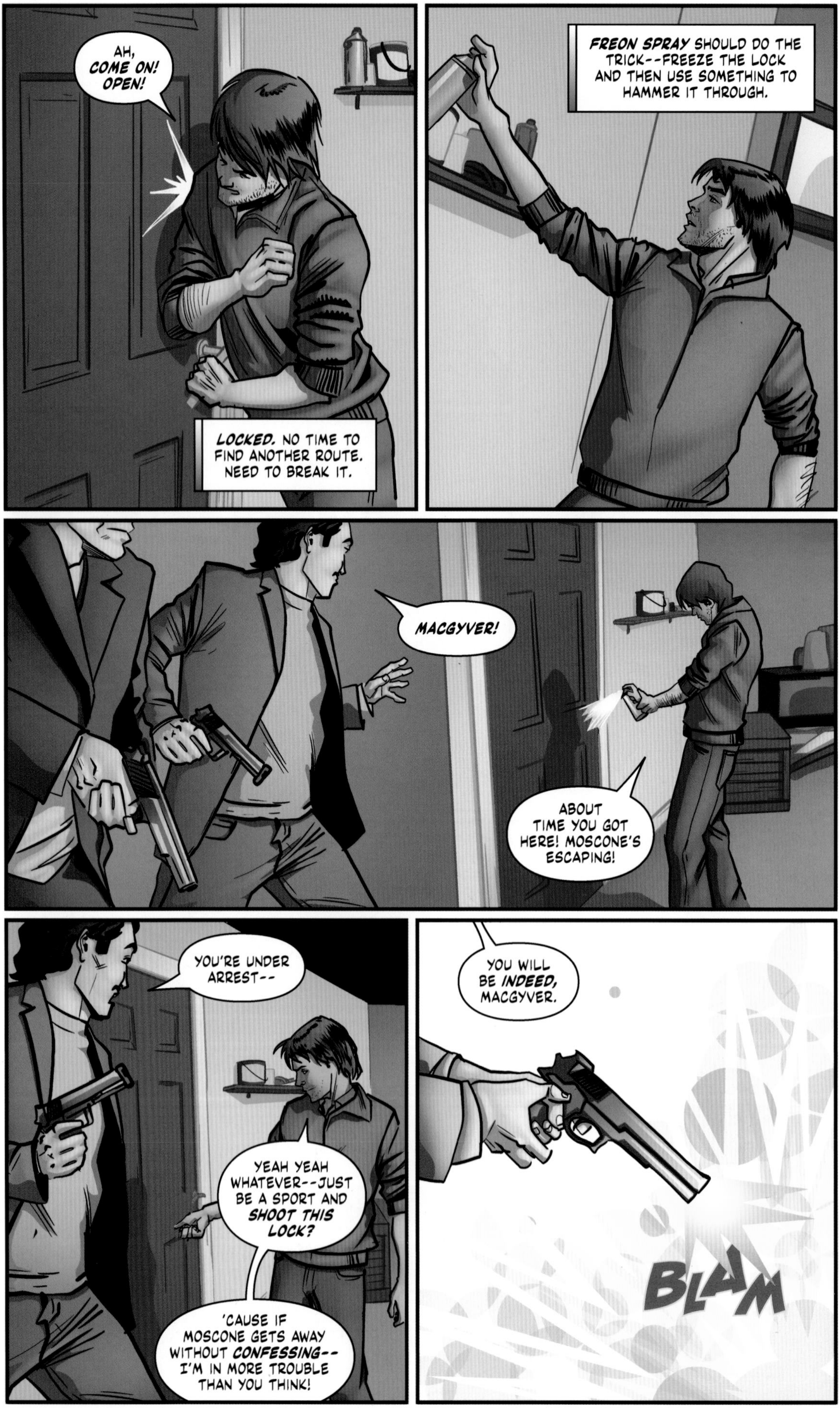
AH, COME ON! OPEN!
LOCKED. NO TIME TO FIND ANOTHER ROUTE. NEED TO BREAK IT.
FREON SPRAY SHOULD DO THE TRICK--FREEZE THE LOCK AND THEN USE SOMETHING TO HAMMER IT THROUGH.
MACGYVER!
ABOUT TIME YOU GOT HERE! MOSCONE'S ESCAPING!
YOU'RE UNDER ARREST--
YEAH YEAH WHATEVER--JUST BE A SPORT AND SHOOT THIS LOCK?
'CAUSE IF MOSCONE GETS AWAY WITHOUT CONFESSING--I'M IN MORE TROUBLE THAN YOU THINK!
YOU WILL BE INDEED, MACGYVER.
BLAM

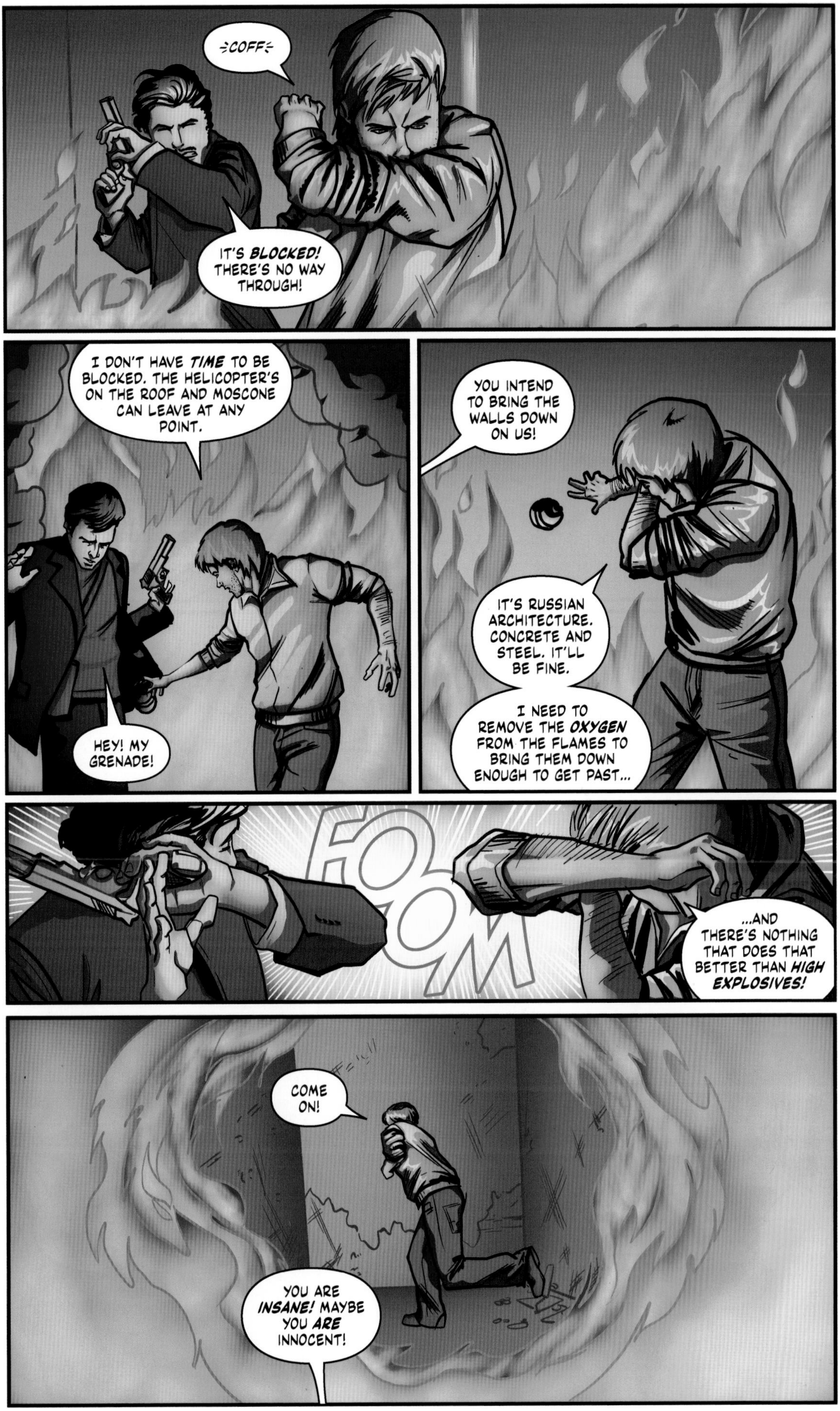

=COFF=
IT'S BLOCKED! THERE'S NO WAY THROUGH!
I DON'T HAVE TIME TO BE BLOCKED. THE HELICOPTER'S ON THE ROOF AND MOSCONE CAN LEAVE AT ANY POINT.
HEY! MY GRENADE!
YOU INTEND TO BRING THE WALLS DOWN ON US!
IT'S RUSSIAN ARCHITECTURE. CONCRETE AND STEEL. IT'LL BE FINE.
I NEED TO REMOVE THE OXYGEN FROM THE FLAMES TO BRING THEM DOWN ENOUGH TO GET PAST...
FOOOM
...AND THERE'S NOTHING THAT DOES THAT BETTER THAN HIGH EXPLOSIVES!
COME ON!
YOU ARE INSANE! MAYBE YOU ARE INNOCENT!

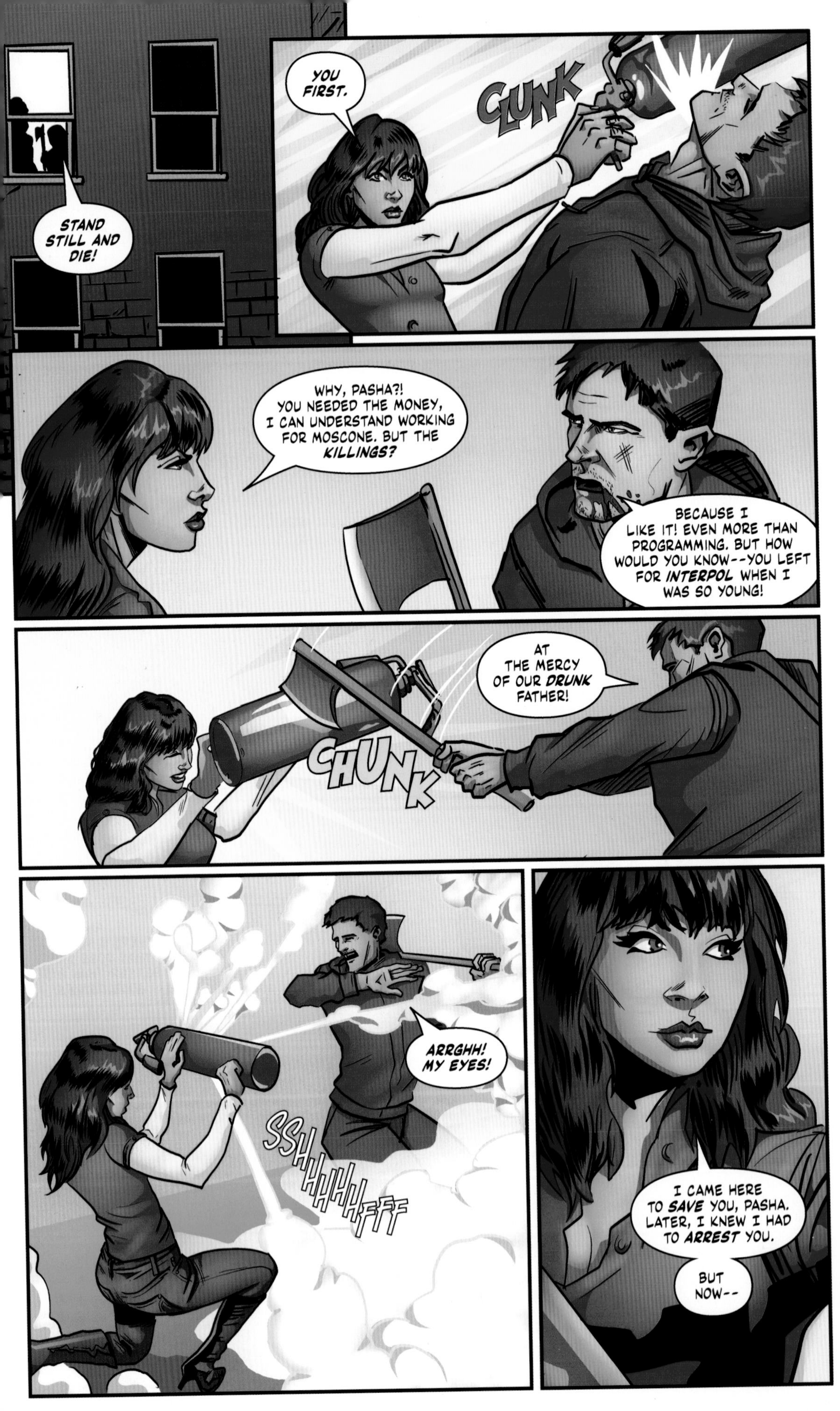
STAND STILL AND DIE!
YOU FIRST.
CLUNK
WHY, PASHA?! YOU NEEDED THE MONEY, I CAN UNDERSTAND WORKING FOR MOSCONE. BUT THE KILLINGS?
BECAUSE I LIKE IT! EVEN MORE THAN PROGRAMMING. BUT HOW WOULD YOU KNOW--YOU LEFT FOR INTERPOL WHEN I WAS SO YOUNG!
AT THE MERCY OF OUR DRUNK FATHER!
CHUNK
ARRGHH! MY EYES!
SSHHHHHHFFF
I CAME HERE TO SAVE YOU, PASHA. LATER, I KNEW I HAD TO ARREST YOU.
BUT NOW--

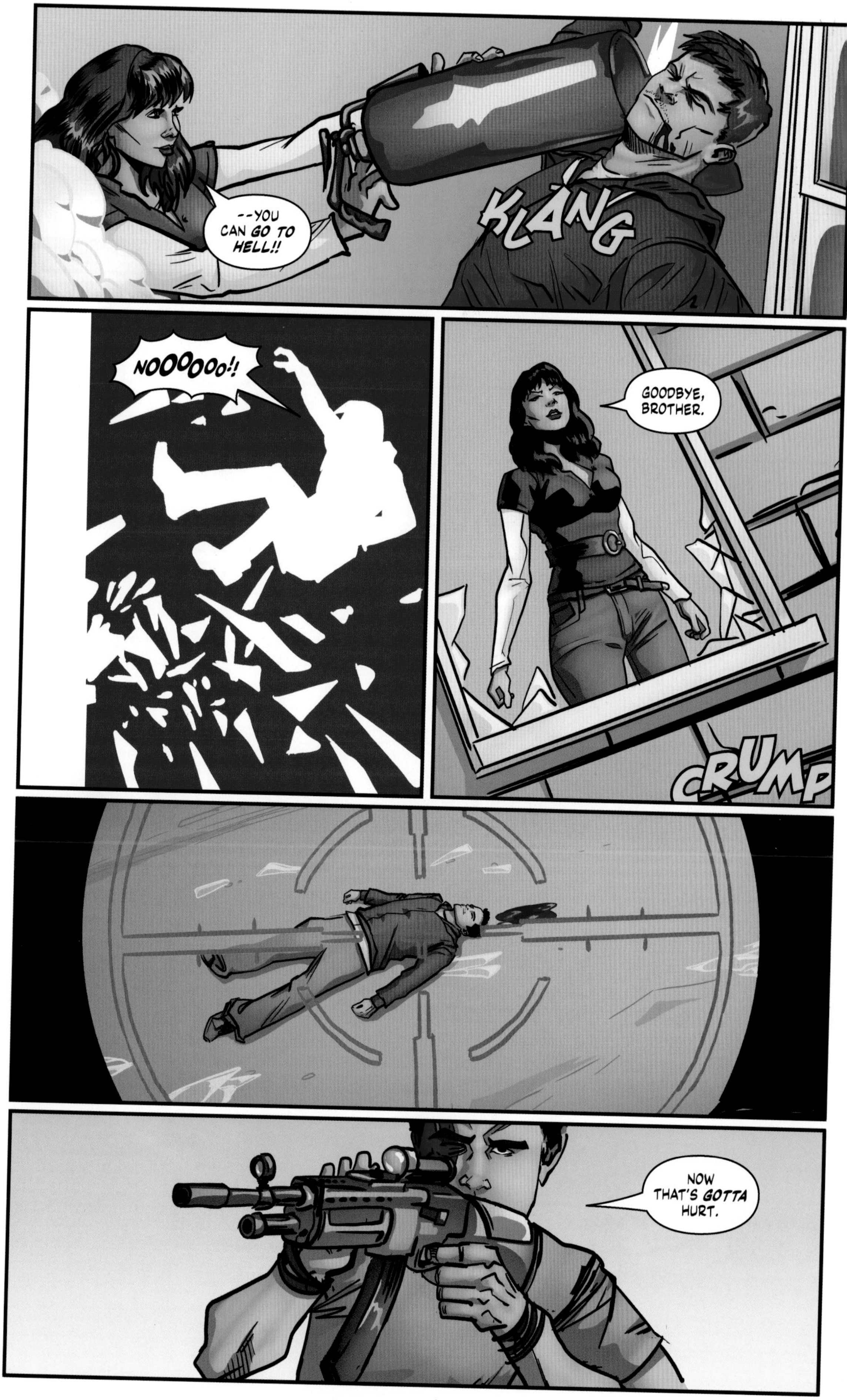
--YOU CAN GO TO HELL!!
KLANG
NOOOOOo!!
GOODBYE, BROTHER.
CRUMP
NOW THAT'S GOTTA HURT.

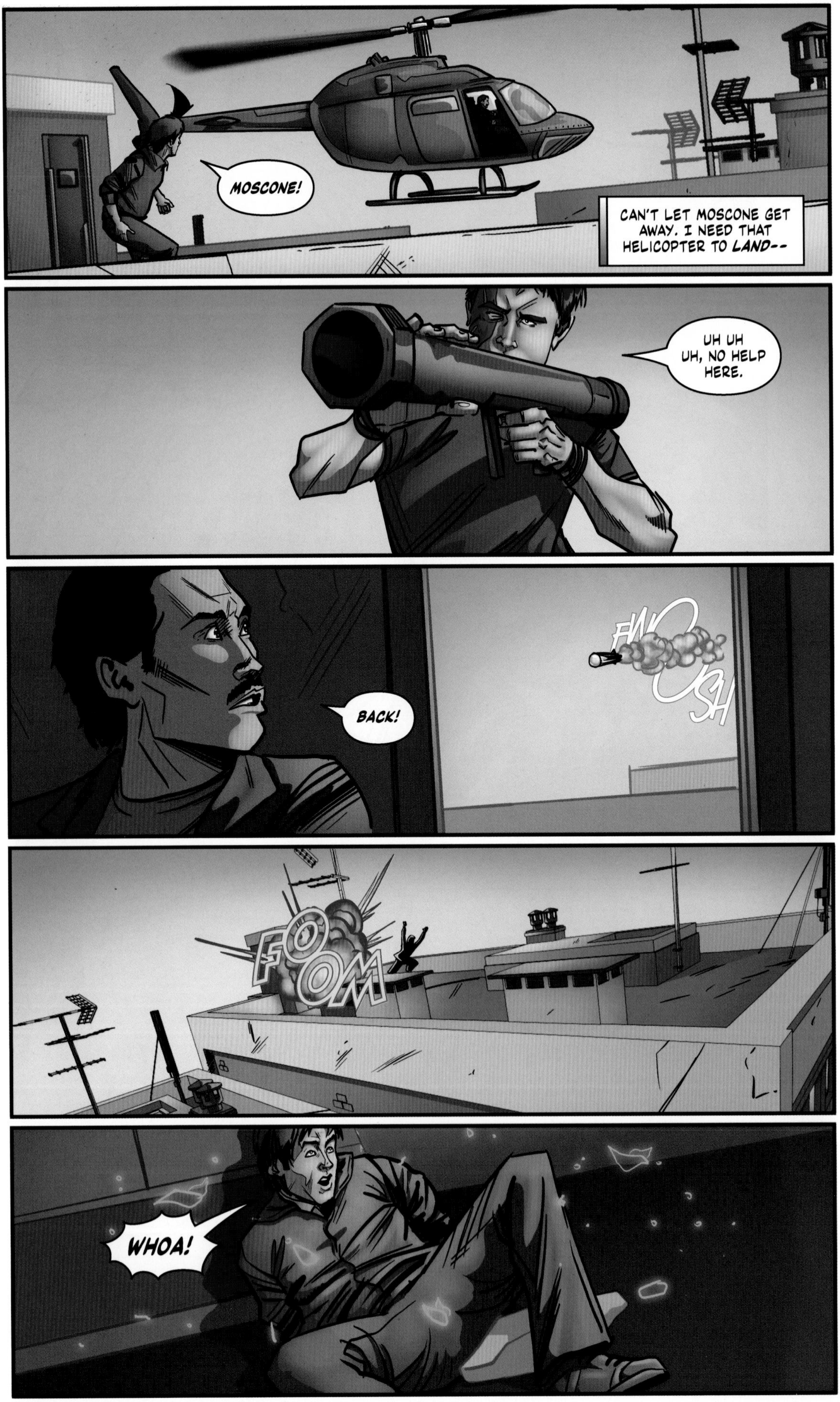
MOSCONE!
CAN'T LET MOSCONE GET AWAY. I NEED THAT HELICOPTER TO *LAND--*
UH UH UH, NO HELP HERE.
BACK!
FWOOSH
FOOM
WHOA!

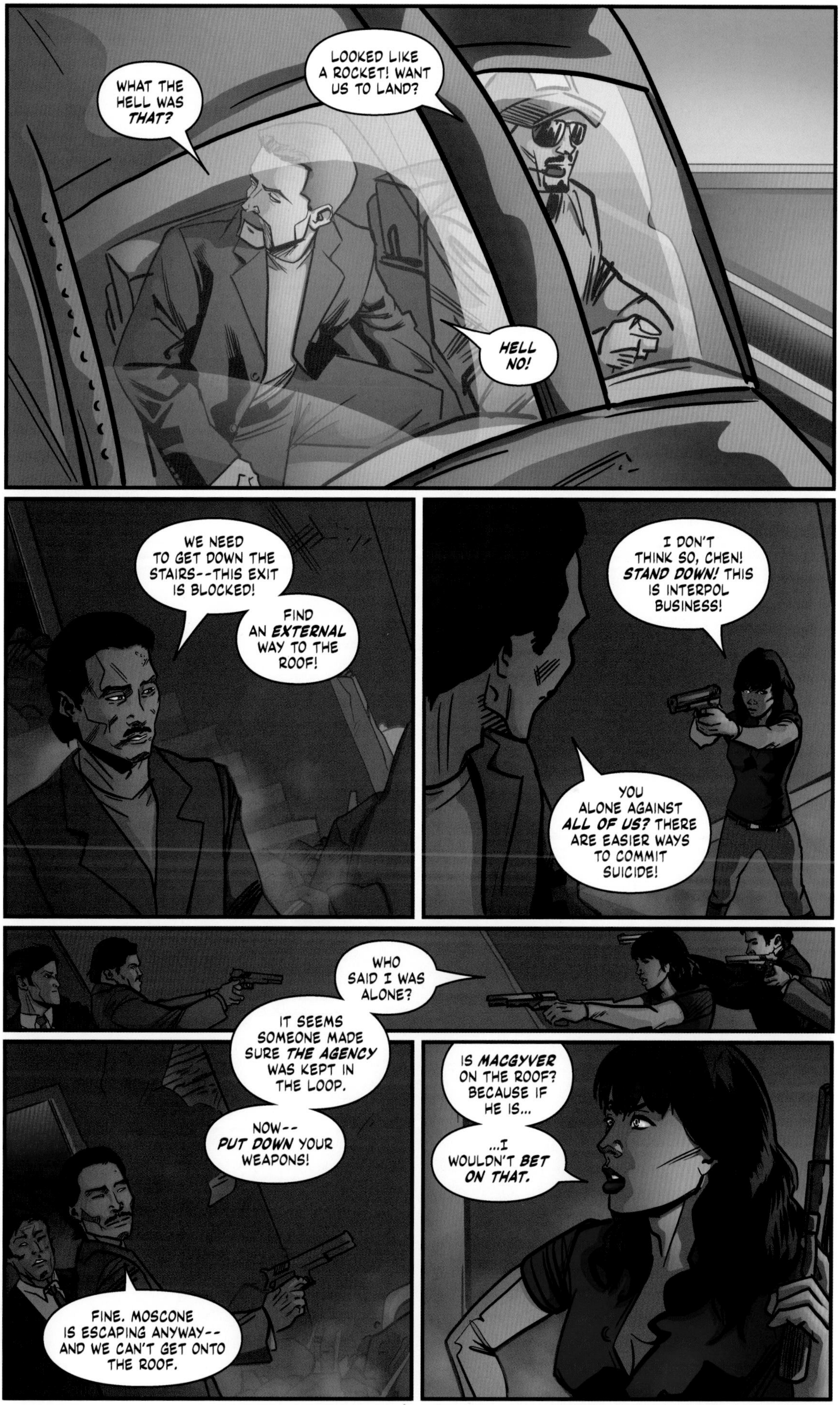
WHAT THE HELL WAS *THAT?*
LOOKED LIKE A ROCKET! WANT US TO LAND?
HELL NO!
WE NEED TO GET DOWN THE STAIRS--THIS EXIT IS BLOCKED!
FIND AN *EXTERNAL* WAY TO THE ROOF!
I DON'T THINK SO, CHEN! *STAND DOWN!* THIS IS INTERPOL BUSINESS!
YOU ALONE AGAINST *ALL OF US?* THERE ARE EASIER WAYS TO COMMIT SUICIDE!
WHO SAID I WAS ALONE?
IT SEEMS SOMEONE MADE SURE *THE AGENCY* WAS KEPT IN THE LOOP.
NOW-- *PUT DOWN* YOUR WEAPONS!
FINE. MOSCONE IS ESCAPING ANYWAY-- AND WE CAN'T GET ONTO THE ROOF.
IS *MACGYVER* ON THE ROOF? BECAUSE IF HE IS...
...I WOULDN'T *BET ON THAT.*

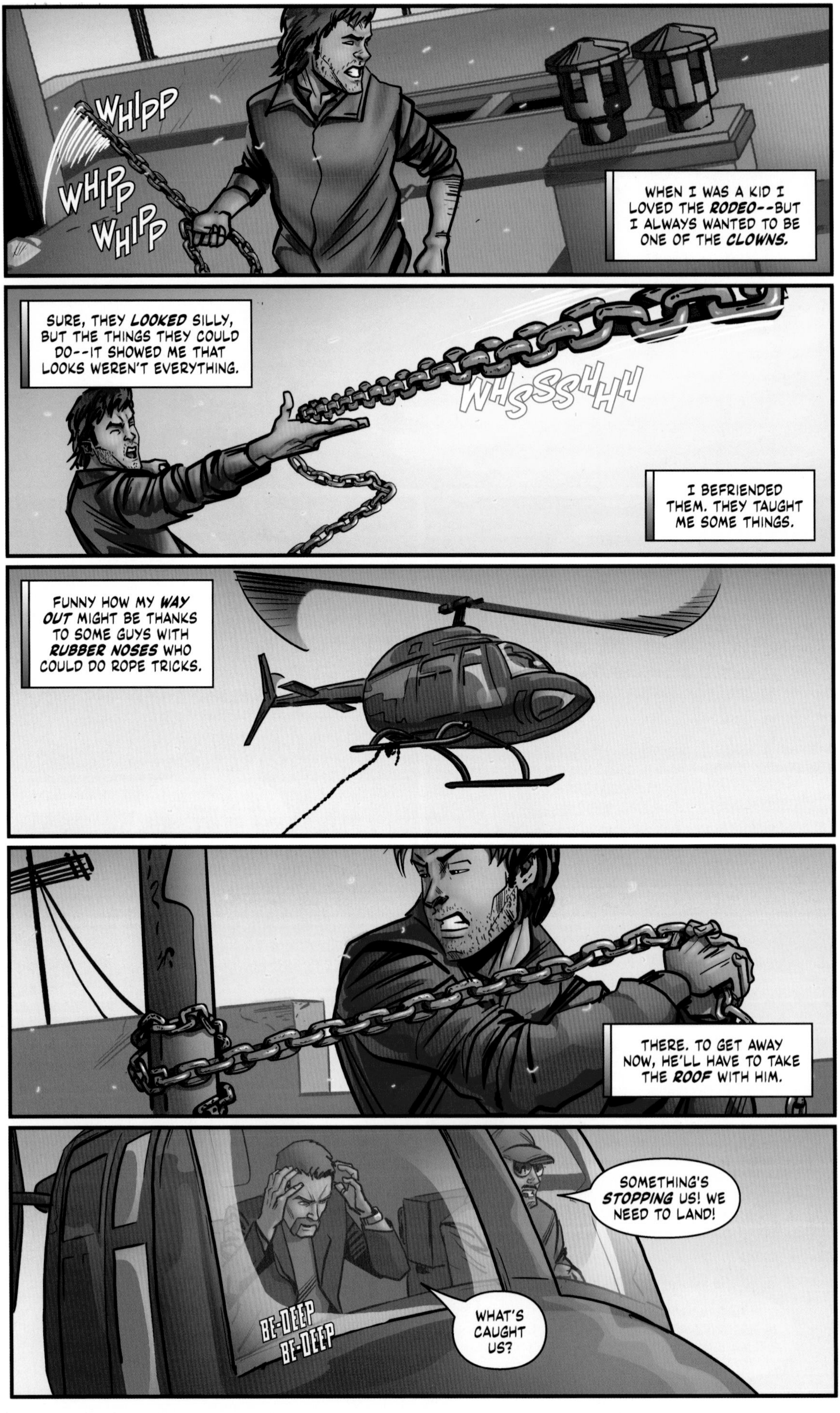
WHIPP
WHIPP
WHIPP
WHEN I WAS A KID I LOVED THE ***RODEO***--BUT I ALWAYS WANTED TO BE ONE OF THE ***CLOWNS.***
SURE, THEY ***LOOKED*** SILLY, BUT THE THINGS THEY COULD DO--IT SHOWED ME THAT LOOKS WEREN'T EVERYTHING.
WHSSSHHH
I BEFRIENDED THEM. THEY TAUGHT ME SOME THINGS.
FUNNY HOW MY ***WAY OUT*** MIGHT BE THANKS TO SOME GUYS WITH ***RUBBER NOSES*** WHO COULD DO ROPE TRICKS.
THERE. TO GET AWAY NOW, HE'LL HAVE TO TAKE THE ***ROOF*** WITH HIM.
SOMETHING'S ***STOPPING*** US! WE NEED TO LAND!
BE-DEEP
BE-DEEP
WHAT'S CAUGHT US?

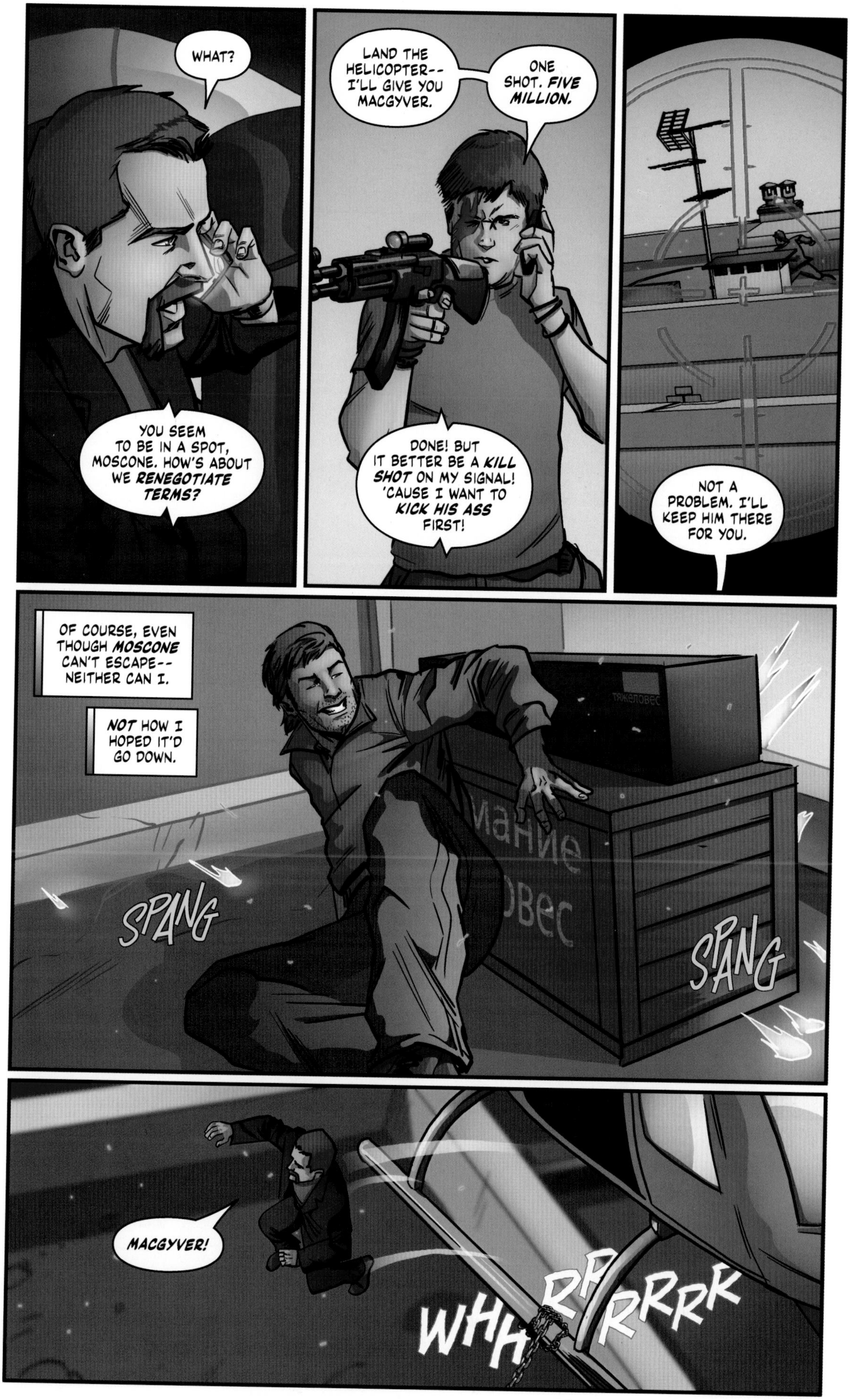
WHAT?
YOU SEEM TO BE IN A SPOT, MOSCONE. HOW'S ABOUT WE *RENEGOTIATE TERMS?*
LAND THE HELICOPTER-- I'LL GIVE YOU MACGYVER.
ONE SHOT. *FIVE MILLION.*
DONE! BUT IT BETTER BE A *KILL SHOT* ON MY SIGNAL! 'CAUSE I WANT TO *KICK HIS ASS* FIRST!
NOT A PROBLEM. I'LL KEEP HIM THERE FOR YOU.
OF COURSE, EVEN THOUGH *MOSCONE* CAN'T ESCAPE-- NEITHER CAN I.
NOT HOW I HOPED IT'D GO DOWN.
ТЯЖЕЛОВЕС
SPANG
SPANG
MACGYVER!
WHHRRRRRK

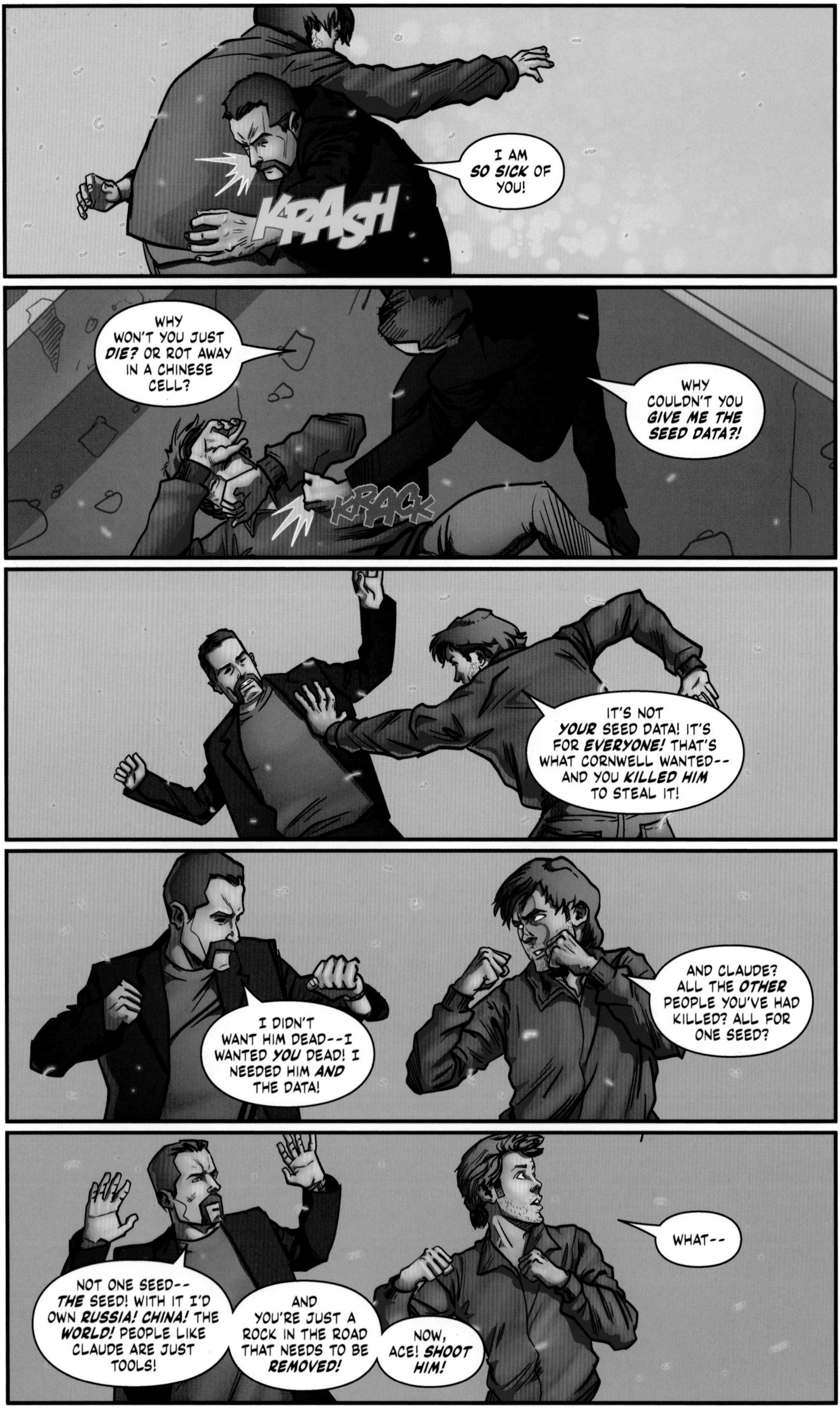
I AM SO SICK OF YOU!
KRASH
WHY WON'T YOU JUST DIE? OR ROT AWAY IN A CHINESE CELL?
WHY COULDN'T YOU GIVE ME THE SEED DATA?!
KRACK
IT'S NOT YOUR SEED DATA! IT'S FOR EVERYONE! THAT'S WHAT CORNWELL WANTED-- AND YOU KILLED HIM TO STEAL IT!
AND CLAUDE? ALL THE OTHER PEOPLE YOU'VE HAD KILLED? ALL FOR ONE SEED?
I DIDN'T WANT HIM DEAD--I WANTED YOU DEAD! I NEEDED HIM AND THE DATA!
NOT ONE SEED-- THE SEED! WITH IT I'D OWN RUSSIA! CHINA! THE WORLD! PEOPLE LIKE CLAUDE ARE JUST TOOLS!
AND YOU'RE JUST A ROCK IN THE ROAD THAT NEEDS TO BE REMOVED!
NOW, ACE! SHOOT HIM!
WHAT--

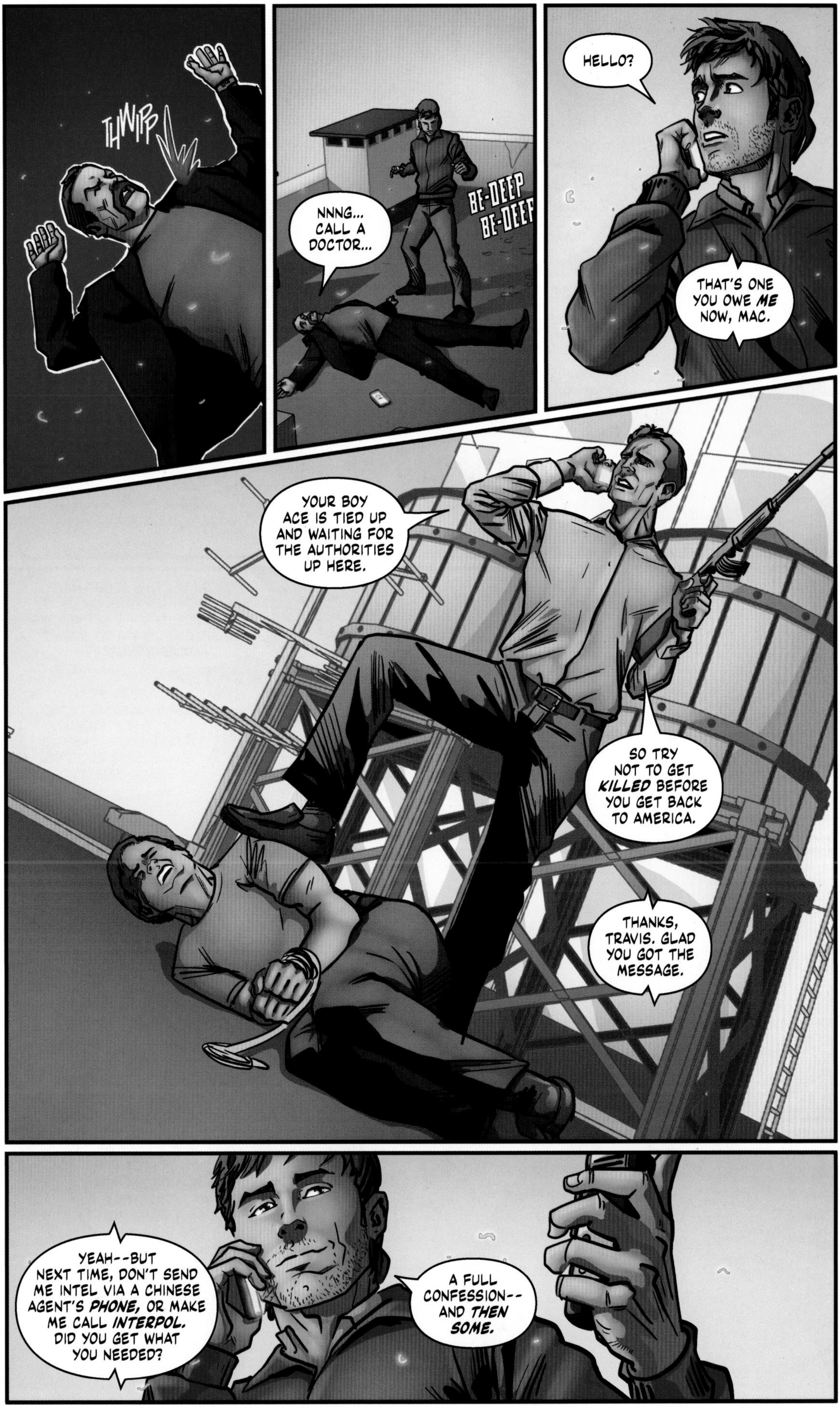
THWIPP
NNNG... CALL A DOCTOR...
BE-DEEP BE-DEEP
HELLO?
THAT'S ONE YOU OWE *ME* NOW, MAC.
YOUR BOY ACE IS TIED UP AND WAITING FOR THE AUTHORITIES UP HERE.
SO TRY NOT TO GET *KILLED* BEFORE YOU GET BACK TO AMERICA.
THANKS, TRAVIS. GLAD YOU GOT THE MESSAGE.
YEAH--BUT NEXT TIME, DON'T SEND ME INTEL VIA A CHINESE AGENT'S *PHONE,* OR MAKE ME CALL *INTERPOL.* DID YOU GET WHAT YOU NEEDED?
A FULL CONFESSION--AND *THEN SOME.*

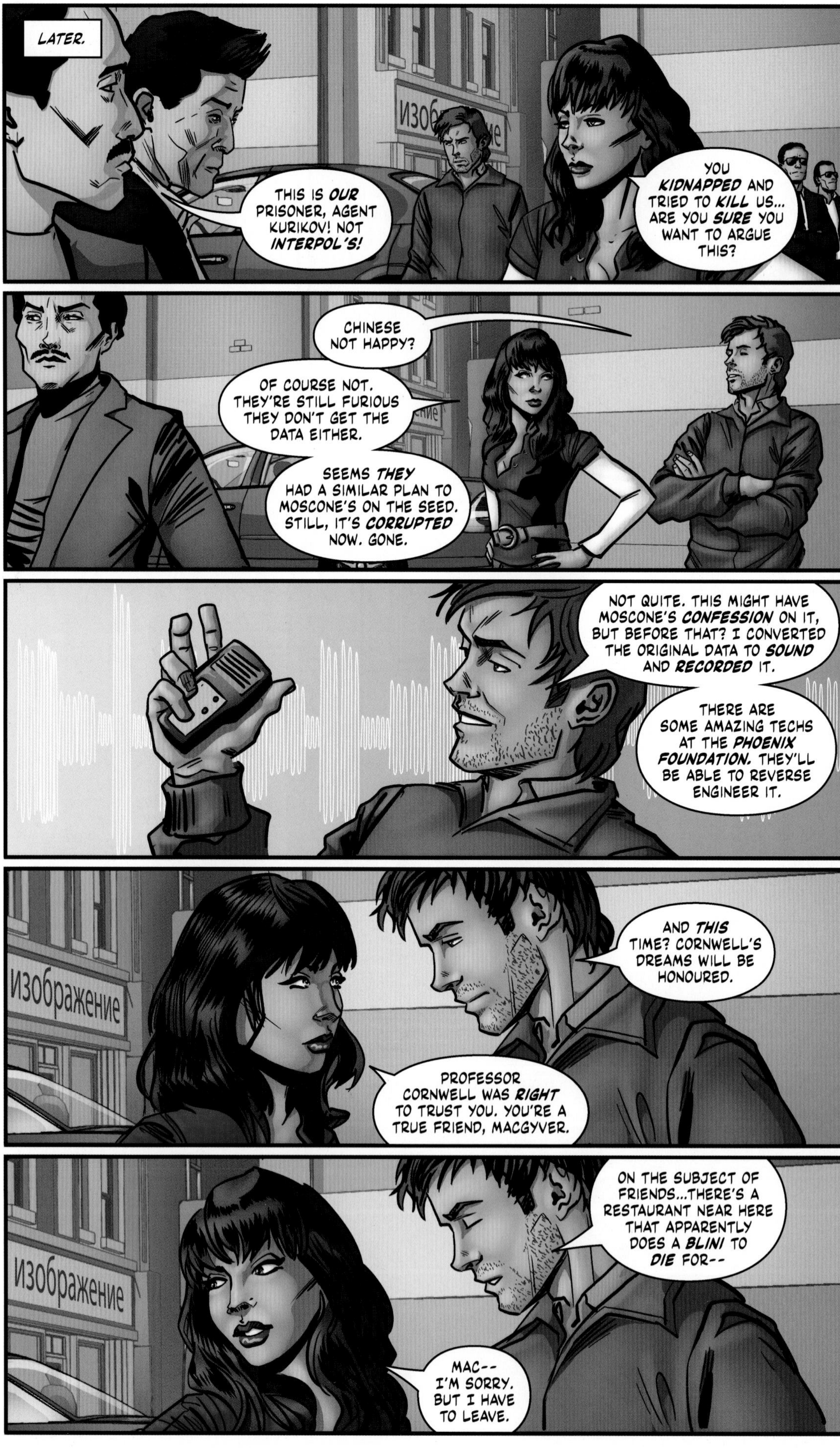
LATER.
THIS IS OUR PRISONER, AGENT KURIKOV! NOT INTERPOL'S!
изображение
YOU KIDNAPPED AND TRIED TO KILL US... ARE YOU SURE YOU WANT TO ARGUE THIS?
CHINESE NOT HAPPY?
OF COURSE NOT. THEY'RE STILL FURIOUS THEY DON'T GET THE DATA EITHER.
SEEMS THEY HAD A SIMILAR PLAN TO MOSCONE'S ON THE SEED. STILL, IT'S CORRUPTED NOW. GONE.
NOT QUITE. THIS MIGHT HAVE MOSCONE'S CONFESSION ON IT, BUT BEFORE THAT? I CONVERTED THE ORIGINAL DATA TO SOUND AND RECORDED IT.
THERE ARE SOME AMAZING TECHS AT THE PHOENIX FOUNDATION. THEY'LL BE ABLE TO REVERSE ENGINEER IT.
изображение
AND THIS TIME? CORNWELL'S DREAMS WILL BE HONOURED.
PROFESSOR CORNWELL WAS RIGHT TO TRUST YOU. YOU'RE A TRUE FRIEND, MACGYVER.
изображение
ON THE SUBJECT OF FRIENDS...THERE'S A RESTAURANT NEAR HERE THAT APPARENTLY DOES A BLINI TO DIE FOR--
MAC-- I'M SORRY. BUT I HAVE TO LEAVE.

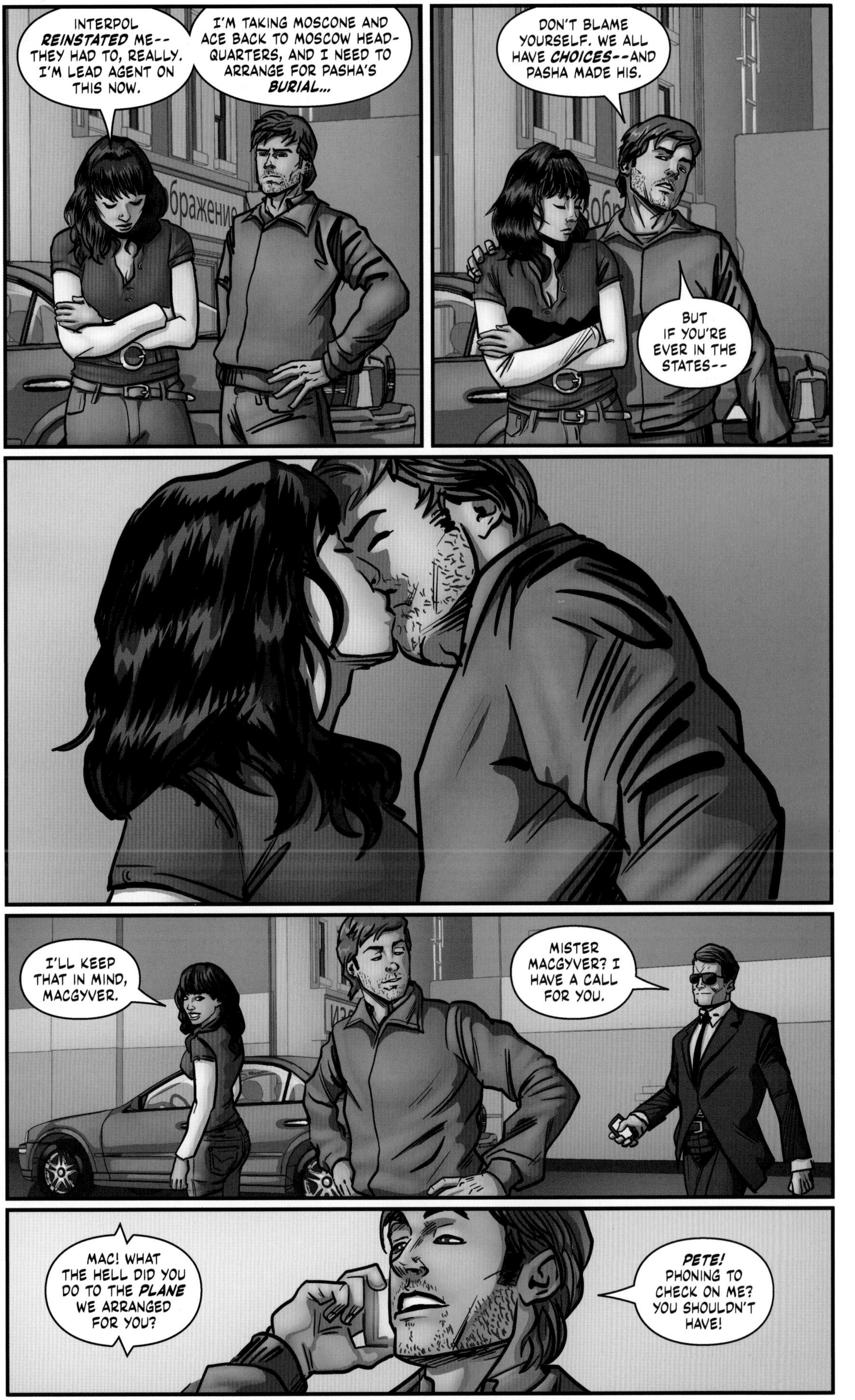

INTERPOL *REINSTATED* ME--THEY HAD TO, REALLY. I'M LEAD AGENT ON THIS NOW.
I'M TAKING MOSCONE AND ACE BACK TO MOSCOW HEAD-QUARTERS, AND I NEED TO ARRANGE FOR PASHA'S *BURIAL...*
DON'T BLAME YOURSELF. WE ALL HAVE *CHOICES*--AND PASHA MADE HIS.
BUT IF YOU'RE EVER IN THE STATES--
I'LL KEEP THAT IN MIND, MACGYVER.
MISTER MACGYVER? I HAVE A CALL FOR YOU.
PETE! PHONING TO CHECK ON ME? YOU SHOULDN'T HAVE!
MAC! WHAT THE HELL DID YOU DO TO THE *PLANE* WE ARRANGED FOR YOU?

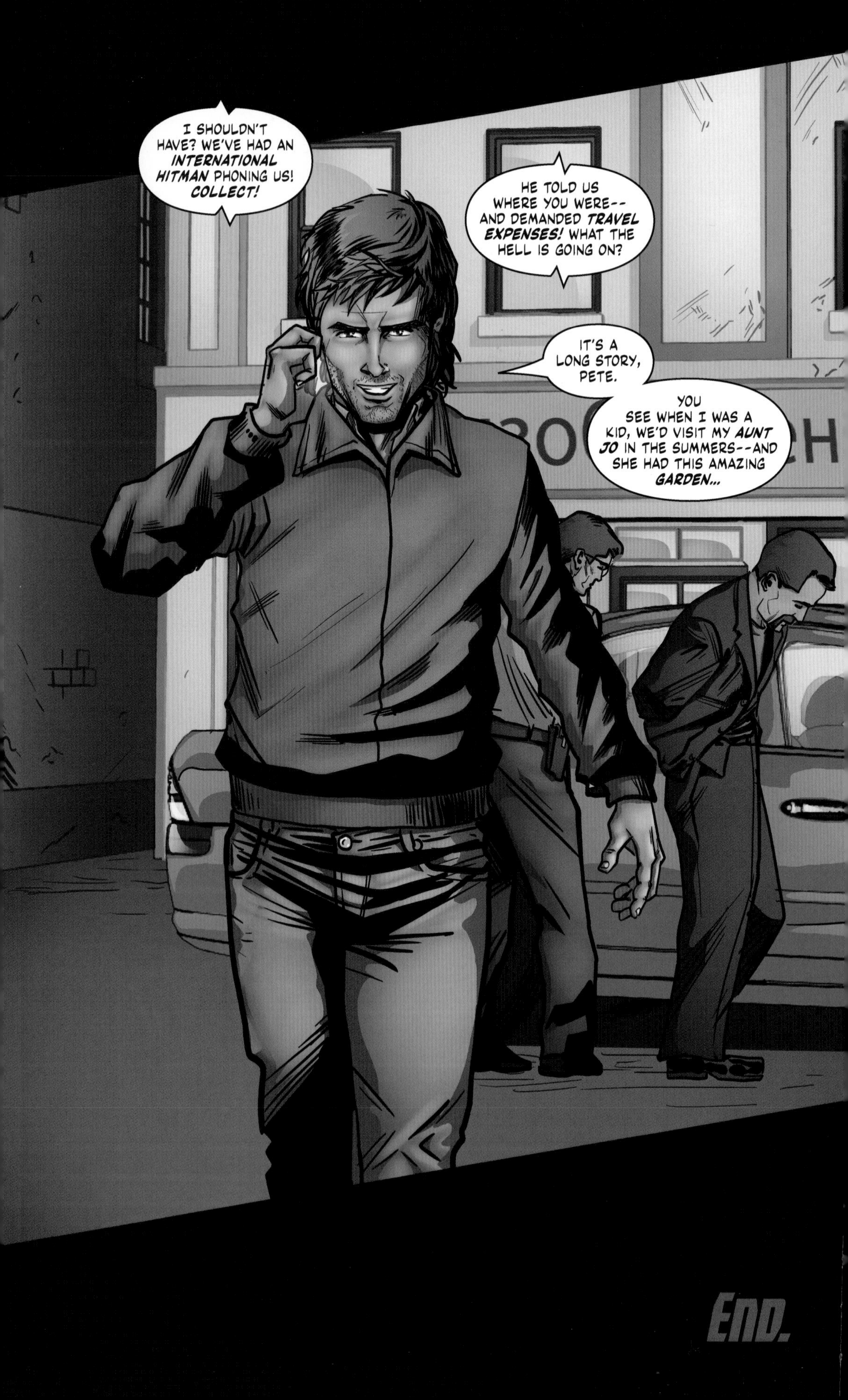
I SHOULDN'T HAVE? WE'VE HAD AN *INTERNATIONAL HITMAN* PHONING US! *COLLECT!*
HE TOLD US WHERE YOU WERE-- AND DEMANDED *TRAVEL EXPENSES!* WHAT THE HELL IS GOING ON?
IT'S A LONG STORY, PETE.
YOU SEE WHEN I WAS A KID, WE'D VISIT MY *AUNT JO* IN THE SUMMERS--AND SHE HAD THIS AMAZING *GARDEN*...
END.

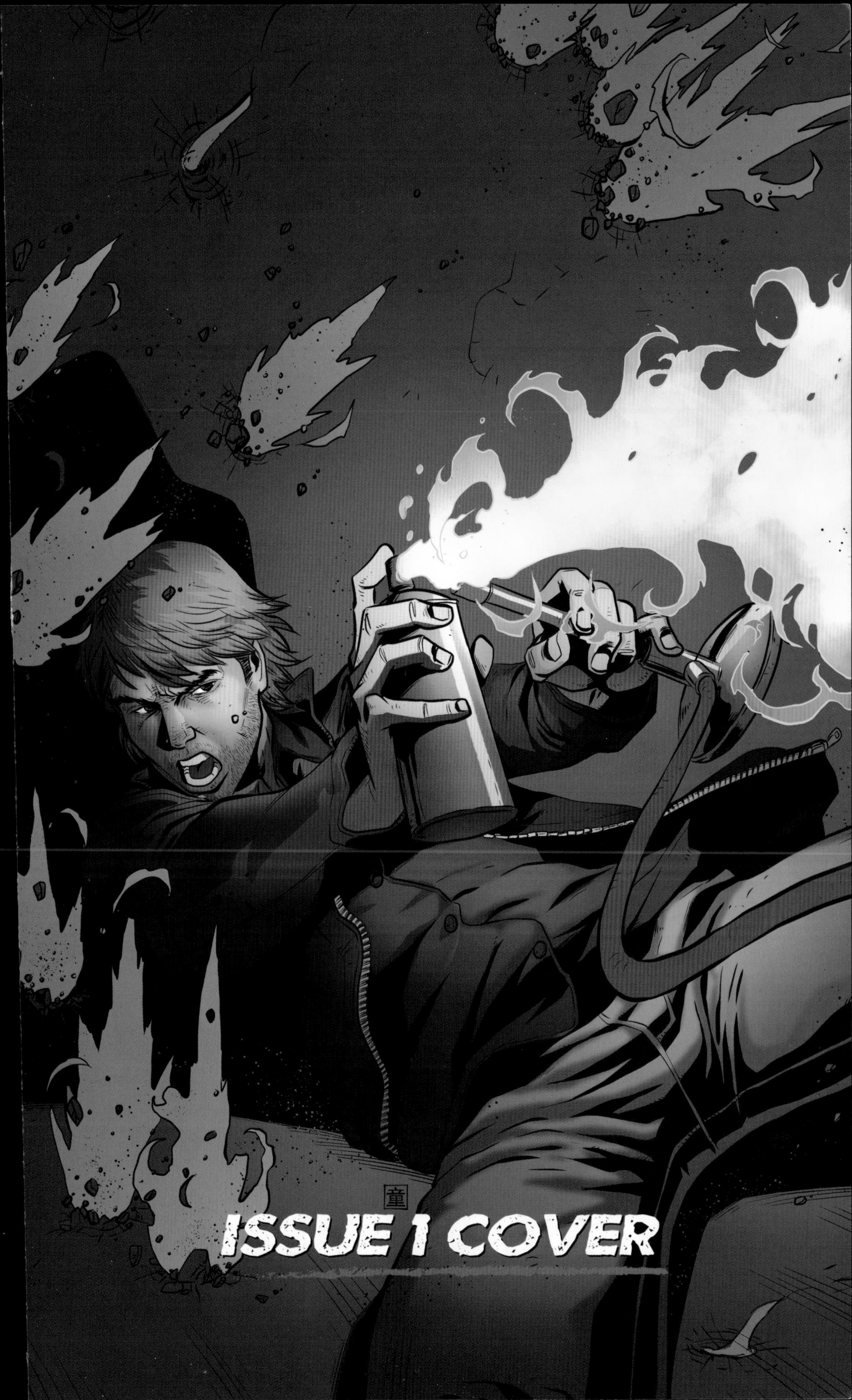

ISSUE 1 COVER

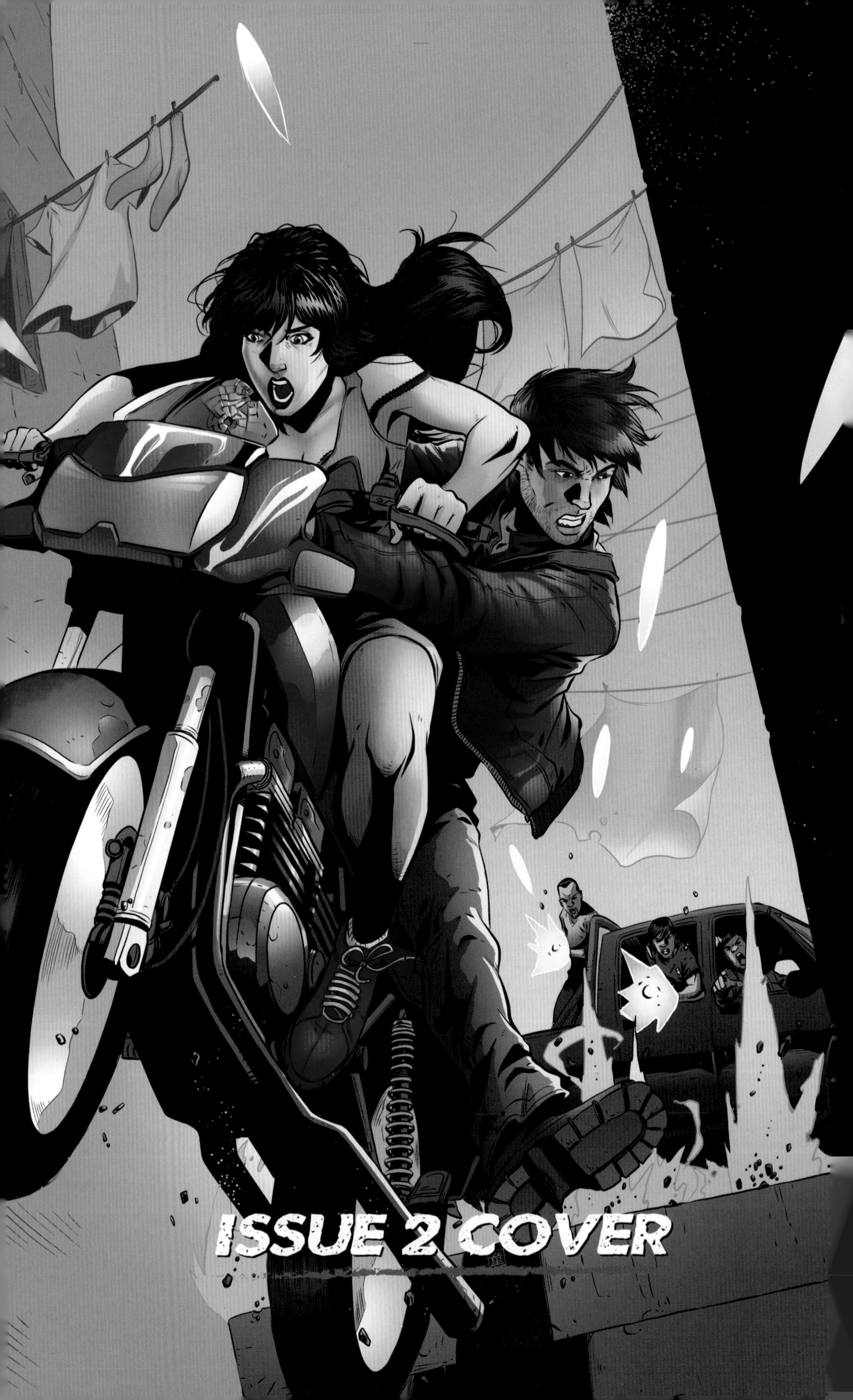
ISSUE 2 COVER

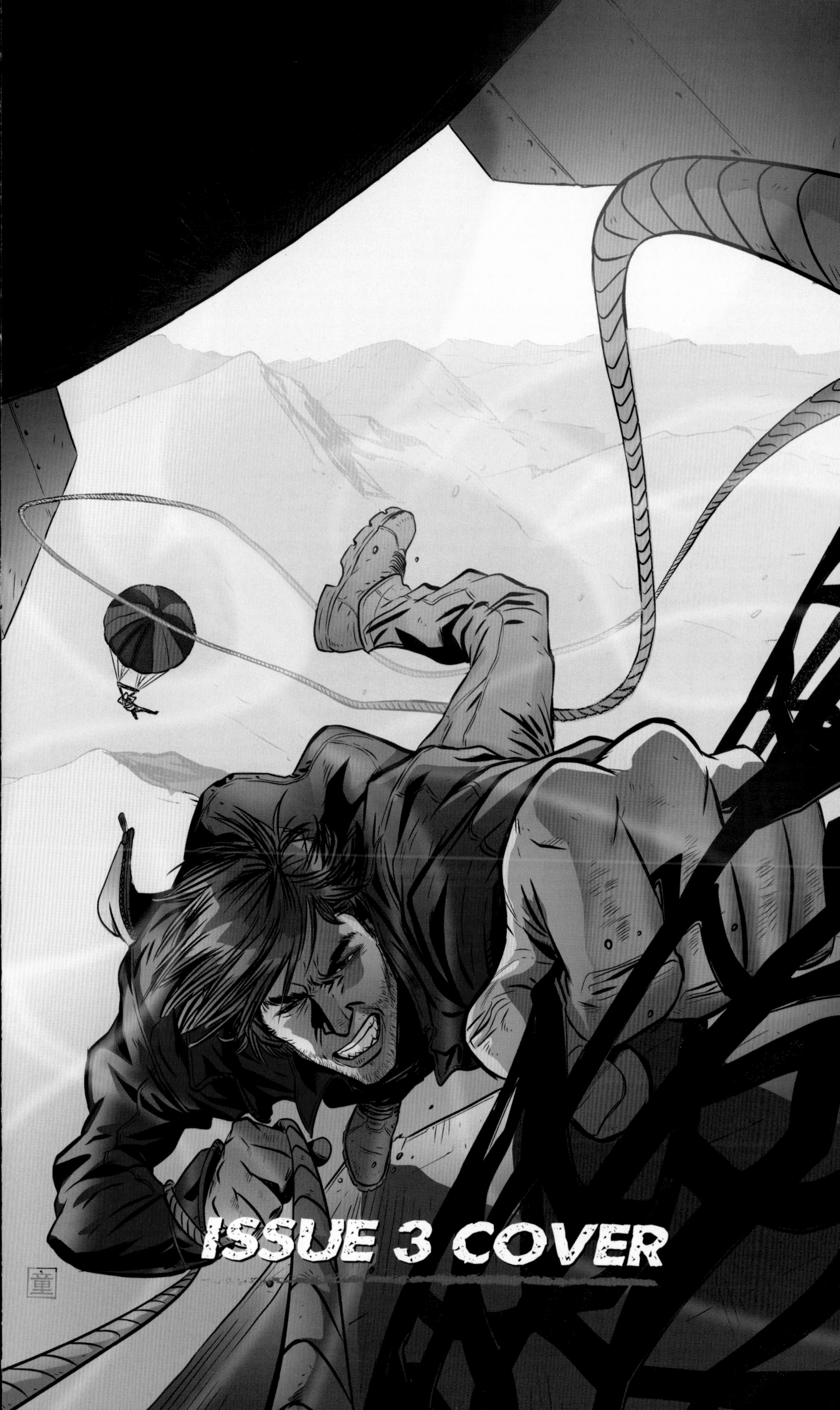

ISSUE 3 COVER

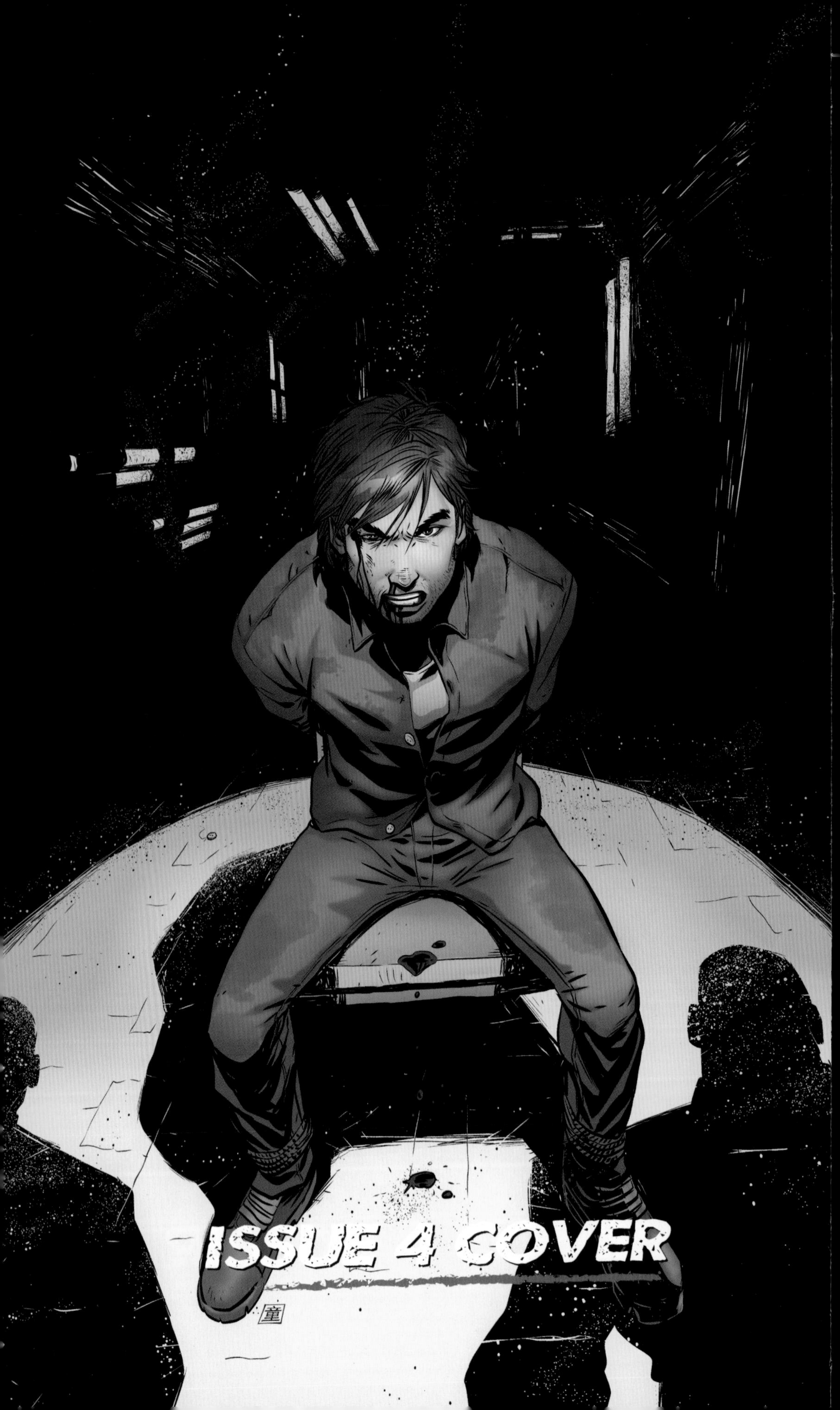
童

ISSUE 4 COVER

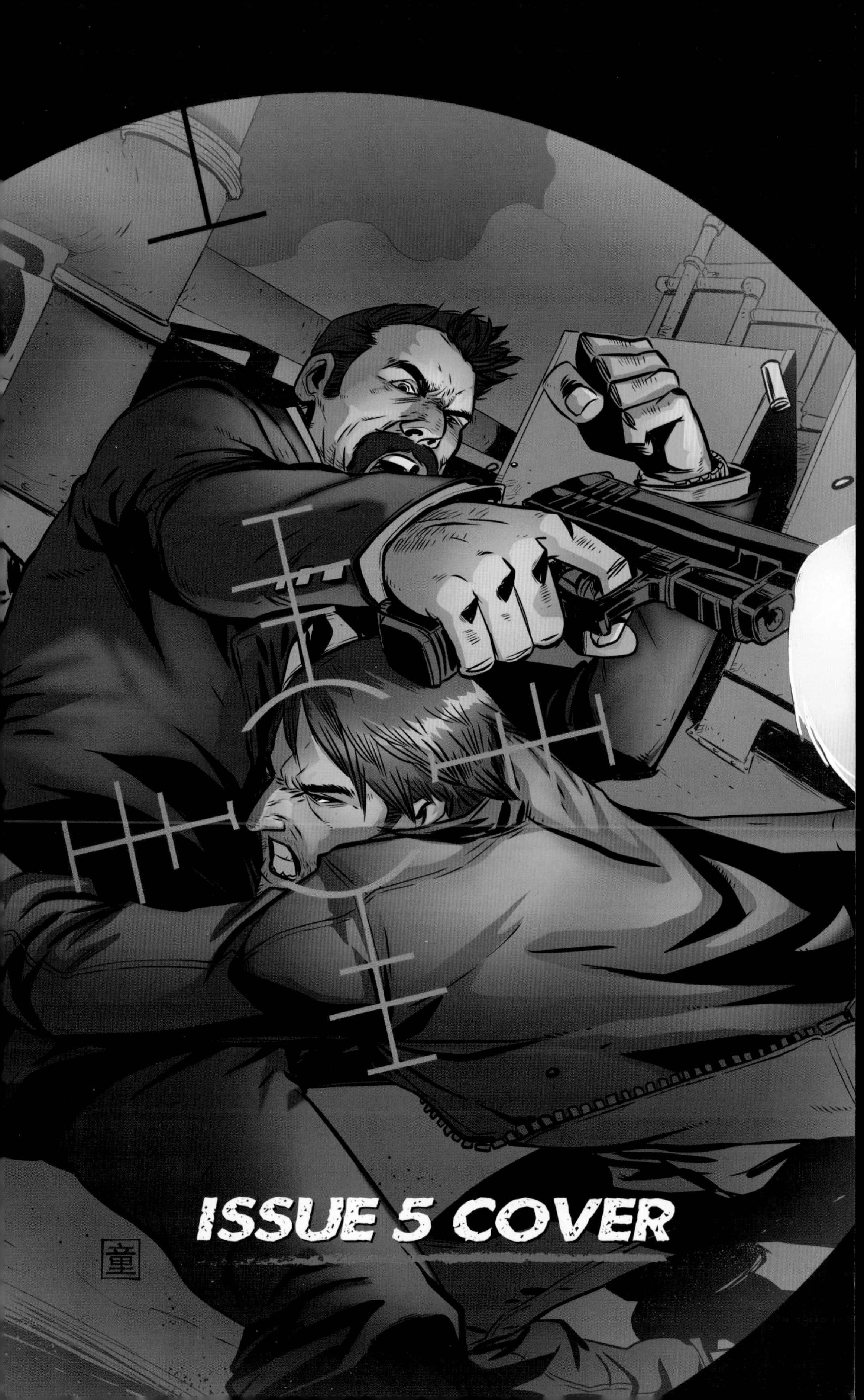
ISSUE 5 COVER
童

MacGyver

BY LEE DAVID ZLOTOFF

It's hard to believe that it's been a generation since MacGyver first whipped open his Swiss Army knife on the cultural horizon. Harder still to believe that his name has joined the dictionary and, over the years since his creation has become a global icon for resourcefulness and invention in the face of adversity. And, most surprising of all, at least for me has been the persistent demand to... BRING HIM BACK, PLEASE!

So, finally bowing to popular demand, in this graphic novel series and in other forms currently in the works, we've dug out the knife, duct tape and the leather satchel to turn MacGyver loose on a whole new world and set of adventures - which has been something of an adventure in itself. In the generation since his debut, as I've travelled the globe and met literally countless Mac fans, the one question that I'm inevitably asked is, *"So where did the idea for MacGyver come from anyway?"* Where indeed? Well, therein lays a tale my friends, no less fraught with surprising twists and turns than any of Mac's missions. And, while in the past I would usually just smile and politely side-step the question, since MacGyver is now making his way back to the present, if not the future - I suppose it's only fair that I come clean and tell the *real* story of how this amazing, enduring and beloved character came to be created. Now, even as I reveal all this, it's very important to remember that television is a collaborative medium with a slew of producers, studio and network executives, and others all piled atop the lone writer - in this case me - not to mention all the directors, actors and hundreds of crew it takes to make a TV pilot much less an entire series. And no doubt they all have *their* version of this story - which could easily, and understandingly, differ from mine. But rest assured, soon enough I will invite them to share their tales as well so the record will be available for all to see. But, as I alone bear the mantle of being the show's 'creator', I can say with Mac - if not the Almighty - as my witness, this is how it happened...

Though I didn't know it at the time, I suppose in some way it all started when I was at a small liberal arts school called St. John's College where, believe it or not I spent four years reading and discussing the great books of the western world; Plato, Homer, Aristotle, you name it. The greatest storytellers and thinkers that ever lived who inspired me to not only learn to think outside the box, but realize that the course of future world opinion was going to be formed as much by film and TV as by great books. So I decided it might be worth giving showbiz a try. And after leaving school I made my way to New York where I eventually landed a job as a dialog-writer for a soap opera called "The Doctors" (to her dying day my loving grandmother was convinced that my regular credit on her TV screen meant that I had *actually become a doctor.* Bless you, Grandma). But it was clear - after an invaluable year of learning to write dialog - that soap operas just weren't my thing so, now expecting my first child, we decided to pack up and relocate to Los Angeles where, you know, the fruit grows on trees in your backyard. *At least we wouldn't starve* I kept telling myself. And we didn't, though for the next few years it was something of a struggle to feed the kids. (Yes, there was soon a second one... and eventually a third... and a fourth. Apparently, I really liked having kids. They were certainly a hellova motivation to keep writing)

So I hustled with whatever writing jobs I could find, when I wasn't doing construction and home repairs to keep bread on the table - until I finally broke through into episodic drama writing as a staff writer. And, man, did I *ever* break through. Because for nearly the next three years, as a staff writer or producer for a number of TV series, I discovered - as did my bosses - that I could crank out decent episodic scripts at a furious pace (which is the name of the game in series writing). And crank I did, practically starting a new script before the ink was even dry on the last one. But after writing like a machine possessed for all that time, I could tell that despite the generous income and the titles I was amassing, I was fast approaching a case of serious burnout. So to avoid both a creative and emotional breakdown - and to spend some real quality time with my young family, since it seemed my kids were having trouble remembering what I looked like, I'd left the series I'd been writing for and took some time and space to go back and just write for myself again, crazy as that sounds. Perhaps not the most recommended of career choices, but the writer in me was clearly in need of some breathing room and, as he'd been damn good to me so far I wasn't about to ignore him and wait until I hit the wall. I'd seen that happen to friends and colleagues and, trust me, it ain't pretty. And here's where the juicy part of this creation story really kicks in. *It was a dark and stormy night...*

Nah, it was actually a weekday afternoon at the office in Santa Monica I'd rented to ignore the siren's call of the biz and just try writing for myself again (with a houseful of kids, writing at home was a non-starter, believe me). Now at first my agent, lawyer and business manager (all of whom got a piece of my income) were generally supportive of this unorthodox shift in direction, saying "Do what you need to, bro, we're here whenever you want us." But given how hard it can be to get a decent writing gig in La-La land, most writers do what they can to hold on to it with both hands, not jump off the carousel, so I could tell my reps were still a little nervous. And after doing my own thing and, as John Lennon put it 'watching the wheels go round and round' for the better part of a year, I could tell they were really beginning to sweat... "Are you *sure* you don't want to just try writing for a paycheck again?" So that afternoon when my agent Marty called yet again, to say he had a great job for me, I felt I owed it to him to listen. "I got a pilot for you - and it's already been sold to ABC, so you don't have to pitch it or anything. It's with Henry

Winkler's company at Paramount. All you have to do is write it. Bing, bang - you're in and out and it's over before you know it. What do you say?"
"What's it called?" I asked.
"It's called *Hourglass*, I think."
"Hourglass, huh? And what's it about?"
"Who cares what it's about? It's a job - Just tell me you'll consider it and let me go make you a great deal, will ya, please?!"
Now, I can't tell you whether this was a moment of weakness or strength - sometimes it's hard to tell with these things - but I said "Okay, sure. Go make the deal. I'll give it a shot."
"Fantastic! Trust me, you won't regret this!" And Marty hung up the phone fast, before I could change my mind. Now I think Marty eventually spent some time in prison, but I'll give him this, he was right about that job. I certainly don't regret agreeing to take that assignment - at least not now anyway.

So it began; I'd just agreed to write something called 'Hourglass' without the slightest idea of what I was in for, and I was in for quite a ride. And, after the usual haggling between my agent and the studio's business affairs department, the deal for me to write their 'Hourglass' pilot was finally made and it was time for me to head over to Paramount TV to meet with the studio execs and the producers to find out what exactly *was* 'Hourglass'. (Since all I'd been able to glean so far was that it was to be a 'single-lead, action/adventure show', "single-lead" meaning one hero instead of an ensemble cast or 'a team'.)

Now 'meetings' in Hollywood are a lot like dating; there's usually a round of 'pre-meeting' calls between the agents, producers and execs to stroke everyone about how excited we all are to be meeting, followed by the meeting itself of course, and then another round of 'post-meeting' calls to determine how the meeting *really* went, and was everyone pleased with the outcome or just pretending that they were. I mean, nobody likes to blow it on the first date, right? And since we already had a deal in place, all involved were eager to see things got off on the right foot. For my part, I was mostly just there to look excited and listen—not a stretch really— since this was *my very first pilot* and by now I was truly curious, and figured I could find a way to have fun writing an action/adventure piece, no matter what it turned out to be. Soon enough then I'm in a conference room with Henry Winkler—by then a huge star thanks to playing 'The Fonz' on *Happy Days*—and his producing partner, the highly regarded director, John Rich, along with the studio execs, Grant Rosenberg and Tony Jonas. (No doubt there were some junior execs and assistants there as well—there are always 'seconds' in these meetings to take notes and learn—but, for the life of me, I couldn't tell you who they were—and hereby offer my apologies to them for the haze of memory that eventually haunts us all). But what was immediately clear in the meeting was how psyched ABC was about this project: "Everyone at the network *loved* it, and bought our pitch *right there in the room!"*
(In the TV biz, that's a big deal; usually the network likes to put on a poker face and say they'll get back to you with their decision). So now I'm genuinely excited. Wow. They bought it in the room. This is awesome. And I can tell everyone at the table smells a hit here. Enough with the suspense; 'Hourglass'—lay it on me!
"So the reason we call it 'Hourglass'", they continue, "Is because every episode happens in *exactly one hour!* Get it? We have a *real* ticking clock. One hour of TV time is *one hour of actual time!* It's a *totally* new concept. Great, huh?" Now my mind is already starting to race a little—and not in a good way—as I smile and nod, trying to wrap my head around this before I come back with the most obvious question...

"Oh, so you want to do a *serial*, is that it? Each episode is one hour of a larger continuing story?" (A concept by the way that nearly two decades later was employed to enormous success on the show *24*.)

"Oh, no", they casually reply, "The network doesn't want a serial. Each show has to be a 'stand alone' episode: a single story from start to finish—all in one hour. And get this; it's *never been done before!* How cool is that?" And that's when **the bomb** went off in my head, because I knew at that instant there was a *very good reason* it had never been done before, which was *it wouldn't work*. This brilliant concept that everyone, including the network—was in love with was *doomed before it could even get off the ground!* And, apparently at the moment, *I was the only one who got that!*
Since it's generally considered bad form to throw up all over your partner on the first date, I'm doing my best not to look horrified—considering I've already signed on to be the writer here—and desperately searching for *anything* that might give me a way to spin this. So I try backing away from the dynamite I've just found in my lunch box and go for another tact by asking, "And the main character in this?— What's he all about?"
"Well, we like to think of him as the court of last resort", they say, "You know, when nobody else can handle the mission, they call him."
"Anything else you can tell me about him?", I press gently, already feeling my fingers slip off the edge of the cliff into the abyss looming beneath me—
"Not really. We sorta thought we'd leave all the rest of that up to you. You know, not to tie you down with too many details or get in the way of your creative process."

And there it was—*I got nothing!* My head's in free fall, my arms and legs flailing in empty space like Wile E. Coyote who's just been snookered off the precipice by the Road Runner—again. Worse still, they're all looking at me, waiting for me to coo with excitement over their beautiful newborn, when I know for a fact it's just a head of cabbage. Nothing to do now but stare at all that dynamite and give it a poke in the hope maybe someone else will realize it's a bomb.

"So in this format of the ticking clock," I ask, "What happens if our hero has to, you know, like go across town or something? Do we just see him travel for all the time it would really take to do that?"
"Oh," somebody jumps in, "He like knows all the bus schedules cold or something. And he could like hop from the back of one bus to another to do that really fast—or something like that, you know?"

I just nod again, realizing now that I've got to get out of there, fast. Because if I poke that dynamite any harder by pursuing such questions, the bomb is definitely going to go off right then and there—which would *not be a good thing at all.* So I quickly swaddle this *thing* in as much bubble wrap as I can muster with the futile hope that maybe I can get it back to my office and figure out *some way* to disarm it. "Wow, cool" I mutter, "This is really something, you know. I'm gonna have to give this all some serious thought. Can't wait to get started, in fact. So if there's nothing else?..." And I beat a hasty exit, and tried not to crush the steering wheel of my car on the drive home—though there might well have been a considerable amount of screaming and cursing; the mind tends to heal itself over time by forgetting such things.

How did I know with such complete certainty that this 'Hourglass' concept was such a non-starter? Well, one of the most amazing—and effective—aspects of storytelling through film (or TV) is the ability to jump instantaneously across space and time. One second you're in location A, the next second you cut to location B, C, D or whatever. And the new location can be simultaneous with the first or an hour, day, month, year or *millennia* later. So now imagine if you will, trying to tell a compelling and satisfying story in one hour *without* that ability. They told me they wanted a single-lead, action / adventure show of 'stand alone' episodes: that is, each show had to be a complete story in itself built around a single, main character and NOT a serial where the story carried over from episode to episode. For example, *NCIS, Bones* or *Castle*, say, are 'stand alone' shows where the character stories may arc over a whole season but each show is a 'case' to be solved in that episode: whereas *Grey's Anatomy* and *Boardwalk Empire* are more 'serials' where the stories carry over from show to show and each episode is just a part of a larger story that arcs across an entire season, sort of like a soap opera. The networks' desire for stand alone series vs. serials in prime time tended to move in cycles, but in the early 80s when I got this assignment, trust me, *no one* wanted a serial so there was no point in even exploring that option.

So if each episode had to be confined to a *single hour of actual time*, that meant my main character - our hero - couldn't really *travel* much at all since it takes, you know, time to go from place to place. He couldn't for instance be in the U.S. in one scene and then be in China or Istanbul or even *another city* in the next scene. And even if I could cut away to, say, the disaster or problem he was going to solve - or some other characters (which I didn't really have either because the show was to be built around our hero), it wasn't going to be very interesting to just watch our guy *travel*, you know? In a show like this you want to see your hero *doing things*, not traveling to the scene. That meant, in order to squeeze the most drama out of any story, it pretty much *had* to take place *in one location*. And our hero would have to *arrive at that location at the start of the episode*. In other words, since traveling for more than a few minutes was out, every show *would have to end where it started*. Needless to say, trying to generate decent action / adventure - on a typical TV budget - while confined to one location was going to take some doing.

To be clear then, under the proposed 'Hourglass' format I would have to completely forfeit the primary ability of film language to jump either space or time since the time *had to be continuous*. And that in turn meant the space - or location - had to be, more or less, unified as well, at least for the purposes of our hero because, if I couldn't jump time, then he would need to be restricted to a fairly tight area or location for the bulk of the story. Because the larger the area of the story, the more time it would take for our hero to get from one place to the other and, unless he was being chased - or racing to get somewhere - that wasn't apt to be terribly interesting to watch. And even racing and chasing can get old after a while. Not to mention that racing and chasing happen to be the *more expensive things to portray on film*, requiring moving the crew and camera multiple times for which you only get a few seconds of actual 'screen footage' for each move. And an easy budget-buster, at least for television. What's more, after a few episodes of that, the audience would soon realize they were going to be more or less

stuck in one place for the *entire hour*. And if they didn't happen to feel like spending the next hour of their lives in that particular setting, all it would take was a little squeeze of their remote and *our show would be gone*.

Still, not impossible. I could easily come up with a bunch of episodes that might fit the bill: the mine cave-in, the locked bank vault, the burning oilrig, the sinking submarine; you get the idea. But, back then, for a series to be considered successful by the studio it needed to run for a minimum of *five seasons*. That meant this concept had to be sustainable for more than just a season or two; it had to work for like *110 episodes!* And no matter how hard I racked my brain to find a way to make the 'Hourglass' concept work - like with extensive flashbacks, maybe of things before the key incident? Or by trying to see the same action repeatedly but from different characters' points of view, (known in the biz as 'Rashoman' style after the Kirosowa film), whatever I considered just seemed so incredibly *restricted* that I couldn't picture how anyone would pull that off for even one full season, much less *five of them*.

Bottom line: I simply couldn't find a way to disarm the bomb I'd been handed, because this 'Hourglass' concept wasn't just a challenge, it was a *fricking straitjacket!* And I at least was not enough of a creative Houdini to wriggle out of it. This then left with me an acute moral dilemma - yeah, I know, morality in showbiz, hard to believe, huh? But there it was. I knew if push came to shove, I could keep my mouth shut, write a single pilot that satisfied the 'Hourglass' criteria, and make it look like this concept would work. And leave the bomb just ticking in the lunchbox for someone else to discover.

But this was my *first pilot*. And in truth, they weren't just asking me to write a single cool episode, but to *create a blueprint for a whole series* - that at least had a shot of lasting five seasons or more, right? And, after a stern talking-to from my better angels, I knew there was no way in good conscience I could pass the buck on this one. So after a few days of personal and creative struggling to make sure I had left no rock unturned, I finally bit the bullet and called Grant Rosenberg and Tony Jonas at Paramount to tell them I just couldn't make 'Hourglass' work... and why. And, despite the fact that we had a deal in place, I would bow out gracefully if need be so they could find another writer if they wanted. Grant and Tony (both of whom by the way eventually went on to be really successful TV producers in their own right) just listened patiently and said they would discuss it internally and get back to me. Certainly not the kind of call one likes to

make, but at least the bomb was out of the lunch box and on the table and ticking away for all to see. Next thing I know, I get a call from Henry Winkler's office: Henry would like to meet with me - *alone*. No agents, no studio execs, no other producers or 'seconds' - just me and Henry, period. Oh, man. *This cannot be good.*

Now it might help you to know that Henry Winkler has a well-deserved reputation for being like the *nicest guy in show business*. I don't mean he just has good publicists or spin doctors, I mean everyone who knows Henry genuinely reports that *he's a prince among men*. He shares his time and wealth with a host of charities, he waits his turn in line despite the fact that he's a major star; he helps old ladies across the street *for real*. Henry doesn't just talk the talk; he walks the walk of 'niceness' *with a passion*. And it dawns on me that, more than likely - I've just managed to piss off the nicest guy in show business! And he wants to see me, alone... now.

That bomb is ticking louder than ever. And as I make that seemingly endless drive to Henry's office, I can just picture my career going up in flames - *what kind of imbecile must you be to invoke the ire of Henry Winkler!* My first pilot deal is going to be my last: no more assignments, no more TV shows... *I will be banished from show business*. So I'm trying like hell not to picture my children starving as I drive through Hollywood, blasting the AC to keep the sweat from soaking through my clothes, and silently praying I haven't just detonated that bomb under myself.

Now Henry's office was on the Paramount studio lot, which is smack dab in the heart of Hollywood. And the traffic there is usually terrible, so I'm really counting on the long crawl across town to rehearse the encounter in my head and get my nerves under control. No such luck.

In some freak occurrence that defies all explanation *there is no traffic*. The roads are *deserted* and you just know *I make every single traffic light*. It's almost as if I'm being inexorably pulled toward his office like it's some black hole from which any escape is hopeless and I will be sucked into oblivion - *forever*. And before I know it I'm inside the studio gates and marching across the acres of parking lots, sound stages and twisting warrens of offices - in the searing southern California heat - so that, by the time I finally locate Henry's office, you could *wring* the sweat from my clothes, my nerves are in wicked knots, and when his smiling assistant chirps, "Would you like something to drink?" it takes a Herculean effort not to ask for a double scotch and instead mumble that a water will be fine, before I'm ushered in to meet my fate.